The State, the Market and the Euro

The State, the Market and the Euro

Chartalism versus Metallism in the Theory of Money

Edited by

Stephanie A. Bell

Assistant Professor of Economics, University of Missouri, Kansas City, US

Edward J. Nell

Malcolm B. Smith Professor of Economics, Graduate Faculty, New School University, US

Edward Elgar

Cheltenham, UK • Northampton, MA, USA

Published by
Edward Elgar Publishing Limited
Glensanda House
Montpellier Parade
Cheltenham
Glos GL50 1UA
UK

Edward Elgar Publishing, Inc.
136 West Street
Suite 202
Northampton
Massachusetts 01060
USA

A catalogue record for this book
is available from the British Library

Library of Congress Cataloguing in Publication Data
The state, the market, and the euro : chartalism versus metallism in the theory of money / edited by Stephanie A. Bell, Edward J. Nell.
   p. cm.
   1. Euro. 2. Money. 3. Monetary policy. I. Bell, Stephanie A., 1969– II. Nell, Edward J.

HG925 .S73 2003
332.4'94—dc21

2002034709

ISBN 1 84376 156 4
Printed and bound in Great Britain by MPG Books Ltd, Bodmin, Cornwall

Contents

Figures

Tables

Contributors

Stephanie A. Bell is Assistant Professor of Economics at the University of Missouri, Kansas City and a Research Scholar with the Center for Full Employment and Price Stability. She has published articles in the *Journal of Economic Issues*, the *Cambridge Journal of Economics*, and the *Review of Social Economy*. Her primary research interests include monetary theory, government finance, social security and European monetary integration. She has an M.Phil. from Cambridge University and a Ph.D. from the New School for Social Research.

Charles A.E. Goodhart, CBE, FBA is the Norman Sosnow Professor of Banking and Finance at the London School of Economics. Before joining the LSE in 1985, he worked at the Bank of England for seventeen years as a monetary adviser, becoming a Chief Adviser in 1980. In 1997 he was appointed one of the outside independent members of the Bank of England's new Monetary Policy Committee until May 2000. Earlier he had taught at Cambridge and the LSE. Besides numerous articles, he has written a couple of books on monetary history, and a graduate monetary textbook, *Money, Information and Uncertainty* (2nd edn 1989). He has published two collections of papers on monetary policy, *Monetary Theory and Practice* (1984) and *The Central Bank and The Financial System* (1995) and another (with Richard Payne) on *The Foreign Exchange Market* (2000), and an institutional study of *The Evolution of Central Banks*, revised and republished (MIT Press) in 1988.

Robert Guttmann is Professor of Economics at Hofstra University (New York) and the Université Paris-Nord (France). He has written widely on money and banking, monetary theory and the international monetary system. Most recently, he has been working on a book entitled *Cybercash: The Coming Era of Electronic Money*, which will be published by Palgrave/Macmillan in 2002. His work has been published in Austria, Brazil, Britain, France, Germany, Italy and the United States.

Eric Helleiner is Canada Research Chair in International Political Economy at Trent University, Peterborough, Canada. He is author of *States and the Reemergence of Global Finance* (Cornell, 1994) and *The Making of National Money: Territorial Currencies in Historical Perspective* (Cornell, 1994), as well as co-editor (with Emily Gilbert) of *Nation-States and Money: The Past, Present and Future of National Currencies* (Routledge, 1999).

Michael Hudson is President of the Institute for the Study of Long-term Economic Trends (ISLET) in New York and London. Among his books on the politics of international finance are *Super-Imperialism: The Economic Strategy of American Empire* (Holt Rinehart, 1972), and *Global Fracture: The New International Economic Order* (Harper & Row, 1979). He formerly taught international economics at the New School for Social Research, Graduate Faculty (1969–72), and has traced the development of international trade and financial theory in *Trade, Development and Foreign Debt* (Pluto Press, 1993). He is editor of the ISLET assyriological colloquia on Debt and Economic Renewal in the Ancient Near East (CDL Press, 2002), Urbanization and Land Use in the Ancient Near East (Harvard: Peabody Museum, 1999), and Privatization in the Ancient Near East and Classical Antiquity (Harvard, 1996).

Perry Mehrling is Professor of Economics at Barnard College, Columbia University, where he teaches courses in both money and finance, theoretical and applied. His book *The Money Interest and the Public Interest* (Harvard, 1997) traces the development of American monetary thought from 1920–1970. His chapter in this volume is part of a larger project to bring the story up to the present. His current major project is an intellectual biography of Fischer Black.

Edward J. Nell is Malcolm B. Smith Professor in the Graduate Faculty of the New School University, and a former Rhodes Scholar. He has taught at Oxford, Wesleyan, the University of East Anglia and the New School, and has been a visiting professor at the Universities of Rome, Paris, Orleans, Bremen and Frankfurt among others. His main work is *The General Theory of Transformational Growth*, but he is also the author of *Making Sense of A Changing Economy, Prosperity and Public Spending* and *Transformational Growth and Effective Demand*. He has written over 75 articles and notes in professional journals and is the editor of *Transformational Growth and the Business Cycle*. He has an apartment in New York City and a house in Woodstock, NY.

L. Randall Wray is a Professor of Economics at the University of Missouri–Kansas City as well as Senior Research Associate, the Center for Full Employment and Price Stability (at UMKC), and Senior Scholar, the Levy Economics Institute. He is currently writing on full employment policy, modern money and the monetary theory of production. He has published widely in journals and is the author of *Understanding Modern Money: The Key to Full Employment and Price Stability* (Edward Elgar, 1998) and *Money and Credit in Capitalist Economies* (Edward Elgar, 1990). Wray received a BA from the University of the Pacific and an MA and Ph.D. from Washington University in St. Louis.

Preface

Edward J. Nell and Stephanie A. Bell

In a paper published in the *European Journal of Political Economy* in 1998, Charles Goodhart revived an old approach to monetary theory – the Chartalist approach – and used it to make a critical assessment of the new monetary system that was adopted by most Western European nations on 1 January, 1999. The importance of his contribution struck us immediately. Could the consequences of abandoning sovereign currencies in favor of the new European currency – the euro – be as grave as Goodhart warned? If so, perhaps the theory of money that underlies most modern macroeconomics is not so well grounded? What determines the value of a currency, and how is the state's power over its currency related to its ability to stabilize prices and employment? How will its power over the currency be affected when the state has little or no fiscal authority? Because these questions are so interesting and because the success (or failure) of the new system has such far-reaching implications (for both theory and policy), we decided to organize a mini conference, dedicated to an analysis of the central themes of the Goodhart paper.

A diverse group of theorists, including a number of economists, a political scientist and a historian, shared their thoughts with a large audience at the New School for Social Research in April 1999. Some tackled the big issues, such as the history and evolution of money, while others chose to focus on more subtle themes. While it would be disingenuous to suggest that the participants reached a bona fide consensus on matters, it is fair to say that everyone considered Goodhart's paper an important and provocative essay. In fact, the participants were so enthused that most of them agreed to prepare a formal manuscript, elaborating on their previous remarks, for this edited volume. A few others, who were unable to attend the conference, also agreed to contribute.

In order to make the participants' remarks accessible, we have reprinted Goodhart's article in the first chapter of this book. In this piece, Goodhart presents a remarkably clear connection between economic theory and practical policy, specifically between two sharply contrasting theories of money – Metallist and non-Metallist or Chartalist – and two equally sharply contrasting approaches to macroeconomic policy.

He refers to the Metallist theory as 'M theory' and associates it with the writings of Aristotle, Locke, Jevons, Menger, von Mises, Brunner and Alchian. According to M theory, money is a *creature of the market*, arising out of individual (or, more frequently, collective) choices, driven by efficiency and utility. Early M theorists tended to argue that money was invented (or agreed upon) by individuals attempting to truck, barter and exchange their way to economic bliss. From their perspective, money is important primarily because it serves as a medium of exchange, which facilitates trade by reducing transactions costs. Then, as trade becomes sufficiently expansive, M theorists tend to suggest that money should be organized to cover Optimal Currency Areas, that is, areas in which trade is regular enough and factors are mobile enough to justify the use of a common currency.

Goodhart refers to the second theoretical approach as 'C theory', which he traces to G.F. Knapp (and to Keynes in the *Treatise on Money*). According to C theory, money is a *creature of the state*. The role of the state is important because money is said to originate as a consequence of the state's demand for goods and services. The state needs all sorts of things, which it obtains by imposing a tax liability, payable in its own IOUs. In order to obtain the government IOUs that are needed to settle tax obligations, the private sector provides the things that the state needs. Thus, C theory emphasizes the relationship between the state's power to tax (and to specify the unit in which these obligations must be paid) and the demand for money (as a means of settling these obligations). It is, therefore, concerned more with money's role as a unit of account and a means of payment than with its function as a means of exchange.

In addition to the theoretical differences, the two approaches are also based on contrasting methodologies. M theory is individualist in its methodological approach. Markets are made up of rational agents, making optimal choices subject to various constraints. Money arises spontaneously as a means of reducing the costs of making and carrying out these choices. The specific thing that is chosen to serve as money is selected because of the particular properties that individuals find desirable (for example the portability and divisibility of precious metals). The money article will be supplied competitively (for a price) and will be demanded in proportion to the volume of transactions. In order to rationalize a fully fledged commodity system, M theorists typically argue that the state emerges (*ex post*) as the entity responsible for vouching for the quantity and quality of the metals used in exchange, thereby resolving the 'identifiability' problem that is supposed to complicate the use of unstamped metals.

C theory takes an institutionalist approach, paying particular attention to social relations and institutional detail. Chartalist theory emphasizes the role that the state, palace or temple has played in the development of early monetary systems. The relevant markets are connected by flows of funds and, of course, flows of goods and services. These flows are facilitated by the issue of credit by traders and banks. Many decisions about prices, techniques, capacity construction and the like will be made by representatives of institutions, and decisions are relevant to planning the future. In the present, the question is whether the resources and labor currently available will be fully utilized, and this depends on factors that can easily move in destabilizing directions. Money is a major part of the picture, because the flows are monetary flows – but money moves because it is spent or lent, and this depends in part on government fiscal policy.

On policy matters, M theory considers the economy to be normally self-stabilizing at an optimal position. Policy interference should therefore be minimal, and chiefly concerned with the prevention of inflation. Fiscal policy is generally ill advised, since the actions of rational agents can preempt or nullify any desired outcome. Moreover, output and employment are considered the determinants of supply-side variables, leaving policymakers with only prices as a viable policy target. Thus, the only effective policy tool will be control over the money supply, which is supposed to allow the monetary authority to promote stable prices.

C theory considers the economy to be volatile and often unstable. Cycles are endemic; asset-booms lead to crashes. This view is consistent with the balance sheet approach implicit in Chartalist theory. Money is at once a credit (asset) and a debt (liability) – and the credits are always trying to get in touch with the debts. Thus, in a monetary production economy, the balancing of cash flows is essential. When the credits obtained by a particular unit are insufficient to service past commitments, financing difficulties can arise. Government intervention is necessary and must emphasize fiscal policy, since only the government can provide the credits that are needed when a rush to liquidity threatens the stability of the financial system. Monetary policy boils down to control over interest rates, which, as a means of stabilizing the macro economy, is not likely to prove useful. As the Japanese experience teaches, even negative real interest rates may have no stimulative effect. And, as the US experience of the late 1970s teaches, interest rates may have to climb to devastatingly high levels before having the desired effect on spending.

With respect to history, M theory presents an *idealized* story. It is not only that the story is abstracted, that is, told with many elements left out, but also that it is told on the assumption that agents had abilities and information – and access to resources – that in the vast majority of cases, they did not have. The story assumes various natural proclivities, such as the propensity to truck, barter and exchange as well as an insatiable desire for material possessions. M theory treats such behavior as rational, and depicts agents as well-informed, self-interested beings pursuing their individual interest with determination and vigor. Although most anthropologists would deny this historical depiction of human behavior, M theorists depart from actual history in favor of the assumption that the behaviors exhibited in propertied, class societies are natural and eternal, and so have always been present, even if subordinated. In their view, it is good enough to speak *as if* the present provides an accurate account of the past.

In contrast, C theory focuses on history and the evolutionary development of institutions. Money, while always representing a social debt relation, changes forms at different historical junctures. Goodhart praises C theory for its ability to look beyond the changing surface phenomena at the common attributes of various money systems. When the state is weak, or when regimes are liable to change suddenly, what serves as money will tend either to be valuable in itself, or readily convertible into valuable articles – coin, bullion, plate. But, when the state is strong, and its continuity assured, the fiat or backing of the state will be sufficient. Indeed, what we have seen since the rise of the nation state is the circulation of national currencies within specific national borders, which as Goodhart emphasizes, is not simply the end result of Gresham's Law. Instead, C theory argues that there is an intimate relationship between sovereign power over money and power over national policy. The importance of this relationship is drawn out clearly in Goodhart's discussion of the euro.

M theory solidly supports the euro. In fact, M theorists not only sanction the design of Optimum Currency Areas but also favor the particular institutional arrangements that have been put in place across the eurozone. Specifically, they applaud the establishment of the European Central Bank as an ultra-independent monetary authority. And, since fiscal policy is generally viewed as ineffective, they also tend to favor the constricting fiscal rules that now constrain national governments. Put simply, they see no fundamental problem with the abandonment of power in the monetary sphere and the concomitant loss of power in the sphere of public policy.

C theorists, on the other hand, emphasize the interdependence of monetary and political sovereignty and, thus, worry that the institutional set-up may be wrong. C theory contends that fiscal policy is both effective and necessary. Without the stabilizing impact of government spending and lender-of-last-resort intervention, there is a good chance the economy will experience lasting spells of rampant inflation and periodic debt deflations. Further, C theory argues that without fiscal backing, the euro (or any other currency) may prove unmanageable.

Each of these themes is taken up in the chapters that follow. There is no need for an overview; the chapters speak for themselves. But it is worth explaining that the chapters are not easily grouped into unique categories. Some authors tried to touch on almost all of the important themes, while others chose to narrow their focus, treating specific problems in greater detail. For example, Mehrling places Goodhart's paper in the context of his entire body of work, showing how his ideas have developed over time. For this reason we placed it first, immediately following Goodhart's paper. The others did not separate neatly into groups. Thus, at first glance, Hudson and Helleiner might seem chiefly concerned with history and institutions, Wray and Nell with the differences between M and C theory, and Guttman and Bell with the implications for the euro. But Hudson and Helleiner also draw out the implications of history and institutions for theory, and Guttman spends the first two thirds of his chapter on the same subjects. Nell contrasts the way institutions worked in different historical periods and argues that theory must reflect such differences in practice; Wray likewise surveys historical practices, while Bell develops theory. Each of the chapters, in fact, covers most of the issues raised by Goodhart. We chose an order of presentation that seemed to allow the discussion to develop. The book ends with Goodhart's commentary and reply.

Edward J. Nell and Stephanie A. Bell

1. The two concepts of money: Implications for the analysis of optimal currency areas

Charles A.E. Goodhart

1. INTRODUCTION

Much of the economic analysis and assessment of the comparative advantages and disadvantages of moving to a single currency, euro, area in Europe has been undertaken within the context of the Optimal Currency Area paradigm. This, in its turn, is the spatial/geographic facet of the currently dominating model of the nature and evolution of money. This latter views money as having developed by a process whereby the private sector has sought to minimize the costs of making exchanges in the process of trading. In this chapter I shall argue, first, that there is a second, alternative approach to the story of the evolution and nature of money, which is historically and empirically more compelling. Next, I shall claim that this second approach is far better able to predict and explain the observed relationship between sovereign countries and their associated currencies than is the OCA model.

There has, in fact, been a continuing debate between those who argue that the use of currency was based essentially on the *power* of the issuing authority (Cartalists) – that is, that currency becomes money primarily because the coins (or monetary instruments more widely) are struck with the insignia of sovereignty, and not so much because they happen to be made of gold, silver and copper (or later of paper) – and those who argue that the value of currency depends primarily, or solely, on the intrinsic value of the backing of that currency (Metallists).[1] A conjoint debate exists between those who have argued that money evolved as a private-sector, market-oriented, response to overcome the transactions costs inherent in barter (let us call them Mengerians),[2] and those who again argue that the state[3] has generally played a central role in the evolution and use of money (Cartalists).

There is little doubt that the M team has assembled the more illustrious collection of economists (plus the endorsement of Aristotle[4] and Locke[5]), and has expressed its analysis in more formal and elegant terms, from the earlier economists such as Jevons (1875), and Menger,[6] via Mises (1912/34), Brunner

(1971) and Alchian (1977b), on more recently to Kiyotaki and Wright (1989) and (1993), plus a host of other eminent economists.

Against them the C team has arrayed a more motley, fringe group of economists, such as Knapp in Germany (1905), Mireaux in France (1930),[7] and (most of) the post-Keynesians in the UK and USA.[8] Nevertheless as Mélitz (1974) and Redish (1992) have noted, the C team approach has also received the support of a large number, probably a sizeable majority, of those in other disciplines, for example anthropologists, numismatists and historians concerned with the origin of money.[9] Whereas the M group has been strong on formal theory, it has been constitutionally weak on institutional detail and historical empiricism. Mélitz is the only current economist, known to me, from the M team who tries to address the anthropological and historical issues presented by the C team.

I shall expand on this discussion in Section 2, and attempt to demonstrate where the M team's model has its main weaknesses, and to provide further evidence, historical and analytical, in support of the C team approach.

The Optimal Currency Area theory (OCA) connected with the names of Mundell, McKinnon and Kenen is a natural extension of M team theory into the spatial, geographic, domain. If the origin of money is to be seen in terms of private sector market evolution, whose function is to minimize transactions costs, then the evolution of a number of separate moneys in differing geographical areas should, analogously, be analysed in terms of private sector market evolution, whose function would have been to minimize some set of (micro-level) transaction and (macro-level) adjustment costs.

Against this, the C team analysts would claim that the spatial determination of separate currencies has almost nothing to do with such economic cost minimization and almost everything to do with considerations of political sovereignty. In Section 3, I shall argue that the C team hypothesis does far better in explaining and predicting historical reality than the M team (OCA) model. Indeed, the discrepancy is so marked, that the continued supremacy among economists of the M (OCA) model indicates how strong remains the attachment of economists to nicely constructed models, whatever the facts may be (the belief that Central Banks not only can, but also do, control the monetary base of their economy is another example of this genre). The comparative paradigmatic success of the M team (OCA) model may also reflect economists' normative preference for systems determined by private sector cost minimization rather than messier political factors.

Much of the discussion of the cost/benefit balance of, and the appropriate boundaries for, the single currency, euro, area within the European Union have been undertaken within the context of the M (OCA) model. If we should reject that model in favour of the C model, as is argued here, this would suggest a need for reconsideration of the issues that arise.

The key relationship in the C team model is the centrality of the link between political sovereignty and fiscal authority on the one hand and money creation, the mint and the central bank, on the other. A key fact in the proposed euro system is that that link is to be weakened to a degree rarely, if ever, known before. A primary constitutional feature of the European Central Bank (ECB) is to be its absolute independence from government (at any level). Meanwhile, the political and fiscal powers of the various European institutions (Parliament, Commission, and so on) at the matching federal level are far weaker (than has been the case in other previous federal states). That, in itself, raises constitutional and political issues, such as what would happen if the wishes of the community, expressed through its various (democratic) institutions, did not coincide with either the objectives or the operations of the European System of Central Banks (ESCB)?

Within the euro area, the main political and fiscal powers are, instead, to remain at the level of the nation state. Historically the nation states have been able, *in extremis* (whether in the course of war or other – often self-induced – crisis), to call upon the assistance of the money-creating institutions, whether the mint via the debasement of the currency, a Treasury printing press, or the Central Bank. Whenever states (as in the USA or Australia), provinces (as in Canada), cantons, *länder*, and so on, have joined together in a larger federal unity, both the main political, the main fiscal and the monetary powers and competences have similarly emigrated to the federal level. The euro area will not be like that.

In particular the participating nation states will continue to have the main fiscal responsibilities; but in the monetary field their status will have changed to a *subsidiary* level, in the sense that they can no longer, at a pinch, call upon the monetary authority to create money to finance their domestic national debt. There is to be an unprecedented divorce between the main monetary and fiscal authorities.

The thrust of the M team's theoretical analysis is that this divorce is all to the good; indeed it is largely the purpose of the exercise. The blame for recent inflation has been placed on political myopia, via the time inconsistency analysis, and the ability of the political (fiscal) authorities to bend and misuse monetary powers for their own short-term objectives. While there is much truth and realism in this analysis, the C team analysts worry whether the divorce may not have some unforeseen side-effects.

2. ON THE NATURE AND ORIGINS OF MONEY

Many economists and historians have noted the severe transactions costs involved in barter, and also the advantageous characteristics of precious metals as a medium of exchange (for example durability, divisability, portability). Clower (1969) is a good example. This conjunction has led numerous economists to construct models showing how the private sector could evolve towards a monetary economy as a function of a search for cost minimization procedures within a private sector system, within which government does not necessarily enter at all. Kiyotaki and Wright (1989 and 1993) provide the current state-of-the-art examples of such models. Menger's work from the *Economic Journal*, 1892, is, perhaps, the most quoted early example.

Apart from their lack of historical support (not that any such has usually been considered to be necessary), the main drawback of such models is that they fail to recognize the informational difficulties of using precious metals as money. As I have previously noted (1989, 34),

> Precious metals in an unworked state have been used as a means of payment in exchanges only under very special circumstances – e.g., in the various gold rushes in California and Klondike – and even then the picture, immortalised, for example, in a film by Charlie Chaplin, of merchants and bar tenders weighing and checking the gold dust before accepting it in payment, suggests that payment in unworked precious metals has more in common with barter than with a monetary payment.

When the ordinary person goes into a jeweller's shop, he (or she) has very little capacity to judge the fineness, or weight, of a gold or silver object put before him. We usually take on trust the jeweller's claim about the carats involved, supported by the fact that the claim is *potentially* objectively and independently verifiable, and that the jeweller's reputation depends on such verifiable claims being upheld.

Nevertheless the cost, and time involved, in such verification is not small. The whole thrust of Alchian's paper (1977b) is that money arises as a result of the existence of a good whose identification costs are low.[10]

But the costs of identifying the quality of either unworked or fabricated precious metal for the ordinary person are high. An individual could, of course, go to a money-changer for expert advice, but that would also involve costs. So such costs were probably higher, for example, than the cost of identifying the value of items in common every-day use, for example salt, corn, nails or even perhaps cattle (most people in a rural agricultural community would reckon to be able to assess the value of a cow).[11] Likewise such costs are again greater than the cost of assessing the value of an item which is acceptable by being part of a set of items needed for some intra-societal functions (for example religious or wergeld); Grierson (1970/1977) is a leading advocate of this latter view (see Appendix A); also see Einzig (1949/1966).

The above argument may appear to be a straw-man; few people argued that precious metals would be used as a medium-of-exchange currency until the identification problem was largely resolved by the technical innovation of a mint process whereby the identification costs could be drastically reduced by means of stamping a quality guarantee upon a coin (see Appendix B). Thus the argument is that a combination of the innate characteristics of the precious metals, *plus* the identification cost reduction allowed by minting, enabled the private sector to evolve towards a monetary system.

Again, however, that analysis is historically flawed. Although, once the idea and technical process is discovered, minting would seem to be as capable of being done within the private sector as any other metal-working process, in practice minting has, in the vast majority of cases, been a government, public sector, operation.[12] Amongst the experts on the historical evolution of minting coins are MacDonald (1916), Grierson (1970/1977), (1979) and Craig (1953). These authorities, in turn, refer to hosts of other earlier writers. In those cases where the mint has been run by the private sector, the government has in most cases both set the standards of fineness and extracted a rent, or seignorage tax, that collected most of the available profits. This concentration of minting under the government's aegis is not accidental. There are two associated reasons why this is so.

First, a mint requires an inventory of precious metals. It will, therefore, act as a magnet for opportunistic theft and violence. It will require protection, and the protector (who wields the force necessary to maintain law and order in the economic system) will therefore be able to extract most of the rent from the system.

Second, the costs of identifying the true value (quality) of the metals included in the minted coin lead to time inconsistency. The mint operator is bound to claim that that quality will be maintained forever, but in practice will always be tempted to debase the currency in pursuit of a quick and immediately larger return.[13] Olson (1996) has described how the development of a secure, dynastic regime reduces time inconsistency in the ruler[14] (see also McGuire and Olson, 1996).

Few inventions are made by government bodies (except perhaps within the military field, for example the Manhattan project). This has also been so in the monetary field. The metallurgical developments and the invention of banknotes, in China and the West, came initially from the private sector. But money's initial role as a means of payment, for wergeld, bride price, religious occasions, and so on (which probably predated money's role as a medium of exchange), and its role in facilitating the fiscal basis of government (discussed further later), meant that government made the monetary process, for example the guarantee through minting of the fineness and at the outset of the weight of the coins, into a pillar of the sovereign state.[15]

There is, as set out by Grierson, a further argument leading to the same conclusion. Society cannot work if violent behaviour is too prevalent. Some people will always be violent. An initial act of violence provokes revenge and a possibly endless feud. Feuds destroy society. One early crucial function of money, wergeld, was to set a tariff whereby (the relatives of) the initial offender could recompense the damaged party. This practice spread to other inter-personal relationships (bride-price, slaves), in some cases before formal markets and the use of money in trade arose.[16] See also Exodus 21: 32 and 35 and Deuteronomy 22: 13–19; 28–29. Kleiman (1987b, 261–87) describes such compensations.

I take it as a maintained assumption that the establishment of law and order involves and requires a governance structure. Others, for example Benson (1990), do not accept that; it is, indeed, a major underlying issue. If law and order, the enforcement of contracts, and the whole infrastructure of settled behaviour that makes markets (and money) work is really independent of the governance structure of our societies, then the M team approach becomes much sounder – the more so, if governments are actually inimical to such necessary infrastructure. But to me, the concept that the existence of law and order is independent of government seems pure (anarchist) wish-fulfilment.

What is remarkable when reading the various histories of minting and currency is the correlation between strong kings (for example Charlemagne and Edward I) and successful currency reforms. Naturally, however, the temptation to debase the currency increases when (external) pressures threaten the continuing life of a government. Thus Henry VIII's debasement was related to war with France and Scotland at a time when 'The Exchequer's poverty was extreme...' (Craig, 1953, p. 108). For a splendid account of how that process (currency debasement) worked in practice, see Sargent and Smith (1995). Glasner (1989 and forthcoming), emphasizes the value to governments facing (military) crises of having control over money creation.

Under the C view of money creation, the collapse of strong government would lead to the cessation, or downgrading of the quality, of minting and a reversion towards barter.[17] Under the M view, once the private sector has estab-lished a monetary equilibrium, thereby much reducing transactions costs, there is no conceivable mechanism within the model which would lead back to barter. Let us look at history. In Japan, for example, 'Rice and fabrics had been commonly used as a medium of exchange after the government ceased the mintage of coins in 958 AD....' (Seno'o, 1996). Also, 'by the end of the tenth century, money circulation ceased and the economy regressed back to a barter economy.' (Cargill *et al.*, 1997).

In Europe, during Roman times, all coins were minted on the state's account; according to Crawford (1970), the fiscal needs of the state determined the quantity of mint output and coin in circulation. As Redish (1992) notes,

Howgego (1990) has recently amplified this view suggesting that there was no one-to-one correlation between state expenditures and new coinage. If the state acquired bullion it might be coined even in the absence of fiscal need. On the other hand, expenditures could be met by older issues, for example, coins received in taxes.

In any case, when the barbarians submerged Rome, strong government disintegrated. Both governments and mints fragmented into weaker smaller units. MacDonald (1916) describes the process (see Appendix C) as does Craig (1953), who also notes that amongst the ruling bodies operating mints at this time were Lords Spiritual, as well as Temporal.[18] With governments being weaker and less secure, their currencies became of lower quality, more likely to be debased, and less acceptable in commerce (much of the minting that occurred was not to finance trade, but for Danegeld and other facets of (military) relationships between power centres). Meanwhile most, but not all, commercial relationships reverted to barter. This decline was halted by Charlemagne and his successor, Louis the Pious.

It is only when a settled and strong government has been established that the authorities can offer both a sufficiently long time horizon and the necessary control to establish a high quality mint. At the same time the creation of money greatly eased and benefited the authorities' fiscal position, as well as much reducing transactions costs for the general public. This may have been so even at the very outset of coinage; as Redish (1992) notes (also see Grierson, 1970/1977),

> Numismatists believe that the earliest coins were produced at Lydia (now Western Turkey) in the mid-seventh century BC. The coins were made of electrum, a naturally occurring alloy of gold and silver. They had a design on one side and were of uniform weight but had a highly variable proportion of gold. In an influential article Cook (1958) argued that these coins were introduced to pay mercenaries, a thesis modified by Kraay (1964) who suggested that governments minted coins to pay mercenaries only in order to create a medium for the payment of taxes. Both interpretations stress the role of the government in the introduction of coinage.[19]

The linkages between the creation of currency and taxation are multifaceted,[20] and the subject deserves a major study in its own right (it is largely because of the domination of the M theory's denial of the importance and necessity of such links for the creation of money, that this has not been forthcoming). First, without money, it would be hard to place taxes on anything other than the production, transport and trade of goods, since only goods (or labour time) could be delivered. Once money exists, poll, income and expenditure taxes, as well as taxes on the production of services become easier to levy. When taxes are received in goods or labour, the balance of goods (and labour) obtained will not be that required for public sector expenditures, so money reduces the transactions costs of governments, *pari passu* with that of the private sector.

By the same token taxes payable in monetary form raise the demand for base money. Since a government obtains seignorage from money creation, this benefits the fiscal position twice over, not only from the taxes levied but also from the seignorage resulting from the induced monetary demand. This was, as Lerner (1954) notes, one of the major reasons for the introduction of Confederate currency by the South in the US Civil War,

> Secretary Memminger saw two immediate and indispensable benefits from levying taxes payable in government notes. First, taxes created a demand for the paper issued by the government and gave it value. Since all taxpayers needed the paper, they were willing to exchange goods for it, and the notes circulated as money. Second, to the extent that taxation raises revenue, it reduced the number of new notes that had to be issued. Memminger's numerous public statements during the war show that he clearly realized that increasing a country's stock of money much faster than its real income leads to runaway prices. They also show that he believed that a strong tax program lessens the possibility of inflation.' (p. 508)

Indeed the imposition of taxes, payable only in money (and not in goods or in kind), has been used on numerous occasions in colonial history for the primary purpose of forcing taxpayers out of a (non-monetary) subsistence economy and into a cash economy producing goods for sale in the world economy; the receipt of extra fiscal revenues was in some cases just a subsidiary motive, as recorded by writers such as Ake (1981), Rodney (1981), and Amin and Pearce (1976).

There is, indeed, a large literature on the use of taxes, payable in monetary form, as a means of driving peasants into a monetary relationship with a capitalist economy. This is not only to be found in the literature on colonial development, but also in the earlier development of capitalism in Europe, for example Hoppe and Langton (1994).

Once the close link between money creation and taxation (and of both to the underlying structure and stability of government) is understood, the move from metallic currency to a fiat, paper, currency becomes much more straightforward to understand. Even if one should accept the M theory of the evolution of metallic coins as money, it is problematic to use that same theory in its pure[21] form to explain why agents should suddenly *all* be willing to jump from using paper notes which were ultimately claims on precious metals (that is private or public sector banknotes convertible into such precious metals) to paper notes which were backed by no specific assets.[22] Instead those notes were, and are, backed by the power of government (for example legal tender laws) and its ability to impose taxes payable (and often only payable) in that fiat currency (as well as legal tender for the discharge of all other payments within the country).

Thus the M-form theory has difficulties with explaining the introduction and use of fiat currency. The C-form theory has no such difficulties.[23] The transition was entirely natural. The interesting questions relate, instead, to the factors determining the historical timing of the switch. The growing power of the nation state and the extra seignorage that could be obtained (particularly the need for such in wartimes) pushed for an earlier adoption of fiat currency. Historical inertia, credibility effects (time inconsistency problems were *always* foreseen and legal tender fiat currency invariably had a bad reputation as potentially low quality money), and perhaps at times concerns about counterfeiting, tended to delay the switch.

Let me conclude this section by pointing out that M-form theory finds it difficult to account for the role, or existence, of money within a general equilibrium model. Money in the utility function, or cash-in-advance models, are proposed, without much conviction. This difficulty is not surprising given that such models also abstract from the existence and role of government. While it is, of course, the relationship between taxation and the demand for money that the C-form theory emphasizes, it should also be remembered that it is the maintenance of law and order, the form and enforcement of contracts, and the whole infrastructure of regulation within society, that allow the epiphenomena of (organized) (private sector) markets to occur at all.

A disclaimer may, however, also be needed. The purpose of this section was to argue, first, that money frequently played an initial means-of-payment role in inter-personal social and governmental roles *before* it played a major role as a medium-of-exchange in market transactions, and second that the relationship of the State, the governing body, to currency in all its roles has almost always been close and direct. But I do *not* claim that the private sector cannot, and has not, ever been able to develop monetary systems without the involvement of state authorities. Perhaps the most likely early historical example of purely private sector monetary systems is the Aztec cocoa bean money (Mélitz, 1974, 129–30), but more recent examples include the cigarette money of POW camps, Radford (1945, 189–201), and the use of vehicle currencies in foreign exchange trading (Swoboda, 1969, and Hartmann, 1994). Several national currencies have in the course of history become widely accepted internationally, for example the Byzantine Hperpyron or 'Bezant', the Florentine Guilder, the Venetian Ducat, and more recently the pound sterling, US dollar and in some countries the Deutschmark, in some cases against the wishes, and without any involvement, of the issuing government. Indeed many economic agents voluntarily hold money issued by a state other than their own, for example US dollars almost everywhere, Deutschmarks in East Europe (see Cohen, 1996). Other examples can be added. Moreover, were the state authorities now consciously to choose to abdicate their monetary role, the void would surely be taken up by commercial institutions.

3. THE M-FORM SPATIAL THEORY, OR OPTIMAL CURRENCY AREAS

If the use of money can evolve through a (search) process of cost minimization, without any necessary intervention by a government, then by analogous reasoning the spatial domain for any one money[24] can also evolve from such a similar cost-minimization search process. The Optimal Currency Area analysis has, indeed, followed that approach. It has, broadly, compared the benefit, in terms of transaction cost minimization, of having a single currency over a wider area against the costs in terms of adjustment difficulties (Krugman, 1993). Those costs depend in part on market imperfections whereby there is imperfect flexibility (either spatial, that is, migration, or in (nominal) wages) in labour markets. The standard litany of factors affecting OCAs then follows, such as size, openness, labour market flexibility, concentration or diversity of production, nature of and specificity of shocks (whether symmetric or asymmetric), and so on.

Note, however, that following M-form theory the functions and role of government do not necessarily, or even usually, enter this list. Under the (pure) OCA theory (Mundell, 1961) there is no reason why currency domains need to be co-incident and co-terminous with sovereign states. There is no reason why such a state should not have any number of currencies from zero to n, and an Optimal Currency Area, in turn, should be able, in theory, to incorporate (parts of) any number of separate countries from one to n. There should under the M-form OCA theory be a divorce between currency areas and the boundaries of sovereign states. Most subsequent OCA applied research has, however, simply taken for granted the initial starting concordance of sovereign governments and currencies, and then applied the standard tenets of OCA theory to the question of monetary union between such countries. But that ignores the 'political economy' factors that made currency areas coincident with countries in the first place, and hence is likely to overlook the crucial political economy factors that will determine the success, or failure, of such unions, including EMU.

Such lack of concern for political economy considerations is not the case with C-form theory. Since under this theory money is intimately bound up with the stable existence and fiscal functions of government in any area, the sovereign government of that area is predicted to maintain its single currency within the area's boundaries.

Which theory has the better predictive and explanatory power? *Si monumentum requiris, circumspice*! In a recent paper, Eichengreen (1996), writes,

Michael Mussa is fond of describing how, each time he walks to the IMF cafeteria, down the corridor where the currency notes of the member states are arrayed, he rediscovers one of the most robust regularities of monetary economics: the one-to-one correspondence between countries and currencies. If monetary unification precedes political unification in Europe, it will be an unprecedented event. (p. 12)

Yet the economics profession has taken little notice of this 'robust regularity' in its assessment of monetary theory (national or international), and in its adherence to the M-form theory of private sector evolution. Moreover, it is difficult to see how several large countries, encompassing regions geographically separate, sometimes at very different stages of development, often with regionally concentrated production, could possibly meet the criteria for OCAs, for example USSR before its collapse, Brazil, Australia, Canada, and even USA.

In how many countries do we find multiple currencies? Prospectively there will be, after 1997, one such country, China, where the Special Autonomous Region of Hong Kong will keep its separate currency (for 50 years). Given the political circumstances of the planned arrangements, this could be described as an exception that proves the rule.[25] In some countries which have suffered hyperinflation, 'dollarization' has occurred, as in Argentina, Peru and – to some extent – Russia, and similarly with respect to the Deutschmark in Yugoslavia (see Petrovic and Vujoševic, 1996, on the Yugoslav hyperinflation of the 1990s). What is remarkable in these cases is how high the inflation tax rate on domestic currencies has to climb before the public switches to an alternative foreign currency – although once such a switch has occurred it does not reverse easily or quickly. And when the public does decide to abandon the inflating domestic paper currency, the alternative, privately chosen, good money can virtually drive out the 'bad' official money (Bernholz, 1989).

There have, however, been a few historical examples where currencies from several states were treated as equally acceptable in all of them. These included the Latin Monetary (Silver) Union (1865–1914)[26] and the Scandinavian Monetary Union (1873–1914).[27, 28] Cohen (1993) has studied the historical cases of such monetary union,[29] and concludes that the economic factors considered in standard OCA theory have little, or no, explanatory or predictive power to explain the varied history of the sustainability of such unions, and that political considerations are overriding.

Only in one single respect does the M-form, OCA theory have much statistically significant explanatory power, and that is that tiny states (principalities like Liechtenstein, San Marino, Monaco and Andorra), will generally not have their own currencies; and that there is some (statistical) tendency for larger states to adopt more flexible exchange rates and smaller states to have pegged exchange rates (see, for example, Al-Marhubi and Willett, 1996). But this is observationally equivalent, to some considerable extent, with the belief that the tiny principalities have very little sovereign power, and are in several cases effectively vassal subsidiaries of their larger neighbour. Consider, for example the two small countries that use the US dollar as currency, Panama and Liberia. Do these satisfy the OCA model, for example with similar shocks and an integrated labour market with the USA, or is the rationale for such currency usage to be found in political history?

It is certainly true that sovereign states have at times chosen voluntarily (and temporarily) to relax part of their sovereignty by committing themselves to maintaining pegged exchange rates against a precious metal, or against the currency of another state. The gold standard was, perhaps, the best and most successful example. But, as Panic (1992) emphasizes, the countries participating in that did so by independent, voluntary choice, each maintaining, and on occasions utilizing, the right to withdraw. Moreover, as Glasner (1989, 39) has emphasized, it can be optimal for a sovereign country to pre-commit to a regime which will ensure price stability (so long as that regime continues), but only if it retains the ability to utilize its independent money creation powers in a crisis.[30]

Perhaps the clearest indication of the relative predictive and explanatory power of the C-form theory comes on the occasion of the break-up of existing federations into separate states, as in the cases of the USSR, Czechoslovakia and Yugoslavia in the 1990s, and Austro-Hungary after World War I, or on the other hand of the unification of smaller states into a larger federal state, for example the USA,[31] Germany[32] and Italy,[33] on their foundation. The C-form theory predicts that the fragmentation of sovereignty will lead to a fragmentation into separate currencies, and, per contra, that unification into an effective federal state will lead to the unification of previously separate currencies.

The M-form theory has nothing useful to offer on this. If the USSR were an Optimal Currency Area before its break-up, it should have presumably remained so afterwards. If Prussia and Bavaria had been OCAs before the unification of Germany, they should presumably have remained so afterwards.

There is, however, one qualification to the above argument. This is that the acts and existence of a sovereign government in a particular geographical domain may serve to make that domain an OCA, whereas had there been several governments in the same domain, it would not have been an OCA. For example, if the existence of a unified-governmental fiscal system should be helpful in mitigating asymmetric shocks affecting regions in that domain, then it would be more likely to be an OCA. Again a sovereign government is likely to impose laws and to encourage behaviour (for example use of a single dominant language) that usually serve to make (labour) markets far more flexible within, than between, such countries. Similarly, the actions taken by such governments can be regarded as idiosyncratic shocks. For such reasons it is possible to argue that some of the explanatory factors determining OCAs could be argued to make them co-incident with sovereign states. Cesarano (1997) argues that the boundaries of the nation state define an equilibrium currency area. Nevertheless, the speed, and the patent political involvement, attending the association of monetary and sovereign fragmentation or federal unification over geo-graphical areas makes it extremely hard to claim that this follows, or was caused by, some kind of private sector evolutionary search process.

What, of course, is remarkable and unique about the move to EMU and the euro is the absence of an accompanying federalization of governmental and fiscal functions. This divorce between monetary (federal) centralization and governmental decentralization at the level of the nation state, especially with the main fiscal functions remaining at that lower, national level, is the source of potential tensions. It was in part to address such tensions that the Maastricht fiscal criteria and the subsequent Waigel 'growth and stability pact' were introduced.

We should ask why M-form theory maintains such a grip (as contrasted with the C-form theory) over most economic thought. For the reasons outlined in this, and the previous, section it can hardly be because it provides a positive explanation of observable events. Compared with the success of C-form theory, the explanatory (or predictive) capacity of M-form theory is nugatory. As Cesarano (1997) also notes, 'The standard theory of optimum currency areas is falsified by the empirical evidence' (p. 57).

One possible rationale is that M-form theory was never meant to be a positive, explanatory theory, but instead a normative theory, of what should be. As one referee commented, 'OCA theory is a normative, not a positive theory'. A weak form of this would be to recognize that, in practice, monetary institutions are inherently and *au fond* associated with considerations of political sovereignty, but that the subsidiary function of M-form OCA theory is to assess the balance of purely economic benefits and costs that this may generate. The problem with this is that the historical record of the association of money creation with the establishment and maintenance of a stable sovereign power is so overwhelming (apart from the case of tiny, and by the same token politically weak, states) that the balance of purely economic benefits and costs entailed by OCA must presumably be of second-order importance.

One implication of C-form theory is that the value of fiat currency will depend on expectations of the future existence of the current government, and the prospective treatment of that currency by a successor government. This suggests that a currency's valuation should be affected both by war 'news' and news on a defeated country's treatment, post-bellum, independently of the past and prospective future rate of expansion of such money supply. This line of thought has been advanced by economists such as Mitchell (1903) and Dacy (1984), but the methodologies used in their exercises could be improved.

A much stronger version of such a normative approach is again to accept that governments have almost always (historically and traditionally) taken over (usurped) the primary role in (high-powered, base) money creation, but to argue, using M-form theory, that this was neither necessary, nor desirable. Governments have often used their money creation powers to support and benefit themselves (via debasement and the inflation tax), though usually when they are weak and/or threatened, especially by war. Clearly access to the inflation tax benefits such governments. Whether it has benefited, or harmed, the public depends on the circumstances, for example the relative value to them of main-taining their existing government. A properly organized system of privately determined money creation could, so it is argued, provide a monetary system with a superior quality. This is the approach taken by economists such as Hayek, many (but not all) monetarists and the Free Banking School. In the absence of any more radical moves in this direction, the separation of the powers of money creation in an independent Central Bank (which under the Maastricht Treaty is required not to take instructions from government(s)), is (usually) seen as, at least, a step in the right direction by M-form theorists.

More generally there has been an overlap between M-form theorists and those who believe that the intervention of government within the economy is excessive, unnecessary (in most cases) and should be reduced. There is, therefore, an (disguised, but not hidden) agenda of M-form theory in advocating a reduced role for the state in economic affairs. By contrast, C-form theorists tend to believe that government intervention is an inevitable concomitant of the operation and organization of our (political) system. And many worry whether the prospective European Central Bank (ECB) may not suffer from a 'democratic deficit'. But that is a larger issue which we shall not pursue further here.

4.   CONCLUSION

OCA theory has little, or no, predictive or explanatory capacity. Unlike C-form theory it is unable to account for the close relationship between sovereignty and currency areas, a relationship that tenaciously persists through the course of the creation, and break-up, of federal states. The empirical weakness of OCA theory, the spatial facet of M-form theory, throws further doubts on the ability and value of the latter to explain the evolution and nature of money as well as C-form theory can. The main advantages of M-form theory appear to be technical, in that it lends itself better to mathematical formalization, and ideo-logical, in that it is based on a process of private sector cost minimization, rather than a messier political economy process. It is, however, a pity to suspect that monetary economics may be driven more by technical and ideological purity than by empirical and predictive capacity.

If, then, the key issue is the (political) relationship between control over money and sovereign power, we need to consider carefully what problems this may portend for the future euro single currency area. In the euro area the tra-ditional historical links between money creation and sovereignty will be broken to a unique extent. Money creation will be the responsibility of a federal body, the European System of Central Banks, intentionally made, by the Maastricht Treaty, entirely independent of government(s), whereas most other fiscal and other powers will remain in the hand of the participating nation states.

ACKNOWLEDGEMENTS

My thanks are due to Philip Arestis, Peter Bernholz, Jerry Cohen, Tim Congdon, Kevin Dowd, Matthew Forstater, Arye Hillman, Ephraim Kleiman, Jacques Mélitz, Allan Meltzer, Warren Mosler, Morris Perlman, George Selgin, Christopher Waller and three anonymous referees of this journal.

APPENDIX A.   GRIERSON'S VIEWS ON THE SOCIETAL ORIGINS OF MONEY

In his pamphlet on 'The Origins of Money' (1977, 1970), Grierson writes (19–21):

> In any case, the generalized application of monetary values in commodities could scarcely have come about before the appearance of market economies, and monetary valuations were already in existence in what Sir John Hicks has felicitously christened 'customary' and 'command' pre-market societies, *A theory of economic history*, (1969), pp. 2 ff. (rise of the market), 63–8 (origins of money). He has to some extent telescoped the invention of money and the invention of coinage, and in my view he exaggerates the 'store of value' element in early money. Nor, if my argument that money antedated the development of the market is correct, is it the case that the standard 'should be something that is regularly traded'. In such societies they provide a scale of evaluating personal injuries in the institution which the Anglo-Saxons termed the wergeld, and it is in this institution that the origin of money as a standard of value must, I believe, be sought.
>
> The practice of wergeld, that of paying a compensation primarily for the killing of a man but the term by extension covering compensations for injuries to himself or his family and household, is most familiar to us in its Indo-European setting....
>
> The general object of these laws was simple, that of the provision of a tariff of compensations which in any circumstances their compilers liked to envisage would prevent resort to the bloodfeud and all the inconvenient social consequences that might flow therefrom.... The object of the laws is that of preventing retaliation by resort to force, and the principle behind the assessments is less the physical loss or injury suffered, than the need to assuage the anger of the injured party and make good his loss in public reputation. It would cost one four times as much to deprive a Russian of his moustache or beard as to cut off one of his fingers.... Karl Menger, in an impressive article on the origins of money published many years ago, argued ingeniously that one would expect monetary standards to be based on the commodities most commonly and easily exchanged in the market, since these would have the maximum saleability. The law codes suggest that while this may be true of money substitutes, it is not true, or at least is not necessarily true, of the commodities used as standards themselves. [NB for detailed references see the original.]

APPENDIX B.   LIMITS TO THE ABILITY OF EARLY MINTS TO GUARANTEE THE QUALITY OF COINS

Although the development of mints provided a major advance in identifying and guaranteeing the quality and weight of coins, several problems however remained. Until a process was found to give coins milled edges, coins could be clipped, and thereby lose weight. Also, as Mélitz (1974, 71), notes,

Through most of the Middle Ages, many individual coins of the same issue differed substantially in weight and fineness. Indeed, prior to the 13th century, coinage methods hardly permitted less than a 5 to 10 percent variation in weight between individual coins struck from the same plate. Thus, accounting prices of different coins belonging to the same denomination and issue often varied. Differences in weight and fineness, along with a host of other factors, like varying admixtures, ordinary wear, clipping, and sweating, continued to produce differences in accounting prices of money units of the same denomination and issue all the way down to the 17th and 18th centuries.

With coins of varying weight, but of a known, given fineness, transactors would have to make a difficult choice between weighing coins, a time-consuming exercise (or of getting a specialist to assess them), or accepting them as equivalent, without weighing, for example by tale, which carried the risk that some (underweight) coins would not be subsequently acceptable. See, for example, Sargent and Smith (1995).

Kleiman (1987a) notes that a defrauded party, when overcharged, could revoke a deal within a certain time span.

Ascertaining the 'right' price of an article was thus supposed to be a matter of, at most, several hours. The only exception was deficient coins, of which it was said: Until when is one permitted to revoke [the deal]? In cities, until one can show [the coin] to a moneychanger; and in villages – until [the following] Sabbath eves.

To understand we have to remember that the coinage circulating in the Roman world of the first two centuries AD was most variegated.

Moreover, it was sometimes difficult to check whether the fineness of the coin was as stated, without complex, and destructive, metallurgical testing. During the Tokugawa Shogunate in Japan, not only was the fineness of the coins never published (see Ueda, Taguchi and Saito, 1996), but also,

In spite of enormous differences in the fineness of the Kobans created by a series of recoinages, the color of the surface did not deteriorate much and the surface generally shines with a golden color. The Kobans of low fineness, namely the Genroku Koban and the Gembun Koban do look slightly inferior in the surface color to other types of Kobans, but other Kobans minted in and after the Bunsei era show just as beautiful a golden color as the high fineness Keicho and Kyoho Kobans even though their fineness is even more inferior.

This phenomenon is produced by the last process in the minting of the Koban called 'color dressing' (color improvement or coloring). This process dissipates the silver element on the surface of Koban by heating it after coating the surface with chemical substances. This process seems to be unique to Japan in the history of minting and we have not heard of any similar instances in other countries....

APPENDIX C.   MACDONALD'S DESCRIPTION OF THE MONETARY DISORDERS AFTER THE FALL OF ROME

In his book on *The Evolution of Coinage* (1916), MacDonald describes the monetary consequences of the collapse of the Roman Empire in the following terms (29–31):

> When Rome fell, the triumphant invaders took over the institution of coinage from the rulers whose power they had destroyed. The earliest money of the new nations was entirely composed of direct, and not always very skilful, imitations of the imperial currency. This was partly because the barbarian chiefs sometimes chose to maintain the fiction that they were merely the vassals of the Emperor of the East, partly because they were aware that their own issues were more likely to be readily accepted if they conformed in outward appearance to what the mass of the population had for generations been accustomed to use. Even after a certain amount of independence had been developed, the confusion that the Empire had bequeathed showed no sign of passing away. On the contrary, once the restraining hand of a centralized control had been removed, the evil tended to become more and more sharply accentuated. The number of persons in whose names coins were struck multiplied rapidly....
>
> Delegation of authority was the pivot on which the whole of that system turned, and the multiplication of mints by which its development was attended did not, therefore, imply – in theory at least – any breach of the cardinal principle that the right of striking money was an attribute of the sovereign power. In point of fact, the penalties that waited on transgressors were more severe now than at any other period of the world's history....
>
> A similar desire for self-assertion was unquestionably operative in the case of the feudal lords generally. But in the majority of instances there was a baser motive present too. The business of minting could be made personally profitable, if one chose to play fast and loose with the responsibility which the possession of the right implied. The usual practice was to call in the current issues from time to time, or to collect a supply of pieces struck by a neighbour, and adulterate the metal or reduce the weight, and then give out a larger number of coins than had been originally received, the nominal value of each being the same but the intrinsic worth considerably less. This money the people had perforce to use, except in so far as they were able to transact business, as they did to a certain extent, through exchanging actual commodities. The hardships they endured in consequence are testified to by many contemporary witnesses. And there were various aggravations. Minting authorities often made exorbitant charges under the guise of dues. Again, bad as the money was, worse was frequently imported from abroad. Lastly, there was 'clipping', a species of fraud which consists in paring the edges of coins in circulation, in order to accumulate silver.

NOTES

1. As noted in Goodhart (1989), Chapter 2, 34. The problems which the switch to fiat money cause for M-form analysis are addressed later in Section 2.
2. After Karl Menger, especially his 1892 paper.
3. The religious authorities also played a major role, see subsequent footnotes (13 and 18).

4. *Politics*, Vol. 1 (circa 340 BC), also see comments by Grierson (1970/77), 9, and footnote 11.
5. *Two Treatises of Government*, Second Treatise, 318–20. Also, in the same vein, see S. Pufendorf (1744), Book V, Chapter 1.
6. In his *Economic Journal* paper of 1892, Menger assembled virtually all the elements of the intuitive analysis that has remained at the heart of the M-form theory. Subsequent economists with similar views have developed more technically advanced and mathematically rigorous models of the same process without much change to its central message.
7. Also see Fontana (1996).
8. Keynes (1935, 3, 4), believed that *fiat* money had to be explained on a Cartalist basis, but there is less evidence on his views of the earlier origins of money.
9. A leading contributor in this group is Grierson. His pamphlet on 'The Origins of Money' (1970/1977), is particularly useful. Also see Einzig (1949/1966) and Polanyi (1957).
10. 'Now, if there is some good in which identification costs are both (a) *low* and (b) low for *everyone*, that will permit purchase of product identification information cheaply from the specialized intermediary expert. If his costs of identifying that offered (money) good are less than the reductions in costs by using the specialist for information about the basic goods, the total costs of identification can be reduced' (p. 117).

   'Costs of identifying qualities of a good are what counts. If costs for some good are low and generally low across members of society, the good will become a medium through which information costs can be reduced and exchange made more economical' (pp. 121–2). Page numbers are from the reprint in *Economic Forces at Work* (1977a).
11. Burns (1927) records that lumps, bars or instruments in copper became acceptable in exchange in the early civilizations such as Egypt, Babylon and China, but that there was sometimes reluctance to switch from the use of cattle for certain quasi-monetary purposes. 'The cattle unit [in Rome] died hard, for twenty years later [circa 430 BC] it was necessary to order by law (the lex Papiria) that payments in copper should replace payments in cattle' (p. 17).
12. 'And let no man have a minter but the King', from the ordinances of Aethelred (Wantage, 1002) reported in Craig (1953).
13. Craig (1953) records that, 'The Chronicle of Winchester records that the current specie of this country was so much debased in consequence of the great number of mints established in difference cities, of which the masters seemed to contend with each other who should enrich himself most at the expense of the public, that it would pass neither in foreign markets nor even in our own' (pp. 27–8)
14. 'Perhaps the most interesting evidence about the importance of a monarch's time horizon comes from the historical concern about the longevity of monarchs and from the once-widespread belief in the social desirability of dynasties. There are many ways to wish a King well, but the King's subjects, as the foregoing argument shows, have more reason to be sincere when they say "long live the King". If the King anticipates and values dynastic succession, that further lengthens the planning horizon and is good for his subjects.

   The historical prevalence of dynastic succession, in spite of the near-zero probability that the oldest son of a king is the most talented person for the job, probably owes something to an intuitive sense that everyone in a domain, including the present ruler, gains when rulers have a reason to take a long run view' (Chapter 2, 25).
15. On this see Gerloff (1952) and Laum (1924).
16. Mélitz (1974, 39–42) accepts that money in its guise of a means of payment for such intra-societal transfers antedated money as a general medium of exchange in markets. But, on p. 77, he *defines* money as a medium of exchange held 'in order to economize on transaction costs in the activity of trading a variety of other types of goods'. My argument is that the means of payment role was (usually) prior in time and helped to facilitate and develop the subsequent more general medium of exchange role.

   The temporal ordering of the various uses of money remains, however, a contentious issue. The Bible (Genesis, XXIII: 16 and XXXVII: 25, 28) indicates that silver was used as a medium of exchange for (large) payments from a very early date. In early history money and religion were often as closely, or more closely, inter-related than money and the state. Temples were the great economic centres of the ancient world. They provided an opportunity to trade, especially at the festivals marking the end of the agricultural season; and having amassed considerable wealth from the gifts of their cult's devotees, they very often became lenders and 'bankers' on a great scale, hence their need for a monetary standard, which probably anteceded that of the State. I am indebted to Professor Kleiman for pointing me in this direction. Also, see Kramer (1963, 75–86).

17. In more recent centuries, however, the alternative, chosen by the private sector has been, instead, to switch from using the inflationary currency of the domestic government to the more stable currency of some other government (see Bernholz, 1989). The existence of such substitute currencies places some (high) upper limit on the potential ravages of the inflation tax.

18. Thus Craig (ibid. 12) writes that, 'Mints run by ecclesiastics on the other hand were proprietary. Only two are known to have survived from the earliest primitive period. The archbishop of Canterbury has two units... The single unit of the abbot of St Augustine's was merged in this property in or before the tenure of the See by the patron Saint of Goldsmiths, St. Dunstan. The saint's three minters were serfs; he was a hard man of affairs who once shocked his congregation by suspending Easter mass until they hanged certain counterfeiters of his coin, whose trial the people would have delayed till Monday out of respect for the day.'

19. This interpretation has not gone unchallenged, as Redish (1992) again notes, 'More recently, Price (1983) has observed that the early electrum coins were privately issued and not issued by states. Further, he argues that the electrum coin, which was of uniform weight but had a highly variable proportion of gold, would have been overvalued if it traded at a uniform value. This he concludes makes it unlikely that mercenaries would have accepted it. Price's interpretation is that the early coins emerged in the context of a gift/exchange economy, and provided a means for standard bonus payments, and that the imprint was used to identify the issuer, not to guarantee the coin's value. Only later, according to Price, with the introduction of gold and silver coin, did coin become a means of standardizing payments. However, Price does not explain why individuals accepted overvalued coins as gifts. Indeed, it is not clear whether these coins had a uniform value and at what point the pieces of stamped metal crossed the line between medal and coin.'

20. Selgin and White (1996) state that 'Government monopoly in issuing currency can thus be understood as part of the tax system.' That is certainly one key facet of the relationships between money and government.

21. Pure in the sense that the move to fiat paper money is also capable of explanation as a private-sector cost-minimization process. Of course, if M theorists are prepared to accept that government had taken over (usurped) the control of the monetary base by then, the rest is straightforward. The abandonment of convertibility into a real, metallic base was an (unhappy) act of government (as is clear from history). What remains, perhaps, at issue between the M and C theorists is how much of the subsequent acceptance of fiat money is due to the power of government, for example to impose taxes (C theory), or to network factors and inertia encouraging people, without prompting from government, to stay with the existing currency (M theory). I am indebted to correspondence with Professor Kevin Dowd for raising this issue with me, and also for sending me his (1995) working paper, with Selgin.

    Quite a number of economists combine the belief that M form cost-minimization search theory explained the initial development of money, but that more recently the state has clearly taken over the provision of fiat currency. So, whether or not they like the result, they accept that C form theory is at present more realistic, see Congdon's (1981) 'Is the provision of a second currency a necessary function of the state'.

22. Ritter (1995) argues that a community could benefit from moving to a fiat money economy if the issuers could commit to limiting the growth of such base money. Quite so, but as Selgin (1997) argues, there is a, probably insuperable, co-ordination problem within society, unless the authorities can *coerce* the residents simultaneously to switch (as with the introduction of the euro in 2002). Moreover fiat currency has, virtually without exception, been introduced at times of war and other crises, when the rate of growth of base money has been high, on many reckonings 'excessive', and certainly *not* subject to any credible limitation commitment.

23. Not surprisingly, Adam Smith understood the relationship between taxation and fiat currency, even before any widespread usage of the latter. Thus Professor M. Forstater, of Gettysburg College, has brought to my notice '...the following sentence on page 322 of the justly famous

Cannan edition of *The Wealth of Nations*: "A prince, who should enact that a certain proportion of his taxes should be paid in a paper money of a certain kind, might thereby give a certain value to this paper money; even though the term of its final discharge and redemption should depend altogether upon the will of the prince." Cannan's "sidebar" (his summary of each paragraph given in the margin) for this paragraph reads: "A requirement that certain taxes should be paid in particular paper money might give that paper a certain value even if it was irredeemable."'

24. Dowd and Greenaway (1993, 1180–9), have described how 'network externalities' will tend to limit the use of money for ordinary retail purposes in any area to a single kind of money, (in which, of course, there will be coins/notes of many values exchangeable at fixed, set ratios). When the quality of money in an area declines sharply (debasement, inflation), residents may turn increasingly to a higher quality money (dollarization). The costs of overcoming such network externalities may make such a switch partly irreversible. The dominance of a single currency in a single area does not, of course, rule out multiple currency holdings near boundaries, nor holdings of foreign currencies by residents for trade, travel and portfolio diversification reasons; on this latter see Cohen (1996).

The proposed joint usage of national currencies and euros during the changeover transition period within EMU 1999–2002 is *not* a counter-example, since the ratio of the value of the euro to the national currency will be absolutely fixed and irreversible. What is, however, new is that this fixed ratio will be highly user-unfriendly (for example 1 euro = 0.876534 National Units; it has been agreed that the rate will be applied to *six* significant figures), and not the standard user-friendly progression of currency values, for example 1, 2, 5, 10, 20, 50... There will, therefore, be serious additional information and familiarization costs involved in the transition. Note that virtually all prior currency reforms involved knocking zeros off existing currencies, for example 1 New Franc = 100 Old Francs. They were often somewhat traumatic for residents; the switch to the euro will be *much* more so.

25. Also see Kleiman (1994, 365–9) for a discussion of the agreement on currency usage in the areas of the autonomous Palestinian authority. Andorra and Namibia also have more than one legal tender.

26. '[T]he union managed to hold together until the generalized breakdown of monetary relations during World War I. Following Switzerland's decision to withdraw in 1926, the LMU was formally dissolved in 1927' Cohen (1993, 191).

27. 'By the turn of the century, the SMU had come to function, in effect, as a single region for all payments purposes, until relations were disrupted by the suspension of convertibility and floating of individual currencies at the start of World War I. Despite subsequent efforts during and after the war to restore at least some elements of the union, particularly after the members' return to the gold standard in the mid-1920s, the agreement was finally abandoned, following the global financial crisis of 1931', Cohen (1993, 191).

28. The Gold Standard did *not* represent an example of such a monetary union. While foreign agents could obtain national currencies at relatively low transaction cost by shipping gold in either coin or bar form, the currency circulation within each participating country was as overwhelmingly national as now (and the gold value of national currencies could, and did, vary between time-varying physical arbitrage points).

29. Amongst current monetary unions, Cohen also studies the CFA and Eastern Caribbean Currency Area. The CFA has been held together by French political, even including military, and financial support, while the populations of the ECCA are so tiny that the entire region is still too small for anything other than a currency board.

30. One useful and illuminating way of thinking about EMU is to regard this as the monetary symbol of a political pact between the two largest countries of Northern Europe, Germany and France, that there cannot and must not ever in future be a serious crisis, let alone a war, in their bilateral relationships. This line of thought comes naturally to C-team theorists and to politicians such as Kohl. It makes no sense, of course, to M-form theorists who see no necessary or desirable connections between monetary and political relationships.

31. 'When the First Continental Congress met in 1775 in Philadelphia, the first order of business was to establish a national currency' (Kohn, 1991, 70). But states' note issues were not then banned, and that plus, of course, reliance on the issue of 'Continentals' to finance the War of

Independence led to major inflation. This led the Constitutional Convention to establish in Article 1 of the Constitution of 1789 that Congress, and not the states, 'shall have power to coin money, regulate the value thereof and of foreign coin', and that 'No State shall coin money, emit bills of credit, make anything but gold and silver tender in payment of debts' (Davies, 1994, 466).

32. In its pamphlet, entitled *The Reichsbank*, which the Reichsbank published on its 25th anniversary in 1900, the opening paragraphs read as follows:

'The newly established German Empire found in the organization of the coinage, paper money, and bank-note systems, an urgent and difficult task. Probably in no department of the entire national economic system were the disadvantages of the political disunion of Germany so clearly defined as in this; in no economic department were greater advantages to be expected from a political union.

Although the customs union (*Zollverein*) had happily united the greater part of Germany in a commercial union, similar attempts in monetary affairs had met with but modest success, and were absolutely fruitless in banking.

The inconvenience most complained of was the multiplicity and variety of the different coinage systems (seven in all) in the different states, also the want of an adequate, regulated circulation of gold coins.'

33. As reported by Canovai (1911, 26),

'The prior political fragmentation of Italy left the country at the beginning of the 1870s with "...conditions of the institutions of issue and the paper currency [that were] abnormal and unorganized, since there was a mixture of institutions, different in nature and privilege, and a hybrid circulation, partly private and partly belonging to the State, which could not truly serve the economic and monetary conditions of the country".'

REFERENCES

Aethelred (1002), Ordinances of (Wantage).

Ake, C. (1981), *A Political Economy of Africa*, Harlow: Longman.

Al-Marhubi, F. and T.D. Willett (1996), 'Determinants of the choice of exchange rate regime', manuscript, April, Claremont, CA: Claremont Graduate School.

Alchian, A. (1977a), *Economic Forces at Work*, Indianapolis: Liberty Press.

Alchian, A. (1977b), 'Why money?', *Journal of Money, Credit and Banking*, 9, 133–40.

Amin, S. and B. Pearce (1976), *Unequal Development: An Essay on the Social Formations of Peripheral Capitalism* (translated from French by B. Pearce), Hassocks: Harvester Press.

Aristotle (circa BC 340), *The Politics*, Vol. 1, Reprinted in English and edited by W. Newman (1887), Oxford: Clarendon Press.

Benson, B.L. (1990), *The Enterprise of Law*, San Francisco: Pacific Research Institute for Public Policy.

Bernholz, P. (1989), 'Currency competition, inflation, Gresham's Law and exchange rate', *Journal of Institutional and Theoretical Economics, Zeitschrift für die gesamte Staatswissenschaft*, 145, 465–88.

Bible, King James Translation (1611),
   (i)   Genesis, Chapters 23 and 37
   (ii)   Exodus, Chapter 21
   (iii) Deuteronomy, Chapter 22

Brunner, K. (1971), 'The uses of money: Money in the theory of an exchange economy', *American Economic Review*, 61, 784–805.

Burns, A.R. (1927), *Money and Monetary Policy in Early Times*, New York: Alfred A. Knopf.

Canovai, T. (1911), *The Banks of Issue in Italy, Banking in Italy, Russia, Austro-Hungary and Japan*, Washington, DC: National Monetary Commission, XVIII.

Cargill, T., M. Hutchison and T. Ito (1997), *The Political Economy of Japanese Monetary Policy*, Cambridge, MA: MIT Press.

Cesarano, F. (1997), 'Currency areas and equilibrium', *Open Economics Review*, 8, 51–9.

Clower, R.W. (1969), *Monetary Theory: Selected Readings*, introduction by R.W. Clower, Harmondsworth: Penguin modern economics readings.

Cohen, B.J. (1993), 'Beyond EMU: The problem of sustainability', *Economics and Politics*, 5, 187–202.

Cohen, B.J. (1996), 'Optimum currency area theory: Bringing the market back in', manuscript, Santa Barbara, CA: Department of Political Science, University of California.

Congdon, T. (1981), 'Is the provision of a sound currency a necessary function of the state', paper presented at a conference on 'Liberty and Markets', organized by the Liberty Fund, Oxford, 24–26 April 1981, reprinted by L. Messel & Co., 100 Old Broad Street, London.

Cook, R.M. (1958), 'Speculation on the origins of coinage', *Historia*, 7, 257–67.

Craig, J. (1953), *The Mint*, Cambridge: Cambridge University Press.

Crawford, M. (1970), 'Money and exchange in the Roman world', *Journal of Roman Studies*, 60, 40–48.

Dacy, D. (1984), 'The effect of confidence on income velocity in a politically unstable environment: Wartime South Vietnam', *Kyklos*, 17, 414–23.

Davies, G. (1994), *A History of Money: From Ancient Times to the Present Day*, Cardiff: University of Wales Press.

Dowd, K. and D. Greenaway (1993), 'Currency competition, network externalities and switching costs: Towards an alternative view of optimum currency areas', *Economic Journal*, 103, 1180–89.

Dowd, K. and G. Selgin (1995), 'On the (non) emergence of fiat money', manuscript, Athens, GA, Department of Economics, University of Georgia.

Eichengreen, B. (1996), 'A more perfect union? The logic of economic integration', *Essays in International Finance*, No. 198, Princeton, NJ: Princeton International Finance Section.

Einzig, P. (1949), *Primitive Money in its Ethnological, Historical and Economic Aspects*, 2nd edn (1966), New York: Pergamon Press.

Fontana, C. (1996), 'The credit theory of Émile Mireaux: *Les miracles du crédit*', paper given at the Money, Macro and Finance Group Conference, London Business School, Manuscript, Leeds, UK: School of Business and Economic Studies, Leeds University.

Gerloff, W. (1952), *Die Entstehung des Geldes und die Anfänge des Geldwesens*, Frankfurt: V. Klostermann.

Glasner, D. (1989), *Free Banking and Monetary Reform*, Cambridge: Cambridge University Press.

Glasner, D. (1998), 'An evolutionary theory of the state monopoly over money', forthcoming in R. Timberlake (ed.), *Money and the Nation State*.

Goodhart, C.A.E. (1989), *Money, Information and Uncertainty*, 2nd edn, London: Macmillan.

Grierson, P. (1977), 'The origins of money', Creighton Lecture, Cambridge, 1970, reprinted and revised in pamphlet form, Athlone Press, University of London.

Grierson, P. (1979), *Dark Age Numismatics*, London: Variorum Reprints.

Hartmann, P. (1994), 'Vehicle currencies in the foreign exchange market', DELTA Discussion Paper, no. 94–13, DELTA, Paris: Ecole Normale Supérieure; also see his Ph.D. thesis (1996), 'Monnaies véhiculaires sur le marché des change', Paris: Ecole des Hautes Etudes en Sciences Sociales.

Hicks, J.R. (1969), *A Theory of Economic History*, Oxford: Clarendon Press.

Hoppe, G. and J. Langton (1994), *Peasantry to Capitalism*, Cambridge: Cambridge University Press.

Howgego, C.J. (1990), 'Why did ancient states strike coins?', *The Numismatic Chronicle*, 150, 1–25.

Jevons, W.S. (1875), *Money and the Mechanism of Exchange*, London: Henry S. King & Co.

Keynes, J.M. (1935), *A Treatise on Money*, London: Macmillan.

Kiyotaki, N. and R. Wright (1989), 'On money as a medium of exchange', *Journal of Political Economy*, 97, 927–54.

Kiyotaki, N. and R. Wright (1993), 'A search-theoretic approach to monetary economics', *American Economic Review*, 83, 63–77.

Kleiman, E. (1987a), 'Just price in Talmudic literature', *History of Political Economy*, 19, 23–45.

Kleiman, E. (1987b), 'Opportunity cost, human capital and some related economic concepts in Talmudic literature', *History of Political Economy*, 19, 261–87.

Kleiman, E. (1994), 'The economic provisions of the agreement between Israel and the PLO', *Israel Law Review*, 28, 347–73.

Knapp, G. (1905), *The State Theory of Money*, London: Macmillan 1924, a translation of the 4th German edition, 1923; 1st German edition (1905).

Kohn, M. (1991), *Money, Banking and Financial Markets*, Chicago: The Dryden Press.

Kraay, C.M. (1964), 'Hoards, small change and the origin of coinage', *Journal of Hellenic Studies*, 84, 76–91.

Kramer, S.N. (1963), *The Sumerians*, Chicago: University of Chicago Press.

Krugman, P. (1993), 'What do we need to know about the international monetary system?', *Essays in International Finance*, No. 193, Princeton, NJ: Princeton International Finance Section.

Laum, B. (1924), *Heiliges Geld*, Tübingen: J.C.B. Mohr.

Lerner, E.M. (1954), 'The monetary and fiscal programs of the Confederate Government, 1861–65', *Journal of Political Economy*, 62, 506–22.

Locke, J. (1960), *Two Treatises of Government*, P. Laslett (ed.), Cambridge: Cambridge University Press.

MacDonald, G. (1916), *The Evolution of Coinage*, Cambridge: Cambridge University Press.

McGuire, M.C. and M. Olson Jr (1996), 'The economics of autocracy and majority rule: The invisible hand and the use of force', *Journal of Economic Literature*, 34, 72–96.

Mélitz, J. (1974), *Primitive and Modern Money: An Interdisciplinary Approach*, Reading, MA: Addison-Wesley Publishing Co.

Menger, K. (1892), 'On the origin of money' (translated from German by C.A. Foley), *Economic Journal*, 2, 238–55.

Mireaux, E. (1930), *Les Miracles du Crédit*, Paris: Editions des Portigues.

Mises, L. Von (1912), *The Theory of Money and Credit*, 1st German edition 1912, English Translation 1934, London: Jonathan Cape.

Mitchell, W.C. (1903), *A History of the Greenbacks*, Chicago: University of Chicago Press.

Mundell, R.A. (1961), 'The theory of optimum currency areas', *American Economic Review*, 51, 657–64.

Olson, M. (1996), 'Capitalism, socialism and democracy', draft of book, Department of Economics, University of Maryland.

Panic, M. (1992), *European Monetary Union: Lessons from the Gold Standard*, London: Macmillan.

Petrovic, P. and Z. Vujoševic (1996), 'The monetary dynamics in the Yugoslav hyper-inflation of 1991–1993: The Cagan money demand', *European Journal of Political Economy*, 12, 467–83.

Polanyi, K. (1957), 'The semantics of money uses, "Explorations"', Vol. 8, 19–29, reprinted in G. Dalton (ed.) (1968), *Primitive, Archaic, and Modern Economics: Essays of Karl Polanyi*, New York: Doubleday.

Price, M. (1983), 'Thoughts on the beginnings of coinage', in C. Brooke, B. Stewart, J. Pollard and T. Volk (eds), *Studies in Numismatic Method*, Cambridge: Cambridge University Press.

Pufendorf, S. (1744), 'On the law of nature and of nations in eight books', G. Mascovius (ed.), Lausanne and Geneva: Marcus-Michael Bousquet.

Radford, R.A. (1945), 'The economic organization of a P.O.W. camp', *Economica*, 12, 189–201.

Redish, A. (1992), 'Coinage, development of', in P. Newman, M. Milgate and J. Eatwell (eds), *The New Palgrave Dictionary of Money and Finance*, 1, Basingstoke: Macmillan, pp. 376–8.

Reichsbank (1900), 'The Reichsbank, 1876–1900', Berlin: 25th anniversary pamphlet.

Ritter, J. (1995), 'The transition from barter to fiat money', *American Economic Review*, 85, 134–49.

Rodney, W. (1981), *How Europe Underdeveloped Africa*, Washington, DC: Howard University Press.

Sargent, T.J. and B. Smith (1995), 'Coinage, debasement and Gresham's Laws', unpublished manuscript (August).

Selgin, G. (1997), 'Network effects, adaptive learning and the transition to fiat money', Department of Economics, University of Georgia, Athens, GA, Work in progress (April).

Selgin, G. and L.H. White (1996), 'An evolutionary fiscal theory of government monopoly in money', Department of Economics, University of Georgia, Athens, GA, Work in Progress, Draft (August).

Seno'o, M. (1996), 'Yamada Hagaki and the history of paper currency in Japan', Bank of Japan, Institute for Monetary and Economic Studies, Discussion Paper 96-E-25.

Smith, Adam (1904), *The Wealth of Nations*, Cannan edition (originally published 1904; reprinted by Methuen, London, 1961).

Swoboda, A. (1969), 'Vehicle currencies and the foreign exchange market: The case of the dollar', in R. Aliber (ed.), *The International Market for Foreign Exchange*, New York City: Praeger pp. 30–40.

Ueda, M., I. Taguchi and T. Saito (1996), 'Non-destructive analysis of the fineness of kobans in the Yedo Period', Bank of Japan, Institute of Monetary and Economic Studies, Discussion Paper 96-E-26.

2. Mr Goodhart and the EMU

Perry Mehrling

Viewed in the context of his manifold other papers and books, Goodhart's 'Two Concepts of Money' (1998) stands out for its embrace of an explicitly extreme minority viewpoint. An economist among historians and an historian among economists, an academic among central bankers and a central banker among academics, Goodhart has in the past engaged both monetarism and Keynesianism without wholeheartedly joining either camp, preferring instead to identify points of agreement and disagreement with both. His willingness seriously to engage also with more extreme views, such as the free bankers on the one side and the post-Keynesians on the other, shows him to be no knee-jerk moderate since here too he finds things to appreciate as well as to criticize. What brings such a man to lump almost everybody else together as Metallists and to proclaim in opposition his own membership in the rather motley camp of Cartalists?

THE MAKING OF AN ECONOMIST

A monetary historian by training and predilection, Charles Goodhart initially formed his views on money from detailed study of the gold standard period preceding World War I. He focused first on *The New York Money Market and the Finance of Trade, 1900–1913* (1969) and then turned his attention to *The Business of Banking, 1891–1914* (1972) in the UK. Here at the beginning of his career he formed the idea, which later experience never gave reason to abandon, that domestic credit fluctuation is more cause than effect of domestic monetary fluctuation. This is so in the United States, despite the inelasticity of currency under the National Banking System, but also in the United Kingdom and despite its position as the center of the international gold standard.

> The great years of the gold standard were remarkable, *not* because the system enforced discipline and fundamental international equilibrium on this country by causing variations in the money supply, but because the system allowed for the development of such large-scale, stabilising and equilibrating, short-term, international capital

flows, that autonomous domestic expansion was rarely disrupted by monetary or balance of payments disturbances (1972, 219).

After a brief flirtation with academia, in 1968 Goodhart joined the Bank of England where for 17 years he continued to develop his views, now by studying the post-World War II system with a special focus on the monetary problems of the UK. His work as an applied monetary economist positioned him intellectually with a foot in each of the two worlds of academic monetary theory and central banking practice. In his textbook *Money, Information and Uncertainty* (1975) he engaged the academics, finding in uncertainty and transactions costs the theoretical justification for money that is lacking in the full Arrow–Debreu equilibrium model, and in Tobin's portfolio adjustment model a usable framework for his applied monetary work. In his collection *Monetary Theory and Practice: The UK Experience* (1984), the audience is central bankers and the papers record Goodhart's part in the Bank's battle against monetary base control in the heyday of monetarism. In both books, Goodhart finds that the post-World War II world operates more or less like the pre-World War I world, but with the extra degree of freedom that comes from a national currency not pegged to gold.

In 1985, Goodhart left the Bank to take up a position as Norman Sosnow Professor of Banking and Finance at the London School of Economics, where he has remained ever since. There he has continued his practice of standing in between the two worlds of academic theory and central banking practice, but with a distinctly different objective. When he was at the Bank, and academic debate was about monetarism versus Keynesianism, there was something for a central banker to engage. Characteristically, Goodhart identified with neither of the opposing camps, but looked instead to the theory of disequilibrium money to find 'a bridge, a *rapprochement*, between the two schools of thought' (1984, 19; Chapter 10). All this changed when the academic center of gravity shifted in a liberal (pro-market) direction, so much so that some academics went so far as to espouse a radical free banking position. A central banker could not easily engage such an argument without being suspected of self-interest. Goodhart moved back into academia and devoted himself to making the positive case for central banking in his next book *The Evolution of Central Banks* (1988).

The argument is primarily historical. It's taken us centuries, so Goodhart tells us, to learn that what banks most need from a banker's bank, namely a microeconomic lender-of-last-resort, can best be provided by a non-competitive, non-profit-maximizing government's bank. Advocates of free banking miss this lesson of history, that central banking is preferable to free banking even from the narrow point of view of bankers' own self-interest. They also miss the additional attractions of central banking from the larger point of view of macroeconomic price stability. Central banking may not provide much leverage over the system, but it makes no sense to embrace a free banking system that offers even less leverage.

Subsequently, Goodhart has used his independent intellectual platform at the LSE to speak out on issues of monetary policy and financial (de)regulation as they arose. Most important for the purposes of this chapter, Goodhart has staked out a position as a skeptic of the EMU, which position has much the same flavor of his earlier defense of the institution of central banking against its radical detractors. Once again there is a radical monetary idea emerging from academia – this time it is the Optimal Currency Area idea (Mundell 1961) – and once again the effect is to threaten the position of central banking – this time the threat is the replacement of national central banking with a European Central Bank and a common European currency. The Metallism versus Cartalism frame of his 1998 'Two Concepts of Money' is recognizably an update of the free versus central banking frame of his 1988 book. Once again Goodhart makes the case, and once again on historical grounds, for national central banking.

What is new is the sense that now Goodhart is in a definite minority, and he knows it. In 1988 he was defending central banking against an extremist minority viewpoint. Now he feels himself in the minority defending against a viewpoint apparently endorsed by the majority.

THE ECONOMICS OF MR GOODHART

So far as I am able to piece it together, Goodhart's model of how the world works is something like the rough sketch shown in Figure 2.1 which shows the circular flow of spending and income connecting with the monetary system through the flow of bank credit. On the real side, bank credit finances spending. On the monetary side, an expansion of bank credit tends to cause an expansion of bank liabilities and hence the money supply, which tends subsequently to put upward pressure on prices. Note how, against the academics, Goodhart sides with central bank practitioners who 'feel that, in reality, there is no alternative for a central bank but to provide the banking system with the cash it needs. The effective choice of central banks is limited to the terms on which such cash is made available' (1984, 15). But the ideas of academics, both Keynesian and monetarist, also come in. In Keynesian fashion, spending decisions determine income, while in monetarist fashion the money supply determines price inflation.

This eclectic mix has something of the flavor of the standard Hicksian IS/LM story, albeit with a horizontal LM curve to capture the endogeneity of the money supply, but Goodhart never embraces the formalism because the underlying structure of his story is different. In Goodhart, the leading role is played by bank credit and that makes it impossible to treat the goods and money markets

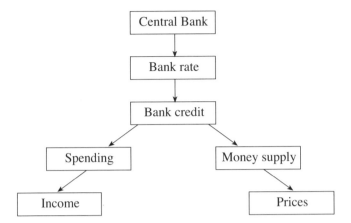

Figure 2.1   How the world works

as different markets. The importance of bank credit comes from the fact that banks are in a position to offer credit to worthy customers whom the open credit markets will never touch. 'The essence of banking lies in the assessment, monitoring and risk-handling of loans in circumstances where information is partial and asymmetric' (1995, 20). In Goodhart's view, it is autonomous bank credit decisions that determine whether the economy expands or contracts on the margin.

Given this view of the world, and presuming that one is concerned with price stability, it follows that one looks for a way to regulate the flow of bank credit. Leaving aside direct credit controls, the principal leverage would seem to come from control of the price of credit, so-called bank rate, though there is some question about how much leverage even this tool affords on account of uncertain interest elasticities. The main problem is the importance of expectations. If, during a boom, expectations are for rising inflation, it may take a very high nominal interest rate to slow a credit expansion. If, during a contraction, expectations are for falling inflation, it may take a very low nominal interest rate to avert a credit collapse. It is a position reminiscent of Ralph Hawtrey (1928) and on that account firmly within the tradition of English central banking.

Additionally, and quite apart from the question of whether or not one can regulate the aggregates effectively, the central bank can provide a backstop source of credit for individual borrowers in time of need. Even if (macroeconomic) price stability proves elusive, (microeconomic) financial stability can be ensured by judicious use of the lender-of-last-resort function. Here Goodhart departs somewhat from the tradition of Bagehot (1873) in his insistence that the point of LOLR intervention is to save institutions, not markets. The reason goes back to the centrality of bank credit, which makes him focus on preserving the key credit relationship between a banker and his clients.

This view of the world begs the question why the central bank can control interest rates, and why it is in a position to act as lender-of-last-resort. As a central banker Goodhart simply knows that it can, but as an academic he recognizes that the question needs an answer. His answer has so far always been the Chartalist answer that the central bank is an arm of the state, from which it inherits the 'power to impart a fiat value on a virtually costless piece of paper' (1975, 11). It is perhaps not a completely satisfactory answer, as we shall have occasion to elaborate below, but it does help to explain why Goodhart has spent so much energy countering the academic advocates of free banking who want to separate money from the state, and it helps as well to explain his skepticism about plans for European monetary union in advance of political union.

Goodhart's position on free banking has developed over time. Initially, so impressed was he by the centrality of the bank credit function that he was willing to contemplate giving up the payments function to a separate payment system operated as a network of collective investment funds transferring variable price shares (as proposed by some of the free bankers). Even leaving the payments system aside, banks would still have a role on account of their credit function, and deposits would still be the natural funding source for that function, so there would still be a role for central banks operating through bank credit (1988). In this respect, it seems fair to say, the extent of bank credit securitization in subsequent years has surprised Goodhart and stimulated him to reconsider his position, as financial deregulation and innovation have reduced the leverage a central bank can exert through bank credit. Now when he writes about the payments system, he insists on 'the need for a Central Bank for the ultimate credibility of a net settlement system' (1995, 346). The urgency with which Goodhart now argues the Chartalist position seems to come from his continuing belief that the central bank still has a lot of leverage if only it will use it. The power of the state to declare what is legal tender represents for him the continuing power of the state to regulate market outcomes.

On monetary union, Goodhart's position has also gone through some development. Twenty-five years ago, he wrote:

> It seems unlikely then that a fixed exchange-rate system can be maintained on any permanent basis until political harmony and social agreement allow the division of burdens within the area and the direction of policy in each major part of the system to be decided by an accepted central *political* process. Once that stage has been reached the next step, to a more efficient single-currency area, eliminating the need for separate currencies, exchange transactions, etc. ..., should be simple (1975, 301).

His point is that, in a single currency system, monetary policy is powerless to buffer regional shocks and one is bound to rely for that purpose on fiscal transfers between regions, which transfers are only possible if the regions are politically and socially unified. Until political and social unification, therefore, it would seem wise to retain the buffering ability of an independent monetary policy in each geographic region.

It is just such wisdom that was ignored in the succeeding decades. In his edited volume on *EMU and ESCB [European System of Central Banks] after Maastricht* (1992), Goodhart sees the new European currency as little more than an expanded Deutschmark, and the new European Central Bank as little more than an expanded Bundesbank (p. 315). Bad enough that the emerging system looks to prevent fiscal adjustment by member states without providing any workable mechanism for fiscal adjustment at the federal level, so that everything depends on the monetary authority. What makes matters worse is that the monetary authority, modeling itself after the Bundesbank, seems determined to focus monetary policy narrowly on price stabilization, which means that nowhere in the system is there any scope for macroeconomic stabilization policy. Even worse than that, it is not even clear that the European Central Bank is prepared to support financial stability by operating as lender-of-last-resort, since it eschews the prudential regulation that goes hand in hand with that function.

Goodhart's concern about the European Monetary Union traces back to the link he draws between state power and monetary stabilization. As he sees things, the move toward monetary union amounts to hobbling state power at the national level without increasing it anywhere else in the system, and the dependable result is likely to be increased instability. Ignoring all the lessons of history, the architects of the new system are apparently placing their trust in market forces, so much so that they cavalierly abandon traditional mechanisms of regulation, both microeconomic and macroeconomic, without embracing any alternative mechanisms.

> Keynes is most assuredly dead. Monetary policy is to be centralised and dedicated to the over-riding primary task of achieving price stability. There is to be little, or no, fiscal stabilisation from the central EC budget...The pressures on national fiscal authorities will be to limit and restrain the response of fiscal deficits to shocks...This will, I fear, cause problems (1992, 297).

METALLISM AND CARTALISM

Goodhart grew up intellectually on the gold standard, but has spent much of his career doing applied monetary analysis of the evolving national money standard system. In this sense, the debate between Metallism and Cartalism has always been with him, in a certain tension between the intellectual habits of his mind and the evidence of his senses. It is that tension that has made him one of the most interesting and insightful monetary economists of his generation, as well as sometimes one of the most difficult to follow. His uncanny ability to see merit in apparently mutually exclusive points of view comes in part, so I suppose, from a lifelong struggle to find an overarching position to resolve the tension in his own thought. In the previous section, it was suggested that the urgency of Goodhart's advocacy for Chartalism can be understood as stemming from his concern about the consequences of the diminished and diminishing power of the state, a tendency caused partly by market forces and partly by political forces within the state itself. That concern explains why he is urging Chartalism now, but it's not why he was urging Chartalism back in 1975. A full understanding of his current view requires abstracting from the current political scene in order to focus more narrowly on the analytical issues at stake.

Looking back to Goodhart's earliest work, it seems clear that study of the gold standard left him with a sense of the importance of distinguishing credit (promises to pay) from money (means of payment). Under the gold standard, gold was the ultimate money. National currencies were convertible promises to pay gold, and national credit structures were built from promises to pay national currency, so everything was ultimately a promise to pay gold. The job of the central bank, narrowly conceived, was to maintain gold convertibility of the national currency, which it did by manipulating bank rate in order to influence the credit superstructure built on top. One effect of successful maintenance of gold parity was a certain internal price stability, not complete stability of course since the value of gold could fluctuate, but certainly no tendency for long-run inflation or deflation. That's how the gold standard worked and, so far as the young Goodhart was concerned, that was how money worked more generally.

The problem was that the collapse of the gold standard, and the exigencies of war and depression finance, left the system with no such ultimate money. Instead, the chain of promises to pay seemed to end with each national currency. Given the breakdown of the international monetary system, national currency appeared to be the ultimate means of payment, not a promise to pay. The job of the wartime central bank was not to maintain gold parity of the currency but rather to maintain currency parity of the war debt by standing ready to purchase whatever debt was not taken up by the market. Even more, state debt hardly seemed to be a genuine promise to pay since what it promised was national currency whose supply the state itself controlled through its control over the central bank. Thus, on the state side of the ledger, there seemed to be no promises to pay, only fiat currency. The concrete experience of war finance ran roughshod over the distinction between credit and money that had seemed so natural in the gold standard period.

The monetary theory that grew up in the aftermath of this experience tended also to blur lines that had formerly been sharp, and to organize analysis on different lines. Money came to be defined not as means of payment but as medium of exchange, a definition that included both bank promises to pay (deposit accounts) and means of payment (currency). The old distinction between credit and money appeared only in weakened form as the (Gurley/Shaw) distinction between inside and outside money. Currency itself was viewed as outside money, which is to say as a kind of paper gold, a fiat currency, *not* a promise to pay some higher order ultimate means of payment.

The tension in Goodhart's thought comes from the conflict between his sense of the naturally hierarchical character of all monetary systems and his observation of the apparently non-hierarchical character of the actual postwar monetary system. We see this tension clearest in his *Money, Information, and Uncertainty* (1975), which can be read as the struggle of a pre-World War I sensibility to come to grips with post-World War II monetary theory. True to his historical training, Goodhart insists in Chapter 1 on the distinction between 'the narrower concept of a means of payment and the broader concept of a medium of exchange' (p. 1, Section A). True to his times, he proceeds to define money in such a way as to include both fiat currency and bank deposits (Section D), thereby muddling the distinction with which he started. In this context, his embrace of Chartalism (in Sections B and C) serves as a bridge between pre-World War I thinking and post-World War II experience. Insisting on the special quality of the state's money (means of payment) allows him to retain something of the older sense of hierarchy (Section B), while recognizing that the pervasive role of the state throughout the system has the effect of flattening the hierarchy (Section C). Here at the beginning, Goodhart's Chartalism serves as a bridging device that allows him to step between the vanished pre-World War I world and the lived experience of his own time.

It was a bridge built originally to help Goodhart communicate from his own shore with an audience largely inhabiting the opposite one. Having built the bridge, however, he proceeded to walk across it and today, 25 years later, the bridge has fallen into disrepair from lack of use. 'Two concepts of money' represents Goodhart's attempt to build it once again, but now from the opposite direction. Today he is the Chartalist building a bridge to the Metallists, not so that he can walk over to them but so that he can lead some of them back over to his own side. That seems to be the intention.

There are some problems with this view of how the current intellectual landscape is organized. Today, war-finance habits of thought are scarce on the ground, to be sure, but that doesn't mean we are all Metallists. Indeed, it's hard to find anyone who traces the value of currency to its metallic backing. If anything we are all Chartalists now, but in a sense broader than that encompassed by the special dictates of war finance or of state-directed economic development, which is to say broader than the classic conception outlined in Knapp's *State Theory of Money* (1905). We are not fiat money Chartalists but rather credit money Chartalists. Today the value of national currency derives in most cases not from the raw power of the State, but from its creditworthiness in commercial terms. National currency is not a fiat currency but a promise to pay.

In an integrated global financial system, the chain of promises to pay does not end with the national currency. At each moment in time, each national currency is instantly convertible into a wide range of financial assets, including other national currencies, and, given a little more time, convertible also into a wide range of goods. In general, the rate of convertibility is not fixed, and this is an important detail, but it should not make us lose sight of the more important fact that today national currencies are commercial currencies. Their (fluctuating) value derives from the calculation of market participants, not the authority of the nation state (and certainly not from any metallic backing).

But if we're all Chartalists now, then why does Goodhart portray himself as practically alone in carrying the Chartalist banner against an overwhelming Metallist multitude? Possibly, and here I am guessing, he recognizes that the emerging modern system looks like being more similar to the pre-WWI gold standard system than the various monetary systems we have had since then. Since that system was Metallist, in the sense that the ultimate money was gold, Goodhart feels justified in classing as Metallists all those who accept the current apparent direction, and especially those who are actively advocating for it. He sees the European Monetary Union as a kind of supranational gold standard, albeit one without even the degree of freedom allowed by the gold points, and one with parities even more irrevocably fixed by the elimination of national units of account (1995, p. 421, fn. 2). This seems a fair characterization, so far as it goes, but is that such a bad thing?

Goodhart worries that the emerging euro standard system will enforce excessive discipline on member states. But certainly he can't be thinking that the euro standard will enforce more discipline than the gold standard, and he himself is on record about the gold standard system emphasizing 'the development of such large-scale, stabilising and equilibrating, short-term, international capital flows, that autonomous domestic expansion was rarely disrupted by monetary or balance of payments disturbances' (1972, 219). Is there any reason to expect less in the modern world? Probably not, and probably Goodhart himself thinks not. His concern is apparently with the increased reliance on capital flows in private markets, and decreased reliance on fiscal transfers through the political system, and that seems to me quite a legitimate concern. I would question however whether the Metallism versus Chartalism frame is very well-suited for bringing that legitimate concern into the forefront.

Taking up the matter that seems closest to Goodhart's central concern, I have to say that it does not seem self-evident to me that the increasing commercial character of state debt and national moneys is a tendency that necessarily marks a weakening of the state. States have always arrogated to themselves the right to designate legal tender, but only financially weak states lacking sufficient tax revenue or access to credit have used monetary issue as a primary means of state finance. Modern states, at least the ones with which Goodhart is mainly concerned, have found that putting their credit on a commercial basis gives them *more*, not less, freedom to pursue their ends. Lest this point be misunderstood, I hasten to add that democratic legitimacy (not budgetary tightness *per se*) appears to be quite the most important guarantor of creditworthiness. What is important in the marketplace is not so much the absolute size of government as the accepted legitimacy of its spending priorities so that taxes can be raised to finance them.

Modern democratic and financially strong states typically treat money issue as the funding source of absolutely last resort, and this is as it should be. Indeed, a main function of the modern central bank (a function of which Goodhart apparently approves) is to keep money issue separate from state finance. Democratic states have gone along with central bank 'independence' because they have come to recognize that the state's credit is a beneficiary of price stability just as much as the private sector's credit. Low inflation risk premia make for low interest rates in commercial markets, for the public and private sector alike.

CONCLUSION

Like Goodhart, Joseph Schumpeter grew up on the gold standard but did his mature work under the national money system. Also like Goodhart, Schumpeter borrowed from Knapp's *State Theory of Money* (1905) to frame his account of the history of monetary economics as, in part, a conversation between Metallism and Cartalism. By Metallism, Schumpeter means 'the *theory* that it is logically essential for money to consist of, or to be "covered" by, some commodity so that the logical source of the exchange value or purchasing power of money is the exchange value or purchasing power of that commodity, considered independently of its monetary role' (Schumpeter 1954, 288). Until the 20th century, so he says, theoretical Metallism of this type was accepted by almost all economists, though there were in all periods some deviants. In accord with the strength of Metallism, analytical advance in economics took place mainly in the area of Real Analysis, and there was very little forward movement in Monetary Analysis. In practical spheres as well, the strength of Metallism tended to stifle advance in money management.

The new century brought shifting focus on all three fronts. Not only did Chartalism begin to enjoy sustained analytical attention, but also monetary analysis rose from a neglected subfield to attain near parity with real analysis, and managed money began to emerge as a viable alternative to laissez faire.

Most of this new discussion took place within the analytical framework of the quantity theory, broadly speaking. In America there was Irving Fisher with his transactions approach, and in Britain Alfred Marshall with his cash balance approach and Ralph Hawtrey with his income approach. The *General Theory* of Keynes (1936) pushed even farther on all three dimensions, and in this respect deserves its status as the paradigmatic accomplishment of its time. The problem was that Keynes, or at any rate his followers, pushed too far.

Generally speaking, Schumpeter saw this shifting focus as a positive development, a chance to pull together developments that had been happening around the margins for centuries, and a chance to consolidate those developments at the center of economics. He was however quite apprehensive about the rapid push for practical implementation in advance of solid analytical progress, and frankly appalled by rejection of hard-won analytical gains of the past. Schumpeter might have been describing himself when he wrote:

> An economist may, for instance, be fully convinced that theoretical metallism is untenable, and yet be a strong practical metallist. Lack of confidence in the authorities or politicians, whose freedom of action is greatly increased by currency systems that do not provide for prompt and unquestioning redemption in gold of all means of payment that do not consist of gold, is quite sufficient to motivate practical metallism in a theoretical cartalist; this does not involve any contradiction. (1954, 289)

Schumpeter worried that his own times were going too far in the shift from Metallism to Cartalism, from Real Analysis to Monetary Analysis, and from laissez faire to managed money.

Today, at the end of the century, intellectual currents are shifting again. Like Schumpeter, Charles Goodhart worries that his own times are shifting too far, but in exactly the opposite direction: from Cartalism to Metallism, from Monetary Analysis to Real Analysis, and from managed money to laissez faire. Schumpeter wrote as a scientist, concerned with preservation of hard-won analytical advance; Goodhart writes as a historian, concerned with preservation of hard lessons of history; both feel keenly the responsibility of defending knowledge against political zealotry. Both feel themselves to be fighting a losing battle against the tide of their times, and that only makes them more determined.

If Schumpeter were alive today, likely he'd be a cautious supporter of the EMU, but not because he favors Metallism, Real Analysis, and laissez faire on analytical grounds. He would, I imagine, see the EMU as quite consistent with the Cartalist spirit of the century. Knapp said that money is the creature of law. What could be more in the Cartalist spirit than a deliberate attempt to establish a new money by law? Schumpeter would however be quite apprehensive about the audacity of such a move, and so would likely look with favor on the manifold restrictions and constraints that have been put in place around it. Schumpeter worried about giving too much freedom of action to untrustworthy political authorities, so he would be happy to see national authorities constrained without corresponding loosening of constraints elsewhere. The point is that Schumpeter, like Goodhart, was a theoretical Cartalist but, unlike Goodhart, a practical Metallist. Their different views on practical policy stem from much the same concept of money, but different concepts of political reality.

This counterfactual encounter of Mr Schumpeter and the EMU may help put the actual encounter of Mr Goodhart and the EMU in context. The counter-factual suggests that maybe different views on the EMU stem not from different fundamental analytical orientations, but rather from different assessments of who can be trusted with what power. Goodhart trusts the old-fashioned nation state and especially its central banking arm, the Bank of England. He doesn't trust the newfangled federal European state and its central banking arm, the European Central Bank. The fact that advocates for the EMU talk the language of Metallism, Real Analysis, and laissez faire only makes Goodhart trust them less. Perhaps he is right not to trust them – he is certainly in a better position to judge than I am. I would only suggest that perhaps they are adopting this language not in the way a scientist would, as a rigidly held conceptual framework to guide scientific analysis, but rather in the way that politicians do, as a more temporary and flexible framework to guide political and social evolution at a particular point in history. It would not be the first time that the boundary between practical and theoretical Metallism has been hard to see. Schumpeter again: 'There is no denying that views on money are as difficult to describe as are shifting clouds' (1954, 289).

REFERENCES

Bagehot, Walter (1873), *Lombard Street: A description of the money market*, New York: Scribner, Armstrong.

Goodhart, Charles A.E. (1969), *The New York Money Market and The Finance of Trade, 1900–1913*, Cambridge, MA: Harvard University Press.

Goodhart, Charles A.E. (1972), *The Business of Banking, 1891–1914*, London: Weidenfeld and Nicolson.

Goodhart, Charles A.E. (1975), *Money, Information and Uncertainty*, London: Macmillan.

Goodhart, Charles A.E. (1984), *Monetary Theory and Practice: The UK Experience*, London: Macmillan.

Goodhart, Charles A.E. (1988), *The Evolution of Central Banks*, Cambridge, MA: MIT Press.

Goodhart, Charles A.E. (ed.) (1992), *EMU and ESCB after Maastricht*, London: Financial Markets Group, London School of Economics.

Goodhart, Charles A.E. (1995), *The Central Bank and the Financial System*, Cambridge, MA: MIT Press.

Goodhart, Charles A.E. (1998), 'The two concepts of money: Implications for the analysis of optimal currency areas', *European Journal of Political Economy*, 14: 407–32.

Knapp, Georg Friedrich (1905), *Staatliche Theorie des Geldes*, Leipzig: Dunker and Humblot; (1928), *State Theory of Money*, abridged English translation of 4th edition, London: Macmillan.

Hawtrey, Ralph G. (1928), *Currency and Credit*, 3rd edn, London: Longmans, Green.

Mundell, Robert A. (1961), 'The theory of optimum currency areas', *American Economic Review*, 51: 657–64.

Schumpeter, Joseph A. (1954), *History of Economics Analysis*, New York: Oxford University Press.

3. The creditary/monetarist debate in historical perspective

Michael Hudson

One way or another, economies are planned. In today's world this usually occurs via the way in which savings are channeled and credit is allocated. The debate over the government's monetary role thus concerns whether elected officials or large financial enterprises are to be in charge of the planning process. At issue is the degree to which financial planning can be permitted to go its own way, independently of government supervision. Behind arguments over the character of money and credit stands this broader controversy over whether banking and finance should be managed by public regulators or left to 'the market', that is, to large global banks and money managers.

Advocates of what Georg Friedrich Knapp called the State Theory of Money (referred to as cartalists in the present set of essays) attribute its value to the government's acceptance of it in payment of taxes or related fees. At the outset of his *State Theory of Money* (1905), Knapp states this basic principle: 'Money is a creature of the law. A theory of money therefore must deal with legal history.' Inasmuch as debt, savings and credit are institutional phenomena, a functional theory must deal with the ways in which savings are channeled to take the form of financial claims on the economy's assets and income. Each economy has its own pattern of channeling credit into the creation of wealth, the build-up of financial claims on existing assets and revenue streams, and the bidding up of asset prices.

Cartalists urge governments to use the finacial dimension of fiscal policy to manage aggregate demand. Within this broad approach, creditary economists urge that credit be steered into the most productive applications, for example to finance real capital formation rather than merely to inflate a stock market and real estate bubble. Monetarists oppose such regulation. Believing that credit functions best when separated from the state, they attribute (and measure) money's value simply to its purchasing power over goods and services, leaving asset prices out of the picture. Their IMF-type austerity policy prescriptions subject wages and commodity prices to debt deflation. But asymmetrically, they tend to favor asset-price inflation, at least when politicians friendly to them are in office. The effect is to polarize economies between income earners and capital-gains beneficiaries.

The history of money has been mobilized to defend each approach. The particular relevance of ancient history lies in the assumption that the first application of any economic practice must represent its natural and inherent function. If it can be shown that money originated in the public sector, the implication is that it is essentially a public phenomenon. But if its use predates intervention by public institutions, then modern attempts to nationalize monetary management seem to be a distortion.

As lawyers or rhetoricians well know, if the facts are not on your side, the preferred tactic is to invent a plausible cover story. Monetarists have created schoolbook exercises to depict neolithic individuals as using money to buy and sell goods and services, and also to make loans. In this view commodity money originated at the hands of such individuals to facilitate their trade and investment by minimizing the transactions cost of doing business. Douglass North (1984), for instance, sees money as having been developed by enterprising merchants seeking a stable measure of value. The designated vehicle was a generally acceptable commodity against which other products exchanged.[1] A corollary is that monetary savings came into being as inventories of virtual commodities (the precious metals) with which to virtually barter for goods and services – or to lend out.

An earlier individualistic view of archaic money along these lines was suggested by Heichelheim (1958), who speculated that the prototypical money took the form of productive capital such as seeds and livestock lent out by well-to-do individuals. If such entrepreneurial objectives were primary, subsequent developments are secondary applications rather than the original and inherent purpose of money.

The individualistic view does not recognize public institutions as playing a positive role. In any event, it is argued, this role arose relatively late. Money based on bank credit resting on the foundation of government debt dates back only to the Bank of England's foundation in 1694. Earlier governments are depicted as interfering with mercantile credit in inefficient ways such as indulging in inflationary monetary policies. An oft-cited intrusion is the debasement of Rome's imperial coinage, foreshadowing the modern world's inflationary monetizing of budget deficits.[2] Governments also are accused of stifling credit by driving lenders out of the market when they restrict the interest rate that can be charged.

In recent years a more historically grounded alternative view of money's early evolution has emerged. A century ago there was a tendency to conflate the introduction of money with that of coinage. A number of monetary historians have attributed the origins of silver coinage in ancient Greece to its role in paying soldiers. A typical practice was for generals to bring minters along on their campaigns to melt down booty from conquered towns to allot among the various ranks of the army, its generals, and the tithe (*dekate*) set aside for the temple to thank the gods for the military victory. In antiquity as today, a major public expense was that of the army, and this monetary means of paying soldiers was in effect a direct form of meeting the public budget through coinage.

In recent years a more historically grounded alternative view of money's early evolution has emerged. Historians of ancient Mesopotamia who deal with cuneiform records – Assyriologists – have found that the monetary role of providing a general unit of account and store of value appears to have been introduced initially in the temples and palaces. This finding supports the cartalist approach by locating the origin of money in the public sector. Thousands of years before coinage was developed, weighed silver was used to keep accounts in Mesopotamia's large public institutions. Under normal conditons the prices administered for internal record-keeping and forward planning were adopted for transactions with the community at large, often by royal decrees of varying effectiveness. The laws of Eshnunna (c. 2000 BC) proclaimed a royal schedule of prices headed by the parity of 1 gur of barley with 1 shekel of silver (also equal to 3 quarts of oil, 6 minas of wool, and so on). The laws of Hammurapi established a similar equivalency of barley and silver. Karl Polanyi has called such systems based on centrally administered prices 'redistributive economies'.

The temples and palaces needed a standard in which to price the flow of rations and raw materials to their labor force (war orphans, widows and other dependents) and workshops. To co-ordinate their account-keeping and forward planning, the Sumerian temples adopted silver as a unit of account. The use of silver and its associated accounting practices by community members outside of these institutions was derivative, and it seems to have started with officials in the royal bureaucracies.

The palaces and temples helped bring market exchange into being, by mediating the production and trade in the major goods marketed – specialized handicrafts, metal working, prestige textiles, raw materials and so forth. And at a time when most production was for self-use, it was mainly transactions within these public institutions that were monetized.

The charging of interest likewise appears to have first developed within the temples, for unlike the case in today's world, the large public institutions were creditors, not debtors. Money served to denominate debts owed to them for the textiles and other products they advanced to merchants to trade for the raw materials needed by southern Mesopotamia, as well as crop payments for the lands they advanced to sharecroppers. From the fourth millennium down through the second millennium BC, long before general taxation came into being (to say nothing of public debts), the large institutions played a major role in the development of debt practices.

The rate of interest was set not by market calculations of profitability, but by ease of calculation in Mesopotamia's calendrically based sexagesimal system of weights and measures. The key measures were divisible by 60, evidently to distribute rations to the dependent labor force for daily use within each standardized 30-day month. The commercial 'silver' rate of interest reflected this system, being set at 1/60th (that is, one shekel per mina) per month, 12/60ths per year. It will be noted that calculation of interest required a monetary measure. Silver was chosen as the monetary commodity, most likely because it was the characteristic contribution to temples.

Mesopotamian rulers recognized the need to maintain standardized monetary weights and measures, and on a broader plane to resolve the problems caused by rural indebtedness. Their approach to managing the debt and payments system was remarkably free of the modern free-market assumption that debts will take care of themselves. There was no idea that self-adjusting mechanisms would lead the economy to accommodate itself automatically to any level of debt. Rulers saw that an overgrowth of debt relative to the ability to pay was a natural tendency as crops often failed, leaving cultivators in danger of forfeiting their crop rights and the land itself to foreclosing creditors. Even in good weather, debts tended to increase beyond the economy's ability to pay.

The experience of Sumer and Babylonia support the Cartalist belief that monetary regulation can be stable over time rather than being inherently disruptive and inevitably being undone by market forces, as monetarists claim to be the case. It is unregulated market relations that appear to be unstable, above all in the sphere of debt relations. What is remarkable is that economic textbooks continue to present individualistic ideas despite the fact that anti-government reconstructions of history fall by the wayside when viewed in the new light of Assyriological studies. To base monetary theorizing on a more empirical documentation of early economic relations, this chapter traces the course of monetary management from Mesopotamia down to the banking controversies of the present century.

My major points are:

1. The monetary use of silver and other metals emerged in the context of the weights and measures developed in the Sumerian temples and palaces as part of their account-keeping and administered prices. Money was a 'public good', used to price rations and other resource flows, to advance handicrafts to merchants, and to consign other activities to managers in the system that F.R. Krauss has called *Palastgeschäfte* (see Renger, 2000).

2. One of the earliest monetary functions was to settle debt balances, starting with those owed to public institutions. Monetary management thus involved debt management. This was linked inherently to fiscal management, as the temples and palaces relied on the income they could

generate themselves rather than taxing their communities. Debts to these institutions included mercantile balances due, and later sharecropping rental obligations owed for the land and other resources that were advanced.

3. The commercial interest rate was set not by market forces but by ease of calculation. The Mesopotamian unit fraction was a shekel (1/60th) per mina per month.

4. Remarkably stable over time, this interest rate did not respond to the market forces that monetarists believe to be inexorable. Also contra monetarist theory, there was no assumption that market adjustment mechanisms would ensure the ability of debtors to pay.

5. There also was no assumption that forfeitures of land rights were efficient. Faced with the problem of how to deal with debts that grew beyond the ability of cultivators to pay, especially in times of crop failure, rulers proclaimed clean slates and restored land to cultivators. This enabled cultivators to resume paying the crop usufruct to the palace rather than to creditors (a large number of whom were royal collectors acting on their own account).

6. In classical antiquity no kings remained to annul debts and restore to debtors the lands they had lost. The Romans narrowed the concept of debt management along lines that today would be called individualistic. They consigned insolvent debtors to bondage, and let a large proportion of society's families be expropriated from access to the land, and hence from the means of subsistence.

7. Landholdings came to be concentrated in the hands of a creditor aristocracy, which used its power to break free of taxation. The ensuing fiscal crisis stripped the economy of money, pushing the Roman Empire into a Dark Age.

8. Bank lending rarely has been associated directly with the production process. In more modern times, banking systems have been founded largely on the basis of national war-debts, starting with the Bank of England. Mercantile credit has financed trade in products already produced, while mortgage lending likewise is collateral-based rather than aimed at bringing new assets into being.

9. In the late 19th century the St. Simonians developed an industrial banking philosophy to steer credit into productive lines to finance new means of production. Deemed 'state socialist', it found its prime expression in the German Reichsbank and other large banks that developed a close relationship with government while building up cross shareholdings in the stocks and bonds of their major clients.

10. Government intervention became most important in the sphere of central banking with regard to foreign exchange rates. In the 1920s, German reparations and Inter-Ally debts focused attention on the incapacity of

debtors to pay their public debts to foreign governments. The international transfer problem was recognized to be distinct from the domestic budgetary problem.

11. Since the 1960s monetarism has emerged as a doctrine opposing government regulation in favor of letting the financial system act as it wishes. To free more revenue to service the debt overhead, it sacrifices economies on the altar of monetary deflation. Claiming that the market adjusts automatically to any given level of debt, monetarism limits the scope of financial theory to regulating the money supply as a means of controlling prices, wages and interest rates. It does not deal with the decoupling of banking from financing tangible direct investment in factories, buildings and other means of production.

12. Denying a positive role for public control of credit, monetarist philosophy sacrifices industry and labor to the economy's *rentier* interests. Instead of steering savings to increase output by promoting direct investment, 'supply-side economics' inflates an asset-price bubble that diverts savings to load down the economy with debt (causing debt deflation), accompanied by asset stripping and downsizing.

To keep this chapter within reasonable bounds I have given end notes for the relevant background support for the above theses in cases where I have covered the material elsewhere.

HOW MONETARIST AND CARTALIST IDEOLOGIES SHAPE THEORIES OF HOW CREDIT SYSTEMS WORK

The Optimal Currency Area theory, recently boosted by granting the 1999 Nobel Economics Prize to Robert Mundell, follows North in viewing the proper role of money as being merely to minimize the transaction costs of doing business, not to play a role in fiscal planning. As Goodhardt (1998: 424) observes, the theory's depiction of economies as spatial/geographic entities rather than political bodies 'was never meant to be a positive explanatory theory, but instead a normative theory of what should be'. It serves as a moral fable intended politically to influence the future, not to explain how the modern world operates, to say nothing of how civilization evolved.

Arguing that money's foundation should be purely commercial and left to the private sector, monetarists advocate a looser confederation that would create money-of-account to serve merely as a measure of value, a denominator. They urge the European Community to make its central bank independent of the democratic process so as to withstand political pressures to use deficit spending to steer the economy. In opposing government activism, they promote the myth that economies are run well under private enterprise but are stifled by public regulation, which is deemed inherently inefficient, while taxes are depicted as an unmitigated burden. No entrepreneurial role of public institutions is recognized, either today or in the past.

This view of history may seem plausible as abstract logic but has little relation to economic reality, except in the sense that George Orwell observed when he wrote that whoever controls perception of the past controls the present, and whoever controls the present controls the future. Economic history and theory are being mobilized politically to shape reality rather than to reflect it.

The Cartalist or 'state' theory deems the essence of money to lie in the sphere of political sovereignty: governments imbue it with value by accepting it in payment of taxes or public fees. It follows that establishment of a regional currency such as the euro is a political act that presupposes a federal parliament to shape the economy by the way in which it collects and spends taxes.

The conflict between monetarists and more institutionally minded economists finds its reflection in Assyriological studies of the ancient Near East. Monetarists view antiquity's development as having occurred along individualistic lines. The German economist Karl Bücher countered this approach a century ago, and his line of criticism was elaborated by the historians and Assyriologists clustered around Karl Polanyi at Columbia University in the 1950s. Since its establishment in 1994 the International Scholars Conference on Ancient Near Eastern Economies (ISCANEE) has continued this tradition.[3]

The Cartalist theory's historical foundation may be strengthened by picking up the record where money and commodity prices are first attested, in southern Mesopotamia (Sumer) in the third millennium BC. The role of money was not yet associated with taxes, to be sure. Independent city-states kept themselves free of taxation as our epoch knows the term.[4] They resisted general taxes as signifying political submission, and hence a loss of freedom.[5] Long before taxes were levied generally on wealth, income or sales, however, public institutions developed money as a measure and store of value. This was particularly the case with regard to long-distance trade and much local exchange, in which Sumer's temples and palaces played a central role as coordinators and as direct producers of handicrafts. They also promoted money's role in settling debts, of which the most important were owed to them for merchandise advanced, user fees, land rent and other charges. It is to these large public institutions that the development of standardized pricing, interest rates and money may be traced.

Knapp's follower Bernard Laum developed a variety of the State Theory of Money in the 1920s. Although he emphasized that the taxing authority is the most important aspect of state power, he believed that this evolved out of tithing as an expression of originally religious sanctification. He proposed that early money in classical Greece and Rome originated as contributions to the temples, above all in the form of food for the communal festivals organized by these institutions. Greek 'spit money' (*oboloi*) and handfuls (*drachmae*) of spits came to serve this role, as did contributions directly in fish and other food-money. In time, Laum theorized, monetary tokens were used as exchange equivalents for the purchase or contribution of such food. [6] This would explain the role played by public oversight of weights and measures, of which money was a logical extension. Religious sanctification of fines would help explain money's role in the law of contracts and modes of foreclosure when debts were not paid.

If gold and silver did not exist, it is hard to imagine people being able to agree so universally on an alternative monetary form. So remarkable a consensus suggests their prototypical sacral function as temple contributions, just as they were used for the sacraments of marriage rings and royal crowns. The role of precious metals as socially acceptable badges of status and success evidently imbued them with a character that prompted traders to adopt them as means of payment.

The temples and palaces are better described as 'public institutions' than as 'the state', set corporately apart from the community rather than controlling it from above. They were endowed with their own land to provide food, and with large herds of sheep to provide wool for their workshops, enabling them to be self-sustaining rather than needing to levy taxes on their communities.

In return, the temples were charged with performing various social welfare functions, including the support of war orphans and widows, as well as crippled and infirm individuals who lacked the strength to support themselves on the land. Most were put to work in the handicraft workshops to weave textiles and make other products. In an epoch when families were basically self-sufficient (making handicrafts for their own self-use), it was the public institutions that produced most specialized high-quality products for market sale. These goods were turned over to 'merchants' belonging to (or at least interfacing with) the temple hierarchy and royal bureaucracy. It was through these individuals that southern Mesopotamia obtained the metals, stone, hardwood and other materials not available in its own rich alluvial soils.

From this commercial function emerged the monetary role of the temples and palaces. By supplying export handicrafts to traders originally in the temple employ, and later land to sharecroppers, the temples acted as early (the earliest?) creditors and *rentiers*.[7]

THE PRE-MARKET ROLE OF MONEY AS A MEANS OF SETTLING DEBTS

A 'stages of development' view of history was put forth in the mid-19th century by the German economists Bruno Hildebrand and Karl Knies, whose ideas were popularized by Wilhelm Roscher and other members of the Historical School. Their idea was that economies evolved from barter to a money stage, culminating in a credit stage. But the actual line of development proceeded in the opposite direction. Archaic debts called for a means of payment in the form of money, as they hardly can be paid without some means of denominating them. Debts also presupposed a system of notation to record them. But the breakdown of the debt and monetary system (along with literacy) led to the barter economy and its shrinkage into self-sufficient estates. This occurred in Rome after its economy polarized and the government, unable to collect taxes from the rich, debased the coinage. The ensuing collapse was not a reversion to primordial barter, but a distress situation that pushed the Roman Empire into the Dark Age.

The linkage between money and debt was forged in the mists of prehistory. Manslaughter and lesser personal injuries seem to have been the first phenomena to be assigned a customary price, and a monetary standard was needed to quantify the magnitude of the obligations to be settled. Goodhardt points to wergeld as a primordial form of debt stemming from personal injury, attested in Ireland's brehon laws, the Saxon laws and other medieval European codes whose compensation schedules called into being various means of denominating and settling debts long before price-making markets developed.

These fines were not market transactions, nor were they determined by supply and demand conditions such as crime rates. In fact, it would be awkward to call their means of settlement 'money', for along with dowries and other 'anthropological'-type payments they consisted of standardized sets of assets such as slave girls or cattle (but rarely consumer 'commodities' or anything as abstract as silver). Such asset groupings tended to be used only for a single designated purpose, not as general purchasing power. Viewed from today's vantage point the definition of money should exclude means of recompense that settled only a single unique type of transaction, and a non-commercial one at that.

What was most important was the idea of payment. The verb 'to pay' originally meant to pacify, to make peace, but as matters evolved, the wergeld and marriage obligations found in the ancient Near East were not ultimately as important as the redistributive exchange found in the large institutions.

Notions of money (and especially coinage) as evolving out of barter as a vehicle to minimize the transaction costs of conducting exchange miss the degree to which trade and the division of labor initially were public phenomena. Sumerian temples performed a role similar to that which anthropologists have long attributed to tribal chieftains – that of mediating exchanges with outsiders. In addition to providing an umbrella institution through which traders could operate, Mesopotamian temples (like the Delphi Temple in Greece) sanctified laws protecting travelling merchants, as well as sponsoring the oath-taking associated with debt and land-transfer agreements. It is on such grounds that

Polanyi criticized monetarist theory for following Adam Smith's ideas of an allegedly universal proclivity to 'truck and barter'.

Most transactions in the third and second millennia BC were viewed as involving debts. When raw materials were provided to a craftsman to make an object, the customer was given a tablet of obligation attesting to the value of the product to be delivered. When temple or palace lands were leased out to sharecroppers, the estimated rental payment was recorded as a debt to be paid. Fees to the palace for water or other services were recorded as debts to be paid on the threshing floor or at some other specified point in time.

The specialization of labor meant that some period of time elapsed between contract and settlement. This led to floating unpaid balances to bridge the gap between the time when resources were provided to the cultivator or craftsman and when the crop was harvested or the handicraft work finished, or between the time when handicrafts were turned over to 'merchant' officials and when they returned with their cargoes of silver and raw materials to repay their backers.

What was needed for money to emerge to settle such obligations were standardized weights and measures, not only for the monetary commodity but also for the products being transferred or scheduled to be delivered. The objective of such measures, rations and other allocation units was to administer the flow of resources through the large institutions. Forward planning was necessary to track their internal flow of resources, and account-keeping to make sure that bureaucrats and others did not take what was not theirs. In addition to assigning prices to the barley rations, oil, wool, copper, tin and other materials flowing through their workshops, Sumer's temples and palaces needed to value the merchandise they consigned to their merchants.

No doubt the production and distribution of each commodity was at first scheduled independently, but a consolidated set of accounts was needed as production and exchange relations became more complex. Any such accounting statement presupposes a common denominator. Barley was one obvious measure because it played a major role in the bread and beer allocated by the large institutions. For traded goods, silver emerged as a standard measure, against which other metals and raw materials were assigned specific price ratios. A dual commercial–agrarian accounting system was consolidated by setting the 'quart' or gur of barley as equal to a shekel-weight of silver. This provided a bimonetary standard (upheld in Hammurapi's laws §51) in which barley could be used to pay silver-denominated debts.

Most of the barley consumed in these institutions was provided by their own landholdings. Under normal conditions the balance was purchased at stable prices from families engaged in sharecropping. Metallic money – especially silver, which functioned as the third-millennium 'money of the world' (to use James Steuart's 18th-century phrase) – developed as an extension of the system of weights and measures. The prices that were assigned aimed at easy calculation in round numbers to provide a set of ready equivalencies, and at stability rather than reflecting shifting supply and demand conditions.

Modern awareness of this proto-market evolution has been discouraged by monetarist ideology claiming that planning is impossible in principle. Viewing public regulation as antithetical to enterprise, this prejudice deems any role of money or credit as part of the planning process to be anomalous. It has been left to Cartalist theory to recognize that in economies whose families were for the most part self-sufficient in essentials, the most important need for money was not to transact exchange but to pay public fees, starting with user fees for water and tools, and for temple services or royal services such as officiating in ceremonies. In time these fees came to include interest charges.

Mesopotamia's public institutions assigned their commercial products, fields and workshops to administrators for fees payable in silver, or barley in the case of sharecropping rents. But these monetary commodities were not yet associated with general taxation. Early temples and palaces were endowed with sufficient land, herds of animals, raw materials and dependent labor to make them self-supporting and, indeed, history's first *rentiers*. What is important to recognize is that money emerged out of these relationships as the common denominator for commercial and land-rental debts, and for calculating interest on them. Early Mesopotamia certainly had markets, in the sense that exchange occurred domestically and over long distances. However, the mode of distribution and pricing did not operate on the supply and demand principles envisioned by monetarist theory. Only in famine conditions did prices rise sharply – for that portion of the crop which passed through the market, mainly from the community's families to the palace. Only gradually was silver used as money in the sense of providing a convenient mode of payment for this kind of exchange.

Along with monetary exchange came crooked weights and measures, attested in Babylonia long before they were denounced in the Old Testament. Temples countered the problem by treating standardized monetary and commercial measures as what today would be termed public goods. Down through medieval Europe, markets and fairs – and money-changing, along with the settlement of mercantile debt balances – were held near temple precincts that provided oversight and sanctions enjoying the respect of buyers and sellers alike.

MONEY, THE CHARGING OF INTEREST AND DEBT MANAGEMENT

The defining characteristic of interest is that it represents a precise fraction, stipulated in advance and accruing with a calendrical regularity. There is no hint of such interest being charged on wergeld-type compensation debts,

marriage debts or other 'anthropological'-type gift exchange. It would be hard
to calculate interest in terms of asset conglomerations comprising slave girls,
cattle and other diverse items as a group. The charging of interest presupposes
a monetary commodity in which payments can be calculated readily as a
uniform fraction of the debt principal. It also requires publicly standardized
and regulated weights and measures, and a public calendar to measure when the
payment of interest falls due. This conjunction of practices is first attested in
Mesopotamia in the third millennium BC.

By presupposing a monetary medium, the charging of interest helped bring
into being a standardized measure of value. In due course, silver functioned as
a common denominator in which to calculate the interest due on mercantile
obligations, as well as prices generally. The earliest interest charges appear to
have been levied on commercial advances. Denominated in silver, sometimes
in gold, copper or tin – all imported commodities in any event and, hence,
involving a temple or palace interface – such charges evidently developed hand
in hand with the emergence of money.

To understand the logic governing how the Mesopotamians set interest rates
(and then dealt with the debt imbalances that emerged), it is important to
recognize that temples and palaces were the epoch's major creditors, and that
the earliest interest rates give every indication of having been developed in
these large institutions. Not only did temples play a major role in organizing the
trade ventures on which interest was charged, but as noted above, these charges
were administered on the basis of ease of calculation reflecting the sexagesimal system of fractions. Based on 60ths, the standard rate of interest was one
shekel (that is, 1/60th) per mina per month, 12 shekels per year – 20 percent in
the decimal system.[8] Rates varied from one region to another, but within
Mesopotamia this core rate remained stable century after century, immune to
the market forces of supply and demand or profit rates that the monetarist anti-
state theory of money claims to be inexorable.

In my reconstruction, mercantile traders received the handicrafts produced
in temple and palace workshops at a stipulated price, to be repaid with interest.
In time, the array of formalities that were needed to establish how the temples
and palaces would share in the commercial gains provided the basis for charging
interest in the agrarian sphere. The reason why rent contracts appear as debt
contracts is that contractual debt formalities had long been in place and were
familiar to Mesopotamian planners. Fees for advancing land, cattle and water
were recorded as debts, and if they were not paid at harvest-time, interest was
calculated at the sharecropping rate. Usually this was a third of the crop,
although there were fairly wide variations, in contrast to the more standardized
20 percent commercial rate for silver loans.

This public-sector nexus of interest charges is not recognized by the anti-
state theory of money. Monetarists depict interest rates as being set by the

debtor's ability to pay out of the usufruct created by using borrowed resources productively, duly qualified for risk (cf. Heichelheim, 1958). This academic approach rarely analyses what happens when the debt burden exceeds the capacity to pay. Bad debts on an economy-wide scale are not supposed to build up in modern equilibrium models. But they always have occurred in economic reality, and are bound to occur when interest rates are determined by 'non-economic' principles such as mere ease of calculation. Problems also inevitably arise when there is no safety valve to release debtors from loans that go bad, as occurs when crops fail or other circumstances that prevent debtors from paying their stipulated obligations.

The question is, who should bear the burden of these bad debts: creditors or debtors? This problem was part and parcel of Mesopotamian monetary, debt and fiscal management.

If interest rates reflected fluctuations in the means to pay, and if the insolvency of rural debtors simply led to their debts being annulled (as occurred when merchants lost their cargoes in transit through no fault of their own), there would be little need for public intervention. But when debts increase by purely mathematical laws regardless of the ability of debtors to pay, some mode of resolution must be developed to prevent economic disorder. Monetarists sidestep this problem by excluding consideration of the debt and payment insta-bilities that were most important in early Mesopotamia.

The rural debt problem had already become serious by the end of the third millennium. When the large institutions leased out lands to sharecroppers, they recorded the anticipated crop yields as debts to be paid at harvest time. In this respect rental obligations were akin to interest payments, as indicated by the word *rentier*. Problems occurred when the crops failed, fields flooded, military hostilities devastated the countryside or cultivators were called away from their land to fight (especially if they were injured, killed or captured). These problems have been part and parcel of rural life throughout history.

Imposing interest charges on the arrears of crop delivery commitments, and on the fees owed to collectors in the royal bureaucracy, quickly increased these debts beyond the ability of many families to pay, as they lived on the margin of subsistence. Forcing them to sell off their cattle, crop rights or other assets pushed them even deeper into debt. In the commercial sphere, merchants ran the danger of losing their cargo at sea or having their overland caravans robbed. Upon taking an oath as to his loss, the merchant's silver-debt to his creditors was annulled. An analogous rural practice is found in Hammurapi's laws (§48; see also §244), which rules that if the storm-god Adad floods a field, the lessor is freed of his crop-debt. But what needed to be dealt with at the society-wide level was how to handle debts when the crops failed on a broad scale, as they tended to do especially in periods of military conflict.

The practice of consigning debtors into bondage probably developed in pre-commercial times. What earlier would have been an extraordinary procedure became more normal in the Old Babylonian period c. 2000–1600 BC. Wives and daughters, sons and family house-slaves were pledged to creditors, and in due course, crop rights on subsistence lands. This undercut the traditional ethic of mutual aid – what today would be called the social safety net – and threatened the viability of city-states to survive militarily, by depriving cultivator-infantry-men of their means of self-support on the land.

Economic order was restored from outside the system, by royal fiat. Having no thought that market forces might produce equilibrium, rulers annulled the overhang of barley debts when these grew too problematic. By announcing that they were serving their local sun gods of justice in proclaiming 'straight order', they claimed religious sanction for limiting the volume of debt to the rural community's ability to pay. It became traditional to proclaim a debt amnesty on the occasion of starting their first full year on the throne (the start of their 'second' year, inasmuch as their reign usually began upon the death or removal of their predecessor at some point during the preceding year).

By leaving commercial 'silver debts' intact, rulers in effect drew the classical distinction between productive and unproductive loans. Productive credit supplies borrowers with resources employed to produce an income able to repay the loan and its interest charges while still leaving something for the debtor. Unproductive loans are consumer loans and tax loans to debtors who cannot make ends meet as it is. To pay off such loans, debtors either must earn income elsewhere (not an easy thing to do in near-subsistence conditions) or relinquish their assets. The first assets to be forfeited or sold were those most needed to maintain economic life on the land: the labor of family members and land-rights to the crop.

Inasmuch as most rural debts were owed to the palace or collectors in the royal bureaucracy, they could be annulled without causing undue economic dislocation. In this way royal debt management (which, under the circum-stances, was also fiscal management) maintained economic viability. Wiping the slate clean of such debts saved the cultivator-army from being deprived of its subsistence lands. These 'restorations of order' also returned to their original families the relatives or slaves pledged to creditors as collateral, and also land and crop-rights they had forfeited for debt arrears.[9] This policy averted debt polarization and foreclosure dynamics of the type that Livy and Plutarch would blame for destroying Roman society in classical antiquity.

No doubt if Milton Friedman had been around to argue the case for Mesopotamia's private creditors, he would have tried to explain to Hammurapi and his fellow rulers that they did not need to cancel debts. If they only would let things alone, matters would adjust themselves to any given level of debt. Governments should stand aside and let local magnates foreclose, on the assumption that their wealth and power signified a superior efficiency to that of small landholders. Higher returns could be obtained in any event by replacing the cultivation of barley with that of cash crops such as dates (or further west, olives) which required less labor. Downsizing thus would seem to be more efficient.

But as far as is known, no proto-monetarist emerged in Bronze Age Mesopotamia to urge rulers to stand aside from debt management and let widespread expropriation occur. Such theorizing would have ignored the social and military problems caused by rural debt. As matters turned out, religion itself played a very different role from that familiar in today's world. Instead of proposing equilibrium theories based on the Lord's invisible hand *à la* Adam Smith, sun gods of justice were depicted as calling for public sanctions against usury, and specifically against unproductive lending. The Jubilee Year of Leviticus 25 used the term *deror* for debt cancellation, cognate to Babylonian *andurarum* employed when rulers of Hammurapi's dynasty and other regions proclaimed clean slates. What changed, to be sure, was the fact that in an epoch when kings had become oppressive, Judaic religion removed from the palace the option to proclaim clean slates, placing the obligation for such policies at the core of the Mosaic covenant.

A hint of where early civilization might have gone if rulers had not proclaimed liberty from debt bondage is provided by what occurred when Rome's aristocracy overthrew its kings. By the time the Republic yielded to the Empire late in the first century BC, a quarter of the population was reduced to bondage. Instead of the privatization of credit policy resulting in equilibrium, society polarized between absentee landlords and landless dependents, pushing Western civilization into the feudal epoch.

According to the monetarist view, what buried Rome was inflation stemming from government spending and adulteration of the coinage, coupled with what Mikhail Rostovtzoff deemed to be over-taxation of the middle class. But what actually led to fiscal and monetary breakdown in every major society from Babylonia through the Roman and Byzantine empires to more modern times was the ability of large property owners to break free of taxes.[10] The Roman treasury was bankrupted by wealthy landowners using their control of the Senate to shift the fiscal burden onto the classes below them. Lacking the means to pay, these classes were driven below the break-even point. As debt deflation drained the economy of money, barter arrangements ensued. Trade collapsed and the economy shrunk into local self-sufficient manor units.

What led to debt deflation was not a popular conviction that wealthy creditors could best run economic affairs. That idea was denied even by the Stoic philosophy to which most well bred Romans adhered as the politically correct ideology of their day. Matters were decided not by economic reasoning but by force of arms. Sparta's kings Agis and Cleomenes were killed by the oligarchy when they set out to cancel the debts of cultivators at the end of the third century BC. A century later matters were sealed when Rome's oligarchy used violence to oppose reforms such as those of the Gracchi brothers late in the second century BC, an episode to which General Pinochet's Chilean coup bears some resemblance.

The aristocracies that overthrew monarchies defended their actions by claiming to protect popular property from arbitrary seizure. The melodramatic story of the rape of Lucretia by the son of Rome's last king played a role analogous to that of Hayek's *The Road to Serfdom* in modern times in opposing state power. But the aristocracies became hubristic in their own right as they took the land by force and by extending loans to strapped cultivators. Without rulers to reverse their foreclosures, oligarchies proceeded to indebt most of society and monopolize the land. The gap between growth in their debt claims and the population's ability to pay ended by disenfranchising much of the citizen-infantry.

Rather than maintaining military power by producing an economic surplus at home, Rome let its internal market be destroyed from within. Driven by its debt deflation and land expropriations, Rome reached outward to conquer foreign territories. Many expropriated cultivators at home found employment as mercenaries as the fiscal character of war was transformed. The Senate used imperial levies of tribute to hire mercenary armies, bringing the entire Mediterranean under the extortionate hand of Roman power. Roman governors and armies paid themselves out of booty seized from the regions they victimized. In the political system, administrative offices were sold to the highest bidder.

Rome did not finance its fiscal deficit by paper credit as could be done under modern banking systems. There was no public debt to be monetized. Rather, private debt drew money out of circulation. As debt deflation dried up the flow of fiscal revenue, the path of least resistance was to debase or 'cry down' the coinage by changing its nominal value. The effect was similar to monetizing the debt.

Between Rome and World War I the major development was the foundation of the Bank of England and subsequent central banks that monetized war debts in the form of loans to the government in exchange for being given a monopoly to create credit-money. The objective was to raise money for governments to defray their military spending, not to fund direct investment in agriculture or industry. In this respect the 'funding system' of public debts via central banks was a pre-industrial policy. But in due course economic writers began to discuss what the best way of shaping the credit system might be.

At issue was whether some forms of credit and monetary systems were preferable to others. Most theorists agreed that credit was most productively extended to private investors. The question was how this should best be done.

19th-CENTURY POLICIES TO CHANNEL SAVINGS INTO INDUSTRIAL LENDING

Neither side in the Cartalist/monetarist debate has spelled out explicitly one of its most important aspects: how should private-sector debt be managed? This question implies the ancillary one of how savings should be channeled. Monetarism has focused almost single-mindedly on the link between the money supply and government debt (seeking to constrain it), while Cartalist and creditary theories view debt financing and credit creation as part of macroeconomic demand management. Both perspectives have major implications for banking and related financial policy.

The preceding pages have traced how interest-bearing debts, money and pricing evolved in the context of a division of labor in the large institutions of Sumer and its neighboring regions. What is striking is how little debt was associated directly with the production process. In my reading, interest-bearing debt appeared initially as trade credit, and mutated into rural usury. Moses Finley has shown how little lending financed direct investment in classical antiquity. Money was advanced to merchants, and also to individuals ranging from poor cultivators to profligate aristocrats, but loans were not made to finance investment in handicraft workshops or other means of production.

Not until the 19th century were attempts made to create an industrial banking policy. In France, St. Simonian industrial philosophy inspired the Periere brothers to found the Credit Mobilier. The idea reached its highest expression in Germany, where the Reichsbank and large private banks developed close linkages with the government and heavy industry. Developing cross-holdings in the stocks of their major customers, these banks undertook much of the planning needed to guide long-term strategic development.

The ensuing debate concerned how governments could best use financial policy to promote industrialization. Although Britain had taken the lead in the Industrial Revolution, banking played little role in funding it. British and Dutch merchant banking extended short-term loans on the basis of collateral such as bills for merchandise shipped ('receivables') and inventories, but did not undertake much long-term lending to finance investment in factories or other direct investment. James Watt and other innovators were obliged to raise investment money from their families and friends rather than from banks. Even today most corporate direct investment is financed out of internally generated earnings, not bank loans. Apart from mortgage lending and auto financing, most bank credit is short-term.

The promise of French and German industrial banking prompted Marx to believe that finance capital would become subordinate to industrial capital. In Part III of his *Theories of Surplus Value* (Moscow 1971: 468) he analysed the tendency of finance capital to grow at compound rates of interest without limit, but then dropped his analysis of this phenomenon on the ground that finance capital, like land rent, was becoming thoroughly subordinated to the dynamics of industrial capital. 'In the course of its evolution, industrial capital must therefore subjugate these forms and transform them into derived or special functions of itself', he wrote optimistically. Although not originally established 'as forms of [industrial capitalism's] own life-process', monetary and banking fortunes would be mobilized to fund economic expansion, just as the land itself was being industrialized into what today is called agribusiness. 'Where capitalist production has developed all its manifold forms and has become the dominant mode of production', Marx concluded, 'interest-bearing capital is dominated by industrial capital, and commercial capital becomes merely a form of industrial capital, derived from the circulation process'. There is no anticipation here of debt dragging down the industrial system.

Nearly all historically minded economists shared this optimistic view of finance capital's subordinate role. The German Historical School and others pointed to the fact that interest rates tended to fall steadily with the progress of civilization; at least, rates had been falling since medieval times. Credit laws were becoming more humanitarian, and the debtors prisons described so graphically by Charles Dickens were being phased out throughout Europe, while more lenient bankruptcy laws were freeing individuals to start afresh with clean slates. Public debts in Europe and North America were on their way to being paid off during the remarkable war-free century 1815–1914. Savers and investors were seeking out heavy transport, industry, mining and real estate to fund, mainly through the bond market. The consensus among economists was that the debt burden would be self-amortizing. Debt problems were curing themselves, by being co-opted into a socially productive credit system.

As matters have turned out, emperors of finance subdued captains of industry. What is striking is how unlikely the prospect of a corrosive and unproductive debt overhead appeared a century ago. When war broke out in 1914, Germany's rapid victories over France and Belgium seemed to reflect the superior efficiency of its financial system. To some observers the Great War appeared as a struggle between rival forms of financial organization to decide not only who would rule Europe, but also whether the continent would have laissez faire or a more state socialist economic system. In 1915, shortly after fighting broke out, the German Christian Socialist priest-politician Friedrich Naumann summarized the continental banking philosophy in *Mitteleuropa*. In England, Prof. H.S. Foxwell drew on Naumann's arguments in two essays published in the *Economic Journal* in September and December 1917 (Vol. 27, pp. 323–27 and 502–15): 'The Nature of the Industrial Struggle' and 'The Financing of Industry and Trade'.

Foxwell quoted with approval Naumann's contention that 'the old individualistic capitalism, of what he calls the English type, is giving way to the new, more impersonal, group form; to the discipline, scientific capitalism he claims as German'. This conclusion followed from Naumann's claim that 'Into everything today there enters less of the lucky spirit of discovery than of patient, educated industry. To put it otherwise, we believe in combined work'. Germany recognized more than any other nation that industrial technology needed long-term financing and government support. In the emerging tripartite integration of industry, banking and government, Foxwell concluded (p. 514), financing was 'undoubtedly the main cause of the success of modern German enterprise'. The nation's bank staffs already included industrial experts who were forging industrial policy into a science. Bankers and government planners were becoming engineers under the new industrial philosophy of how governments should shape credit markets. (In America, Thorstein Veblen voiced much the same theory in *The Engineers and the Price System*.)

The political connections of Germany's bankers gave them a voice in formulating international diplomacy, making 'mixed banking ... the principal instrument in the extension of her foreign trade and political power'. But rather than recognizing the natural confluence of high finance, heavy industry and interventionist government policy, English common law opposed monopolies and other forms of combination as constituting restraints on trade, while Britain's medieval guilds had evolved into labor unions that had embarked on a class war against industrial employers. Germany's historical form of organization was the professional guild developed at the hands of masters, leading to industrial cartels.

Foxwell's articles implied a strategy of capital working with governments to undertake military and diplomatic initiatives promoting commercial expansion. The economic struggle for existence favored growing industrial and financial scale, increasingly associated with government support. The proper task of national banking systems was to finance this symbiosis, for the laws of economic history were leading toward political centralization, national planning and the large-scale financing of heavy industry.

The short-term outlook of English merchant bankers ill suited them for this task. They based their loan decisions on what they could liquidate in the event of loan default, not on the new production and income their lending might create over the longer run. Instead of taking risks, they extended credit mainly against collateral available for seizure: inventories of unsold goods, money due on bills for goods sold to customers but not yet paid for, and real estate.

British bankers paid out most of their earnings as dividends rather than investing in the shares of the companies that their loans supposedly were building up. This short time horizon forced borrowers to remain liquid rather than giving them the leeway to pursue long-term strategies. Foxwell warned that British manufacturers of steel, automotives, capital equipment and other heavy industry were obsolescent largely because the nation's bankers failed to perceive the need to extend long-term credit and promote equity investment to expand industrial production. By contrast, German banks paid out dividends (and expected such dividends from their clients) at only half the rate of British banks, choosing to retain earnings as capital reserves and invest them largely in the stocks of their industrial clients. Viewing these companies as allies rather than merely as customers from whom to make as large a profit as quickly as possible, German bank officials sat on their boards and extended loans to foreign governments on condition that these clients be named the chief suppliers in major public investments.

Although Britain was the home of the Industrial Revolution, little of its manufacturing had been financed by bank credit in its early stages. Most industrial innovators were obliged to raise money privately. England had taken an early lead in stock market promotion by forming Crown corporations such as the East India Company, the Bank of England and the South Sea Company. Despite the collapse of the South Sea Bubble in 1720, the run-up of share prices in these monopolies from 1715 to 1720 established London's stock market as a popular investment vehicle for the Dutch and other foreigners as well as for British investors. But industrial firms were not major stock issuers. The stock market was dominated by railroads, canals and large public utilities. In fact, Britain's stockbrokers were no more up to the task of financing industrial innovation than were its banks, having an equally short-term frame of reference. After earning their commissions on one issue, they moved on to the next without much concern for what happened to the investors who had bought the earlier securities. 'As soon as he has contrived to get his issue quoted at a premium and his underwriters have unloaded at a profit', complained Foxwell, 'his enterprise ceases. "To him", as the Times says, "a successful flotation is of more importance than a sound venture"'.

Much the same was true in the United States. Rejecting the methodical German approach, the Anglo-American spirit found its epitome in Thomas Edison, whose method of invention was hit-and-miss, coupled with a high degree of litigiousness to obtain patent and monopoly rights. America's merchant heroes were individualistic traders and political insiders who often operated on the edge of society's laws to gain their fortunes by stock-market manipulation, railroad politicking for land giveaways, and insurance companies, mining and natural resource extraction.

Neither British nor American banks were technological planners for the future. Their job was to maximize their own short-run advantage, not to create a better and more productive society. Most banks favored large real estate borrowers, along with railroads and public utilities whose income streams could be easily forecast. Manufacturing only obtained significant bank and stock market credit once companies had grown fairly large.

THE MONETARIST ATTACK ON PUBLIC PLANNING

Industrial banking principles imply a distinction between 'real wealth' and 'paper wealth' in the form of loans and securities that represent claims *on* tangible assets. To prevent financial systems from loading economies down with debt without helping create the means to pay, it is necessary to distinguish credit to finance direct investment in new means of production from speculative banking and stock market promotion that merely inflates asset prices. This distinction might well form the basis for a more industrially oriented financial regulation. But like other investors, most banks and stock market investors want to be left alone to make money as quickly as possible. Their opposition to regulation is responsible for some of the most serious blind spots in monetarist economic philosophy.

Prior to the early 1960s most observers viewed the trend of history as leading society to take control of its evolution. Economic thought aimed at refining the ways in which governments might plan their fate. Most countries adopted Keynesian macroeconomic planning to 'fine-tune' their economies. France pursued *planification*, while England nationalized many industries. But what was being 'fine tuned' was GNP. This broad measure drew no distinction between wealth and overhead. During the Vietnam War decade the inflation that ensued as America pursued an economic policy of both 'guns and butter' led to a reaction that sought to limit the authority of government planning generally. So well funded was this anti-state ideology – and so silent the response by social democrats – that it soon achieved censorial power in the world's universities, finance ministries and central banks.

Monetarism achieved its first international victory in Chile in its 1973 military coup. Free-market economists did not endorse the idea of a free market in ideas, to be sure. All economic and social science departments were closed down except for those at the Catholic University, which had established close ties to the University of Chicago. Having blocked dissent, the monetarists let supporters of the military form financial conglomerates that ran deep into debt to buy the nation's public companies, stripping them bare and leaving the economy to be swept by a wave of bankruptcies in 1981–82.

A more politically respectable neo-liberal regime gained office in England behind Margaret Thatcher in 1979, and in 1981 Ronald Reagan brought in his backers to dismantle public oversight in the United States. Deregulation of America's S&L industry led to a real estate bubble and collapse of the Federal Savings and Loan Insurance Corp. (FSLIC), increasing the federal debt by half a trillion dollars on its way to being quadrupled. Reagan's advisors rewrote the nation's racketeering laws to permit takeovers by corporate raiders who repaid their backers by emptying out the bank accounts and pension fund reserves of targeted companies, selling off their divisions, cutting back on R&D and other long-term investment, and downsizing the labor force. The fact that the leading practitioners were sent to prison did not prevent a growing portion of revenue hitherto declared as profits and wages from being earmarked to pay interest on the economy's debt load. The stock market soared as a result of raiders borrowing the money to 'take companies private' and then carving them up to repay their backers.

While environmental deregulation opened the floodgates to abuses that lay the groundwork for future clean-up costs, a parallel phenomenon was occurring in the form of debt pollution as business, personal and mortgage debt levels soared. The issue of high-interest 'junk' bonds to fund corporate takeovers did not fund much new tangible investment. The allocation of savings was deregulated, and savers then were bailed out following problems suffered by the economy when savings were badly channeled. Government intervention and heavy new public borrowing were coming not through regulation, but via the need to clean up the financial bubble spurred by deregulation.

But monetarists only criticized public debt levels. Government spending was to be cut back for programs other than to reimburse savers for the bad loans their banks and S&Ls had made. This 'value-free' financial philosophy meant that social values of the sort supported by Keynesian macroeconomics were to be replaced by government support for financial and real estate speculation. In Britain, monetarist concerns led to constraints being placed on the Public Sector Borrowing Requirement (PSBR) in order to limit the degree to which the public sector could issue bonds or other securities. The intention was to restrict the government's ability to promote full employment by running into debt and thus increasing the tax burden caused by interest payments to bondholders and other creditors.

A political conflict erupted over what most people thought had long been settled: whether economies should be planned by elected representatives in the public interest, or by financial institutions seeking their own gains. One of the factors that re-opened this issue in Britain was the degree to which public enterprise had become dysfunctional. Strong union control of the British Labour Party after World War II helped make that nation one of the world's most socialist (and highly taxed) economies. The Labour Party platform called for managing the economy in the interests of long-term development guided not by pecuniary gain-seeking but by industrial engineering principles as steered by public officials. But instead of financing new direct investment, Britain maintained employment by bureaucratic regulation and by the government itself serving as the employer of last resort.

The financial conditions for industrial modernization were neglected as Labour party planners left financial concerns to the bankers. The Treasury agreed to self-imposed guidelines that limited the public sector's ability to run deficits. Borrowing by government enterprises was counted as part of the deficit rather than as a separate category of 'productive debt' to finance tangible investment (as distinct from consumption or welfare spending). Public enterprise was left without a means to raise new investment funds, especially after the Labour government submitted to IMF austerity planning in 1976. The upshot was that the Treasury denied the nationalized steel industry and other leading public enterprises access to the credit they needed to enable them to modernize and remain competitive in the world economy.

This straitjacket left only one option to enable companies to raise the required funds. They were sold to private buyers, who were free of the Treasury's public borrowing constraints. In this way British privatization reflected not only monetarist narrow-mindedness, but also a loss on the part of socialist planners of the classical distinction between productive and unproductive credit. No politician advocated making an exception to the Public Sector Borrowing Constraint in the case of funding direct investment for public enterprises. And in New Zealand and Australia, local Labour Party policies were even more restrictively monetarist and neo-liberal, leading to stock market and real estate bubbles that seriously disrupted their economies.

What is remarkable is that despite the fact that economic ideology at both ends of the political spectrum had come to ignore the financial logic of industrial development, Britain had developed an alternative. In 1930 the Macmillan Committee, which included Keynes as well as the trade union leader Ernest Bevin, recognized the need for long-term industrial financing. Although Bevin himself did nothing to put the report's recommendations into effect when he became a leading member of the postwar Labour government, an institutional structure was put in place by the Borrowing (Control and Guarantees) Act of 1946. Echoing the Defense Legislation of 1939, the Act's loan guarantees might have promoted industrial credit by enabling banks to lend to small companies for capital purposes. But this 'small print' of the financial law seems never was used, and Mrs Thatcher's Conservatives repealed the Act in 1985.

By this time the Chicago School's anti-government economics had won a public relations coup by capturing the hearts and minds of the Royal Swedish Academy of Sciences. To popularize monetarist views under the seemingly objective banner of science, the Academy awards its annual Economics Prize to academics seeking to strip economics of its historical and institutional dimension. A caricature of economic science is promoted that opposes public taxation and regulation of wealth on technocratic grounds of economic efficiency, whose scope is narrowly construed in a rather asocial manner.[11]

The 1999 Nobel Prize was given to Robert Mundell, largely as an endorsement for his politically narrow version of the euro. His proposal for a limited
currency union reflects the monetarist view of money as being created by private
traders for their own convenience, without any need of intercession (to say
nothing of management) by public institutions. A single currency simply would
save 'menu costs', that is, the inconvenience of prices having to reflect currency
shifts and the transaction fees entailed in making payments from one country
to another within the European Community.[12]

As his colleague Arthur Laffer points out, 'Mundell's impact on the practical
world of real politics can be seen in Reagan's America, in Thatcher's Britain,
in the renaissance of Chile and Argentina, and in Jacob Frankel's monetary
policy in Israel.'[13] Exactly! Awarding him the Economics Prize endorses
monetarist austerity of the sort that has loaded economies down with debt as an
alternative to taxing finance and real estate, while shifting the fiscal burden
onto labor. Mr Laffer adds: 'Many in the profession called him a kook. Today
they call him a Nobel laureate.' One may ask what the difference is, in view of
the fact that the Nobel awards have helped redefine 'economic science' in such
a way as to strip away the social and institutional dimensions needed to guide
governments in regulating economies.

Monetarist policy works through central banks and finance ministries to
restrict regulation of the euro to so narrow a range as to shift economic planning
to the financial sector. By making the Economics Prize a vehicle to counter
social democratic regulation, the Swedish Academy evidently hopes to see
Europe integrated on the basis of finance capital dominating governments, not
the other way around. The preferred model seems to be the looser European
Free Trade Association (EFTA) created by the Nordic countries and England in
the late 1950s as an alternative to the European Community. Little recognition
is given to the virtues possessed by the industrial banking and strong government
activism of continental Europe and postwar Japan. Today's *fin-de-siècle*
cynicism has given up belief in society's ability to steer itself better than can be
done by its wealthiest members at the top of the pyramid increasing the degree
of economic polarization via their control of finance, insurance and real estate.

Dressed up as positivist economics, monetarism is an anti-government
ideology, yet it implies its own form of national planning. Russian government
bureaucrats recently (1999) complained that IMF conditionalities were as
intrusive as was the pre-1990 Communist planning. The difference is that the
IMF program is not an industrial strategy, but favors financial interests at the
expense of labor, industry and the government's fiscal position.

The past half-century has seen an ideological war fought over whether
planning should be done by governments or by financial engineers in the
banking, insurance and stock-brokerage industries, and their representatives in
the central banks and finance ministries. If government agencies do not take

the lead, these financial institutions will fill the decision-making vacuum. It is no exaggeration to say that today's monetarist evangelism represents the most radical proposal to restructure society since antiquity. Never before has there been a call to dismantle government as such. Every social philosophy and religion in history, as well as most political and economic theory has been developed to help guide public regulation to raise living standards and increase human happiness.

Why then should the Economics Prize be viewed as an acceptable badge of science rather than as an ideological attempt to remove global planning from governments and turn it over to financial institutions? Neoclassical economists redefined international economics as a mere exercise in location theory. This excludes the seemingly self-evident 18th-century definition of nations in terms of distinct national policies. Viewing countries abstractly in terms of labor/capital ratios, neoclassical economics assumes that the immobility of labor and capital across national borders will maintain differing ratios. Mundell pointed to the well-known fact that labor and capital are fluid across national boundaries, but avoided the touchy subject of how national policies made economies different from each other.

A trade theory dealing only with the spatial economics of location leaves out of account the laws and institutions that distinguish economies from one another – the broad social scope recognized already in the 1770s by writers such as Josiah Tucker.[14] Monetary and credit systems define nations, and these systems rest on fiscal systems and their related legal framework. Creditary and Cartalist theories acknowledge this linkage, but monetarism does not. Mundell's theorizing implies that there is, in effect, only a single world economy, a view complementary to Margaret Thatcher's statement that 'There is no such thing as society', but only individuals.

There is method to this narrow-mindedness. There will be no difference in social institutions from one nation to another if there is nothing for governments to do but abolish their laws. At this point the world would be duly globalized under the gospel of monetarism, more or less what the MAI calls for.

To promote such a world, monetarists assume that deregulation will work automatically for the best. Turning economics into a set of euphemisms serving the financial sector, the role of theory becomes that of depicting an economic future in which it would seem reasonable to abolish regulatory and tax power. This objective is given a patina of historical rationalization by speculating about how money might have developed somewhere in the universe, but monetarists have little to say about how it actually evolved on earth. Their theorizing is best characterized as a science fiction story about a planet where individuals develop economic relations without finding any need for government, palaces or temples. Such 'virtual reality' is anachronistic with regard to the past, and unhelpful in understanding the present.

The objective of monetarist theory, of course, is to influence the future. Deeming governments inherently incompetent, monetarists seek to gain control of them only to dismantle them, except for their role as guarantors of the financial sector's savings. Bondholders and creditors are to be bailed out from the problems caused by monetarism's neglect of the mathematics of compound interest increasing the debt burden more rapidly than the economy's ability to pay. Money managers and financial institutions ('the market') are to be left alone to shape economies without government regulation ('interference'). Government power is to be countered primarily by freeing wealth-holders ('savers') from taxation. This will reduce public funding, unless governments borrow the money, in which case the resulting deficits and growing public debt will add to the economy's interest charges. The gains of creditors and other *rentiers* are treated as additions to social welfare (GNP), not as a subtrahend achieved at the expense of interest- and rent-payers. It is almost as if credit becomes a veritable factor of production.

But if the creditary position is right, all money today is debt-money, and cannot exist without taxation and a foundation in public debt and monetary management. (The IMF's Special Drawing Rights [SDRs] are convertible into the national debts of its member countries, led by the United States.) The political issue concerns who is to pay the taxes to cover the interest charges on this growing public debt.

THE FUTURE OF THE EURO

Will Europe create a currency on the basis of economic and fiscal consolidation in a federal union as strong as that of the United States of America? The result would be a United States of Europe, a prospect welcomed as little by American geostrategists as it is by Sweden and other Nordic countries. The alternative is for Europe to consolidate itself as a Thatcherite economy run by financial planners.

If euro-money is government debt-money, a political body is needed to provide consent by the taxpayers to decide how to spend the money against which bonds are issued, and whom to tax to pay the interest on these borrowings. That is the principle of 'no taxation without representation'. But as matters stand, the European Parliament is subordinate to national parliaments, and economic policy is limited by the Maastrict Treaty's financial straightjacket limiting the ability of governments to manage their debt and fiscal systems by deficit financing. This poses the danger that the European Community may be as politically and financially neutered in its policy-making ability as EFTA was.

The monetarist belief that a financial system can be created without government control of international payments has a highly political implication: dollarization of the international monetary and debt system will relinquish control to America. At issue is Europe's financial independence, for just as national credit systems are based on government debt, so the global monetary system rests on the foundation of a single nation's debt, that of the US Government. The world's central banks hold their reserves in the form of US Treasury securities, that is, loans extended (not entirely voluntarily) to the US Government. This enables the United States to lower taxes on its own citizens while obliging foreigners to finance the resulting deficits. Europe is threatened with being placed in the position of Japan and much of Asia. If its central bank reserves are not recycled into loans to the US Treasury, the euro will tend to be forced up against the dollar, just as were Europe's exchange rates during America's Vietnam War years and, more recently, Japan's yen was forced up against the dollar.

Never before have economies provided resources to a nation in the way foreign central banks have provided America with a unique affluence since the world went off gold in 1971.[15] Under today's US Treasury bill standard, global financial management has become centralized in the hands of a single national government. For debtor countries outside of the United States, reliance on foreign lending generates payments to US and other foreign financial institutions for creating credit that any nation could create in principle, but not in practice, given today's geopolitical realities. Meanwhile, dollarized borrowings by non-dollar economies run the risk that currency depreciation will sharply increase the domestic-currency costs of servicing foreign debts. This is what happened to Asia and Russia (and to Brazil) after the currency runs of summer 1997 and 1998.

What seems remarkable is that while banking systems based on public debts have had an inflationary bias, especially in times of war or economic depression, international credit now seems to be deflationary, except for the United States. For the European Community to avoid this fate it is necessary for its central bank(s) to keep reserves in a medium other than US Treasury bonds or IMF Special Drawing Rights invested in such securities.

STABILIZING THE ROUBLE

Without the ability to tax or borrow enough to finance public spending, monetary policy is bound to be ineffective. The Cartalist premise accordingly is that the basis for a viable monetary policy must be a sound fiscal policy. Russia's debt crisis illustrates the extent to which modernizing a national credit system needs to go hand in hand with fiscal restructuring. To do this – and to escape from austerity by erecting a credit system on a solid tax base – Russia needs to re-roubalize its economy.

The question is, what backing should exist for such credit? The Duma has discussed basing the rouble on a system of natural resource taxation to collect the rental revenue generated by Russia's fuel and mineral wealth, its public utilities and land. This revenue might be retained within the Russian economy by creating a 'rent-rouble' backed by a rent-tax levied to finance a creditary system aimed at promoting industrial investment and employment.

The monetarist alternative has been to sponsor the privatization of these natural monopolies. Under US/IMF direction their rental revenue is being sent abroad in the form of interest, dividends and capital flight. In 1996, the IMF insisted that Russia remove its capital controls and export taxes on oil and other minerals. This plunged the budget into deficit and shifted the tax burden away from the resource rents sought by global finance capital, onto labor. The effect was to downsize the economy and load it down with domestic and foreign debt. In 1999, Russia re-imposed its export tax on fuels and minerals. This stabilized the federal budget, and also domestic prices and the exchange rate, by saving the rental revenue of land and natural resources from being remitted abroad.

Monetarist regimes tend to run into foreign debt in order to sustain capital flight, while domestic public borrowing saves the financial and real estate interests from taxation. In Russia, the politically well-connected classes have used their power to avoid taxation, and have been backed by the IMF and World Bank in this policy. The government ran into debt essentially so that it would not have to tax the enterprises being privatized to insiders and flipped at a markup to foreign buyers.

After savings were wiped out in the 1991–92 hyperinflation, only foreigners were in a position to buy the public utilities and natural resources being sold off. Rather than taxing the economic rents generated by the fuel and mining companies and other natural monopolies that were privatized, the government burdened industry and labor to such an extent as to push the economy into a state of collapse. As the economy became increasingly dependent on imports, life was sustained largely by foreign borrowing. Under the US Treasury-bill standard in international finance, dollar credits were created, but by America, not Russia. In fact, more US paper currency now circulates in Russia and other countries than in the United States itself. For Russians, interest charges on dollar credits mount up in hard currency, imposing a chronic drain on the balance-of-payments.

Monetarism's pro-creditor deflationary bias deters it from acknowledging that too little money may aggravate under-employment conditions, as David Hume and Josiah Tucker recognized in their discussion of the quantity theory of money in the 1750s and 1760s. The monetarist approach worries only about inflation, which it blames on federal budget deficits rather than on the balance of payments buckling under pressure of foreign debt service and capital flight caused by monetarist policies.

The standard monetarist way to stabilize the balance of payments is to reduce the money supply and raise interest rates to attract foreign loans ('capital inflows') and to sell off public enterprises to foreign investors. Over time, however, such borrowing and asset sales lead to more than offsetting outflows of interest and earnings. High interest rates deter new direct investment at home, making lending and speculation more lucrative.

Monetarist austerity programs also fail to distinguish between productive and unproductive ways of channeling savings. Monetarism rejects such a value judgment in principle, out of fear that it might provide a basis for government regulation. The source of government power is its authority to make, enforce and interpret laws, but monetarists would cut back this regulatory power, as they did under Pinochet after 1973, Thatcher and Reagan after 1980, and Boris Yeltsin after 1991.

Where regulatory agencies survive, they are to be staffed with opponents of regulation who simply will refrain from enforcing existing laws. The effect is to increase government liability to pay for the backwash of debt pollution and the related clean-up costs caused by deregulation (for example in the United States by Danny Wall, placed in charge of deregulating the S&L industry in the early 1980s). This causes crises that are cited as reflecting a need for yet more monetarist policies, and so on ad infinitum as the situation gets worse and worse (except for domestic speculators and foreign investors).

NEEDED: A CREDITARY ECONOMICS

The major use of money in today's world is to pay for stocks and bonds, mortgages and other loans, not goods and services. Each day the value of financial payments passing through the New York Clearing House equals that of nearly an entire year's GNP. Much the same is true in London, Paris, Frankfurt and Tokyo. Yet when monetarists relate the money supply to prices, they only refer to goods and service prices and wage levels, not asset prices for real estate and securities. The upshot is that they miss about 99 percent of what credit is used for.

This blind spot stems from monetarism's focus on the *bête noire* of commodity price inflation and wage inflation, and its antagonism toward government debt financing except for the bailout of savers. By opposing the government's role as planner, regulator, would-be economic stabilizer and employer-of-last-resort, monetarists cast their lot with the large financial institutions against labor and against government responsibility for employment and the uses to which credit is put. Attention is diverted from the financial, insurance and real estate industries to the relatively small fraction of payments that involve the economy's final goods and services. This short-sightedness serves the financial sector by excluding it from the sphere of analytic attention and hence potential regulation. The logic at work is that what is not analysed may not be seen, and what is not seen will run less of a chance of being regulated.

Monetary phenomena are best understood in the context of overall debt relations and the value of collateral that the financial system can monetize. Russian experience demonstrates how such arrangements tend to arise spontaneously. A few years ago the nation imposed austerity by restricting currency and bank credit to what the central bank held in foreign-currency reserves. (Unfortunately, the more dollars the central bank borrowed, the more it provided to politically well connected banks to speculate against the rouble. Little foreign credit got into the domestic money supply to alleviate Russia's depression.) This caused a problem of widespread non-payment, and inter-enterprise debt ballooned.

The Energy Ministry coped with this breakdown by organizing about 1500 enterprises into a clearinghouse co-operative, the Energy Payments Agency. This provided a roundabout way to collect payments for sales of electricity, gas and other energy sold by the Ministry's hydropower plants, coal-powered plants, nuclear power stations and other energy producers to enterprises whose underlying credit-worthiness was sound. First, the Energy Payments Agency created a commission to evaluate their assets. It determined that the companies had attachable assets of 200 billion roubles as of 1997 (equal to about 800 billion roubles in 1999 prices). Based on this potential collateral value, the Energy Ministry provided guarantees for inter-company payments by members of the clearing system, insuring their mutual obligations through a corporately distinct agency.

The system works as follows. Suppose a machinery company consumes electricity, and sells products to an automotive company. The Energy Ministry's electricity and coal companies buy machinery, and pay in energy. The automotive company also buys machinery, and pays in promissory notes backed by its sales of autos to other firms. The machinery company pays its energy bill in the form of IOUs from its automotive customer, and so forth. The resulting financial clearings are organized as a set of multilateral barter deals.

A Cartalist would say that what gives this clearing arrangement its credibility is the ability of members to use their balances to pay their debts to the Energy Ministry. Government sponsorship helps establish the use-value of the credit balances that circulate as means of settling inter-enterprise debts. The agency's certificates of indebtedness resemble the bills of exchange issued by English banks early in the 19th century, except that no interest is charged. (Clearinghouse members are charged an entrance fee of 300 000 roubles, but the clearing agency is not allowed to make a profit. It is only supposed to act as a service agency.)

Despite the fact that clearinghouse balances are used to settle bills (that is, debts) among enterprises, these credit balances are not included in Russia's money supply statistics. Part of the logic at work may be that the bills are only semi-liquid, being transferable among clearinghouse members but not marketable generally, as no viable capital market presently exists and Russia does not have a banking system as such. Indeed, a major intent of the Energy Payments Agency is to avoid having to deal with the Yeltsin regime's pseudo-banks. The ability of members to bypass these banks in settling their mutual bills on each other saved them from suffering losses in the August 1998 meltdown. Had they built up bank balances for this purpose, their deposits would have been wiped out in the general insolvency and fraud that followed in the wake of the capital flight financed by the IMF's dollar loans.

The irony is that what was not included in the money supply (the Energy Payments Agency clearings) served as viable credit, while what monetarists counted – bank deposits and cross-loans to related conglomerate operations by the oligarchs – proved not to be viable. One thus may ask how relevant money supply statistics are, relative to broad credit and flow-of-funds statistics. The moral is that inasmuch as 'money' narrowly defined represents only a small part of the overall credit supply, monetarist theory must give way to a broader, creditary analysis.

The Energy Payments Agency sought to provide more general liquidity to its members by issuing its own notes to investors. Under normal conditions the proper role of government would be to provide legal support for such a credit system. But rather than welcoming the clearinghouse as a healthy arrangement, monetarist advisors threatened it by policies that favor foreign investors. Focusing on foreign-investment and foreign-loan laws, the Yeltsin regime's IMF and US advisors provided a firm legal basis only for dollarized loans and other foreign credit, all but ignoring the creation of a workable body of domestic credit legislation. This asymmetry led the Energy Payments Agency to contemplate going so far as to borrow in dollars from foreign investors as the only available means of providing sound legal protection.

While the IMF helped foreigners extract money from the Russian economy, it did little to organize a credit system that could operate independently of foreigners. The monetarist system promoted international dependency, not autonomy. In conjunction with pressure from the United States to dollarize economies that have been stripped of their domestic assets to pledge as collateral, this policy favored non-Russian over domestic credit creation. It also created a foreign-exchange risk by posing the danger that the rouble's fall against the dollar might vastly increase the economy's debt burden.

Representing mainly US Government initiative, the monetarist system subordinated Russian finance to control not by local officials but those of the United States and the international organizations it controls. This global system threatens to be mediated by the currency and credit policies of a foreign government (that of the United States) operating via an international intermediary (the IMF) and local client oligarchies such as the Yeltsin Family. How ironic an upshot for monetarist ideology that started out ostensibly as anti-governmental!

The fact that most assets in the West are bought on credit provides a similar argument for a broad creditary analysis. About 70 percent of US business loans consist of mortgage financing to purchase the economy's largest asset, real estate. As for the volatile stock market, it is so heavily fueled by credit that the entire stock value of some new Internet companies changes hands a number of times each day. Currency speculation, corporate takeovers and financial arbitrage involve webs of borrowing and lending via the economy's financial institutions.

These creditary phenomena have broad implications for the quantity tautology of money, $MV = PT$. Anything that can be collateralized is potential credit – the gamut of stocks, bonds, mortgage liens and other debt instruments that can be collateralized by the banking system and financial markets. Under the creditary approach, 'M' should be represented by the entire credit supply, and 'P' should signify the price of assets – stock market, bond and real estate prices – as well as commodity prices. 'Q' should refer to the volume of assets (A) as measured by clearinghouse volume, or perhaps a weighted volume of transactions in these assets as compared to the much smaller volume of trade in final goods and services. As prices for the latter are derivative and much smaller in economic importance, they might almost be dropped altogether. In this formulation, Credit × the ever-tautological 'V' = PA, that is, a weighted index number for asset prices multiplied by the volume of transactions 'A'.

The potential volume of credit is determined by the prices of the marketable securities or real property pledged as collateral. This makes the flow of credit essentially a function of asset prices (subject to reserve ratios, and so on), which in turn are determined by the flow of credit. This mutual interaction calls for the analysis of the credit system and the asset prices it supports (or fails to support) to start with the overall flow of funds. The parallelism or 'feedback' between savings and debt is critical to tracking the rate at which prices for real estate, stocks and bonds rise or decline.

This creditary approach makes clear that when governments manage interest rates, they attempt in the first instance to manipulate prices for bonds (and secondarily for stocks and real estate). Through their role as collateral for the credit system, these assets determine the economy's potential credit supply, which in turn determines asset prices. Commodity prices are affected in a more indirect manner.

The way in which savings are recycled will determine whether savings and credit are channeled to bid up prices for land and real estate already in place, inflate prices for financial securities (claims *on* wealth) or finance direct investment in tangible capital formation. Each type of financial intermediary – banks, pension funds, mutual funds, money market funds, insurance companies and so forth – has its own pattern of recycling savings. S&Ls and savings banks channel their deposits into the mortgage market, and most bank loans also are made against real estate. Savings inflows into mutual funds and pension funds are directed mainly into the stock and bond markets, while money-market inflows are invested largely in short-term commercial paper. New tangible investment is financed mainly out of retained corporate earnings, reflecting the degree to which modern credit systems remain decoupled from the direct investment and production process.

One of the major concerns to policymakers should be the shrinking degree to which savings are used to finance production and employment as compared to bidding up real estate and stock market prices. In the 1980s much credit took the form of high-interest 'junk' bonds to finance corporate raiders who reimbursed their backers by emptying the corporate pension fund reserves and selling off divisions, squeezing out more cash flow by paying their business bills more slowly and laying off workers. While monetarists endorsed this 'greed is good' philosophy on the logic that higher payouts signified improved economic efficiency, *ipso facto*, others called for a more responsible public regulation to steer savings along more socially productive lines. Hyman Minsky warned that the economy was becoming like a Ponzi scheme, borrowing new money just to pay interest on its debts.

Borrowing money became easier as inflation was concentrated in the real estate and financial markets rather than in the product and labor markets on which monetarist theory focuses almost uniquely. By 1990 the financial system's distinguishing feature had become the combination of asset-price inflation and debt deflation. As savings were decoupled from financing new production and employment, investment in corporate takeovers (euphemized as mergers and acquisitions) was more likely to lead to downsizing than to new direct investment. Credit was extended to finance transfers of asset ownership (and in the process, to inflate asset prices) without necessarily increasing tangible capital formation. Interest and amortization charges on this credit – the economy's growing debt overhead – were recycled into new lending, inflating the financial bubble even as they deflated the 'real' economy's product and labor markets.

A circular flow was at work that bypassed these labor and product markets altogether. When borrowers (corporate executives financing mergers and acquisitions, raiders, speculators, real estate developers, arbitrage fund managers and so forth) use borrowed funds to acquire properties, they bid up asset prices but, in the process, load real estate and corporate enterprise with debt. A rising share of revenue must be diverted to pay interest. This deflates the 'real' economy, but asset prices nonetheless rise. They rise not because their earnings prospects improve, but because of abundant credit. Mortgage lending fuels a real estate boom even though rental income may stagnate, while the stock market booms and price/earnings ratios rise even though reported earnings are flat. (The greatest stock-market gains recently have been registered for Internet companies running losses rather than reporting profits.) Rising asset prices increase the value of collateral that can be pledged, providing the basis for yet more credit to keep an economy-wide Ponzi scheme going.

As long as borrowers are able to pay their contractual interest and carrying charges out of capital gains on this asset-price inflation, the process seems potentially infinite. It is not necessary to pay this debt service out of current income, as long as the debtor is making sufficient returns in the form of capital gains to increase his credit line. (He may, for instance, keep current on his debts by selling off part of his holdings as they rise in price.) The cycle is maintained as the payment interest and dividend charges are recycled to become a growing source of loanable funds. To the extent that this pattern of recycling holds down interest rates, it supports stock and bond prices (and real estate prices), enabling the financial system to collateralize yet more new lending in an expanding process.

In the past, over-extensions of credit drained money from the financial system, causing crises in which securities were liquidated at falling prices. If borrowers themselves did not bid up the price of credit, the central bank would raise interest rates to stem inflationary pressures. The most important monetary constraint of all was imposed by the fact that the credit pyramid rested on a commodity-money base comprised of gold (and sometimes silver) bullion. But since 1971 this constraint has been removed. Since the 1980s, Federal Reserve policy has come to welcome monetary expansion to the extent that it fuels a financial bubble (making electorates feel rich) but does not spill over into product and labor markets to inflate commodity prices and wages.

Meanwhile, international reserves for the world's central banks are being supplied by growth in US public debt. This makes debt-money the foundation of international credit, and also makes the system highly political in character. Monetarists are uncomfortable at acknowledging this realm of policy interests (at least as long as they are in power), as this leads implicitly into a Cartalist analysis.

Monetarists also have little to say about how capital gains for real estate, stocks and bonds may occur without spurring new tangible investment, and indeed while trends for 'earned income' (wages and profits) actually are falling for most wage-earners. Most seriously, the neoliberal 'value-free' approach favored by monetarists treats any given form of recycling savings as being equal in economic and social value to any other form, as long as the financial returns are the same. Cartalists and creditary economists are more interested in how savings are allocated as between new loans (that is, debt financing), the purchase of existing equities, and new capital formation. This policy concern leads them to focus attention on how to shape the tax and regulatory systems to encourage some forms of investment as being preferable to others, with a view to maximizing growth in employment, output and earned income.

What is ironic is that in the end the debt overhead aggravated by monetarist policies probably will have to be resolved in the way it usually has been: by inflation. This is just what monetarists claim to be fighting against. It will come about because monetarist austerity (debt deflation IMF-style) is needlessly drastic. After the inflationary blow-off or wiping out of debts through widespread bankruptcy or outright cancellation, one may expect monetarism to be replaced by a creditary doctrine that subordinates debt relations to the goal of achieving society's overall economic potential.

The problem is, how much of this potential will be destroyed, human lives shortened and economies stifled in the interim, in a vain attempt to squeeze out more gains for the *rentier* interests supported by monetarism. Their gains have become losses to the rest of the economy. To prevent such losses, one can only hope that the euro's managers will provide leadership by example.

SUMMARY

What is the relevance of ancient history? Does it matter today? Evidently opponents of public regulation believe so, for they have made great efforts to construct scenarios that appear logically consistent as far as they go, but only at the price of excluding consideration of how history actually evolved.

A key role of money throughout history has been to provide a means of settling debts. This monetary function predates market exchange. Indeed, when early exchange, production and rental contracts first developed, in Bronze Age Mesopotamia, they typically took the form of debt agreements. As interest came to be charged on such debts, especially in the agricultural sphere (classical usury), rulers were charged with annulling agrarian and other personal debts when they became overgrown.

One of the stated reasons for awarding the Nobel Prize to North was his unhistorical idea that money was developed not by public institutions, but by individuals to grease the wheels of commerce. The implication is that economies can be run by private enterprise without governments needing to play a role. This was not early antiquity's world-view. Mesopotamian policy was followed by biblical law in recognizing that debt relations, if left alone, tended to polarize economies to the point of instability. Public authority, backed by religion, was needed not only to act against fraudulent and illegal behavior, but also to provide oversight of debt from above the economic system as such.

A study of early monetary and debt history may serve as a mind-expansion exercise to see how wide a range exists for economies to be structured. It also raises a question as to why monetarist theorists have chosen to popularize a hypothetical 'as if' world, speculating about how money, debt and credit might have originated in a kind of parallel universe that stands at odds with the actual historical record. The economic historian can only conclude that monetarist ideology subordinates historical understanding to its political agenda of opposing government activism, privatizing public enterprise and cutting taxes.

Linking their theorizing to the philosophy of economic individualism, monetarists advocate that the monetary base should consist of commercial rather than government credit. Yet their analysis neglects the broad range of marketable financial securities that may be collateralized to create credit. It is the market value of these securities that supports the credit superstructure, not merely bank deposits and reserves invested in government debt.

Urging lower tax rates, monetarists hardly can be expected to attribute the value of money to its use in paying taxes. Reflecting their views, limitations on the range of fiscal policy – in particular on the power to run up a public debt – are written into the rules governing the euro's management. This constraint limits the ability of governments to use deficit financing as a macroeconomic and monetary management tool. However, Europe's central banks are committed to support the value of savings and, hence, the growing volume of loans into which these savings are channeled. In the end, this task may prove to be impossible. It also entails the moral hazard of bailing out savers. America's FSLIC crisis showed how this threatens to increase public debt and taxation in unprecedented ways. In this respect monetarist opposition to government power seems hypocritical. While opposing government regulation in the interests of labor and social welfare, it endorses government taxing power to bail out the financial sector from the consequences of the economic bubble to which monetarism's short-sightedness is contributing.

Financial historians will recognize the relevance of the creditary/monetarist debate to the bullionist controversy in early 19th-century Britain between the Banking (monetarist) School and the Currency (creditary) School. My use of the term 'Cartalist' in this chapter implies a creditary approach to the financial system, encompassing debt management as well as fiscal and commodity-price management. My emphasis is on the financial dynamics at work to determine the flow-of-funds pattern of recycling savings, not merely on the fiat character of monetary management. This vantage point leads naturally to the analysis of who (or what institutions) will control the ability to create credit, who will be the major beneficiaries of this social monopoly, and how the economy's profits and asset-price gains will be used.

ACKNOWLEDGEMENTS

I wish to express my gratitude to Geoffrey Gardiner and Stephen Zarlenga for their helpful comments. My remarks regarding Russia's Energy Payments Agency are based on information provided by its credit analyst Lubov Vasilyeva Surkova and Duma member Vyachislav Zvolinsky at his Duma offices in Moscow on November 3, 1999.

NOTES

1. North, Douglass (1984), 'Transaction costs, institutions, and economic history', *Journal of Institutional and Theoretical Economics*, no. 140. See most notoriously Fritz Heichelheim, *Ancient Economic History, from the Paleolithic Age to the Migrations of the Germanic, Slavic and Arabic Nations* (1958: 54f.).
2. Rather than taxing the wealthy families who traditionally bore the major fiscal burden, Rome struck coins of decreasing commodity-worth when the tax proceeds were insufficient to cover the military costs of empire and related public spending, on bread and circuses. (There was as yet no paper debt-money.) Monetarists argue that this could not have occurred if coinage had been kept out of state hands, but Cartalists reply that it was the oligarchy that created the fiscal crisis by breaking free of taxation. (Most monetarists endorse tax cutting on grounds of economic efficiency.)
3. I survey the literature in 'Karl Bücher's Role in the Evolution of Economic Anthropology', in Jürgen Backhaus (ed.), *Karl Bücher: Theory, History, Anthropology, Non-Market Economies* (Metropolis Verlag 2000), and 'Roscher's Victorian Views on Financial Development', *Journal of Economic Studies*, Vol. 22 (Spring 1995). See especially Karl Polanyi, Conrad M. Arensberg and Harry W. Pearson (eds), *Trade and Market in the Early Empires: Economies in History and Theory* (New York: The Free Press, 1957). The major ISCANEE publications are *Urbanization and Land Ownership in the Ancient Near East*, ed. Michael Hudson and Baruch Levine (Cambridge, MA: Peabody Museum [Harvard] 1999), and *Privatization in the Ancient Near East and Classical Antiquity*, ed. Michael Hudson and Baruch Levine (Cambridge, MA: Peabody Museum 1996). Both volumes deal with debt and monetary issues, and provide a relevant bibliography. The most relevant colloquium for the present discussion is *Debt and Economic Renewal in the Ancient Near East*, ed. Michael Hudson and Mark Van De Mieroop (Bethesda, MD: CDL Press, 2002).
4. In place of general taxes, landowners bore the direct obligation for what is one of the largest fiscal expenses in modern economies: military service, including the equipment and horses for the aristocratic cavalry members. In Athens the largest landholders bore the *leitourgoi* costs of staging of dramatic festivals and outfitting naval triremes or municipal gymnasia. See Michael Hudson, 'Land Taxation in Mesopotamia and Classical Antiquity', in Robert Andelson, ed., *Land-Value Taxation Around the World* (New York: Robert Schalkenbach 1998:17–35).
5. By about 2600 BC, Sumerian military leaders are found demanding tribute from conquered peoples. Leo Oppenheim, *Ancient Mesopotamia* (Chicago 1972) describes the Kassite Babylonian *kudurrus* that freed localities from centralized royal power to levy taxes. Regarding Greek opposition to general taxes see A.M. Andreades, *History of Greek Public Finance* (Cambridge, MA: Harvard University Press, 1933).
6. Bernard Laum, *Heiliges Geld* (Tübingen: J.C.B. Mohr 1924) and 'Geschichte der öffentlichen Finanzwirtschaft im Altertum und Frühmittelalter', in Wilhelm Gerloff and Fritz Neumark, eds, *Handbuch der Finanzwissenschaft*, 2nd edn (Tübingen 1952), pp. 211–35, esp. 216. The

British anthropologist Arthur M. Hocart elaborated the sacral origins of money. See also William H. Desmonde, *Magic, Myth and Money* (New York 1962).

7. Johannes Renger observes ('On Economic Structures in Ancient Mesopotamia', *Orientalia* 18 [1994]: 201) that 'In Sippar during the later part of the Old Babylonian period merchants (*tamkaru*) acted as entrepreneurs receiving wool from the palace for which they had to give silver at a later date. Such transactions are often described as purchase on credit (*vente a credit, Kreditkauf*).' Merchants were early on associated with the temples, and were subordinate to the chief trader. In some cases they received rations, 'certain proof that he was in the service of the community. Moreover, he had the use of a team of donkeys belonging to the temple, no doubt in view of his travels', notes Henri Frankfort (*Kingship and the Gods* [Chicago 1951]: 67). 'The fact that Enlil, the chief god of Nippur, bore the epithet "trader of the wide world", and that his spouse was called "merchant of the world", is an indication of the role of the Babylonian temples in the exchange of goods. When Ur-Nammu, the first king of the Third Dynasty of Ur, attempted to reestablish the former lines of communication after the troubles of the Gutian occupation, "he ordered the commercial navigation and gave the ships sailing to Magan (the present Oman) again into the hand" of Nanna, the chief god of Ur.'

8. I give a full discussion in 'How Interest Rates Were Set, 2500 BC – 1000 AD: *Máš, tokos* and *fænus* as metaphors for interest accruals', *Journal of the Economic and Social History of the Orient* 43 (Spring 2000): 1–24.

9. The most elaborate such proclamation on record is the Edict of Ammisaduqa, translated in James B. Pritchard, *The Ancient Near East*, II (Princeton 1975): 36–41. I briefly review the logic in 'The Economic Roots of the Jubilee', *Bible Review* 15 (Feb. 1999): 26–33, 44, and treat the subject in detail in my forthcoming *Bronze Age Finance, 2500–1200 BC: How Mesopotamian Traditions of Debt Cancellation Shaped Judaism and Christianity*.

10. I trace the dynamics in Robert C. Hunt and Antonio Gilman (eds), *Property in Economic Context* (University Press of America, *Monographs in Economic Anthropology* 14: 1998): 139–69. An earlier and longer version is in 'Land Monopolization, Fiscal Crises and Clean Slate "Jubilee" Proclamations in Antiquity', in Michael Hudson and Kris Feder (eds), *A Philosophy for a Fair Society*: 33–79 (London: Shepherd Walwyn 1995).

11. I provide a general commentary in 'The Use and Abuse of Mathematical Economics', *Journal of Economic Studies* 26 (Spring 2000).

12. See for instance his 1973 article, 'Uncommon Arguments for Common Currencies'.

13. Arthur B. Laffer, 'Economist of the Century', *Wall Street Journal*, Oct. 15, 1999.

14. I trace the changing concept of international economics in my history of theories of *Trade, Development and Foreign Debt* (London: Pluto Press 1992).

15. I trace this development in Chapter 2 of *Global Fracture: The New International Economic Order* (New York: Harper & Row 1977), and trace its roots in *Super Imperialism: The Economic Strategy of American Empire* (New York: Holt Rinehart & Winston 1972).

REFERENCES

Goodhart, Charles (1998), 'The two concepts of money: implications for the analysis of optimal currency areas', *European Journal of Policital Economy*, 14: 407–32.

Knapp, G. (1924 [1905]), *The State Theory of Money*, London: Macmillan, a translation of the fourth German edition.

Renger, Johannes (2000), 'Das Palastgeschäft in der altbabylonischen Zeit', *Interdependency of Institutions and Private Entrepreneurs (proceedings of the second MOS Symposium* (A.C.V.M. Bongenaar, ed.; Istanbul: Nederlands Historisch-Archaeologisch Institute): 153–83.

4. Some limitations of the Chartalist perspective: A comment on 'The two concepts of money'[1]

Eric Helleiner

Why have most nation states sought to maintain their own homogeneous and exclusive currency? As Charles Goodhart notes, Optimum Currency Area theory has limited power to predict the way in which the spatial organization of currencies coincides with the borders of nation states. He suggests that the weakness of the theory stems from its link to 'M theory' which associates the origins of money with private actors' efforts to reduce transaction costs. More accurate, he suggests, is the Chartalist view – 'C theory' – which asserts that the spatial organization of money has much more to do with considerations of political sovereignty which are related to the link between money creation and the fiscal needs of sovereign states.

I have spent the last few years examining the historical origins of the practice of organizing money on a 'one state, one money' basis. Currencies that are homogeneous and exclusive within the territorial borders of a state – what we might call 'territorial currencies' – were created for the first time during the 19th century. As I describe briefly below, a study of their creation certainly endorses the Chartalist view that states have played a central role in the evolution of money. At the same time, however, I argue that this history also highlights how the *reasons* for state intervention in the monetary realm are more complicated than Chartalist theory acknowledges. I highlight three specific limitations of C theory in this respect. First, the fiscal concerns highlighted by C theory were often more closely linked to the kinds of transaction costs issues that M theory highlights than to the issues of money creation that Goodhart highlights. For this reason, I suggest that Goodhart may be drawing too sharp a contrast between C and M theories. Second, C theory neglects the way that concerns over private transaction costs also often drove state policy. The fact that these concerns were frequently linked to broader political goals of state power and national sovereignty provides another reason not to overstate the contrast between 'political' and 'economic/transaction cost' explanations. Finally, the focus in the debate between C and M theory on transaction costs and fiscal motivations ignores altogether two other important reasons why state authorities created territorial currencies in the first place: the desire for macro-economic control, and the goal of bolstering nascent national identities. After explaining these points, I conclude this short chapter by highlighting the importance of these points in understanding the issue with which Goodhart begins his article: European monetary union.

NATION STATES AND THE CREATION OF TERRITORIAL CURRENCIES

The processes that led to the creation of territorial currencies in the 19th century provides important support for Goodhart's view that states have played a major role in the historical evolution of money. As Viviana Zelizer puts it, this new kind of monetary structure resulted only from the 'painstaking and deliberate activities of public authorities'.[2] One such activity involved the removal of foreign coins from domestic circulation. In monetary systems around the world before the 19th century, foreign coins had frequently circulated alongside domestic coins and often made up the bulk of the coinage used within a country. Governments had often sought to prohibit their use, but these efforts had usually been limited and ineffective. Beginning in the 19th century, however, much more elaborate and successful initiatives were undertaken to remove such coins and establish monetary 'sovereignty' in this area. These initiatives were often expensive and time-consuming, involving massive efforts to locate and dispose of foreign coins in circulation across the entire national territory.

During the 19th century, many states also began to bring a greater degree of homogeneity to the money that was issued domestically. Private issues of money – very common before the 19th century – began to be either outlawed or brought under the strict regulation of the state. Much more systematic efforts were made to counteract counterfeiting, a practice that was often very extensive in monetary systems before this. State authorities also undertook elaborate initiatives to improve the quality and homogeneity that they issued. These involved not just the centralization of mints and note-issuing facilities as well as the introduction of a single monetary standard in places where several had previously co-existed. Equally important were the withdrawal of old, worn money on a more regu-larized basis and the application of new industrial technologies to production of coins and notes to create a more uniform high quality.

The construction of territorial currencies through these various state activities took place at quite different speeds in different countries throughout the 19th century. In most countries, it was a gradual process that was spread out over a number of decades. In many countries in Latin America, some parts of Europe

and the British Dominions, it was not in fact completed until the interwar period
of the 20th century. And of course many countries in Africa and Asia were only
able to establish national currencies once they emerged from colonial status in
the years following the Second World War.[3]

Why did it take until the 19th century for states to begin to 'territorialize'
money? A key precondition was the emergence of centralized and powerful
nation states in this era. The centralization of authority which characterized the
new 'nation state' enabled state authorities to assume sole authority over the
issuing and management of money. The consolidation of the domestic monetary
order thus often took place only after dramatic political transformations helped
to consolidate modern centralized nation states, such as the Meiji Restoration
in Japan, the civil war in the US, or the Mexican revolution.

Equally important was the nation state's 'infrastructural' power to directly
penetrate domestic society and influence everyday life.[4] Only once a direct link
between the state and domestic society had been established did state authorities acquire the capability to regulate effectively the forms of money used by
the inhabitants of its territory. The development of nationwide policing
structures in the 19th century, for example, enabled the state to enforce legal
tender laws in a comprehensive fashion for the first time. The expansion of the
state's role in the emerging national economy during the 19th century also gave
it new powers to influence the forms of money they used simply through proclamations concerning which forms of money would be accepted at public offices
and which would not. These proclamations had important results only because
the state's role within the daily economic life of the people it governed was
deepening with the spread of national networks of post offices and railway
stations as well as national military conscription and the emergence of consolidated taxation systems.[5]

The new nation state's infrastructural power also enabled a wider use of
token forms of money – especially subsidiary coins and paper money – which,
in turn, helped to foster the 'territorializing' of currencies during the 19th
century. As Anthony Giddens highlights, the acceptance of token forms of
money on a mass scale was helped along partly by the fact that state authorities now had the ability to regulate the forms of money used by the population
effectively.[6] He also suggests that people's 'trust' in this new kind of money
was strengthened by the emergence of representative government and other
political changes which brought about a closer relationship between state and
domestic society in this era of the new nation state. Token coins and notes
encouraged the creation of territorial currencies partly because they were less
likely to be accepted abroad; their value depended not on their intrinsic metallic
value but on some knowledge of the trustworthiness of the government that
issued them. In addition, with a monetary system based on token forms of
money, state authorities stood a greater chance of being able to create a

monetary system in which all the forms of money issued existed in a fixed relationship to each other over time. Monetary systems that were heavily dependent
on full-bodied coins also often experienced flight of currency and considerable
upheavals when the relative market values of the metals that made up these
coins changed.

THE INTERCONNECTION BETWEEN FISCAL GOALS AND TRANSACTION COSTS ISSUES

The central role of states – or more specifically nation states – in creating territorial currencies beginning during the 19th century gives strength to the
Chartalist theory that Goodhart supports. But it is still necessary to explain *why*
state policymakers chose to use their new power to create this kind of currency
structure during this period. According to Goodhart, a Chartalist perspective
emphasizes that states intervene in the monetary system because of their desire
to control money creation to service their own fiscal needs.[7] Goodhart contrasts
this 'political/fiscal' explanation with M theory's more 'economic' perspective that focuses on the private sector preferences to reduce transaction costs.

To be sure, the growing fiscal needs of states played an important role in
driving the reform of monetary structures during the 19th century. Fiscal
pressures associated with modern warfare encouraged some governments to
unify the issuance of paper money under state control. Important developments
in areas such as the combating of counterfeiting also sometimes emerged during
wartime as states resorted to the large-scale use of token forms of money for
the first time for financial reasons.[8] Fiscal needs associated with costly 'late
development' strategies – subsidies to industry, large public works projects,
and the building of a modern bureaucracy – after the mid-19th century also
played some role in encouraging various monetary reforms that territorialized
money in that era.

But the link between fiscal needs and the territorialization of currency should
not be seen only in the context of the goal of monopolizing money creation.
Equally, if not more important, in many countries were concerns about what we
might call the 'fiscal transaction costs' of modern government. In their
exhaustive history of the fiscal practices of governments, Carolyn Webber and
Aaron Wildavsky note how the 19th century was a period of dramatic fiscal
reforms.[9] Governments began for the first time to centralize their capacity to
collect taxes and spend money in keeping with modern forms of fiscal planning
and budgeting. This more rational and centralized fiscal administration was
capable of mobilizing and distributing resources on a much more efficient and
large-scale basis. For this reason, its creation was seen as crucial – more so

than the control of money creation in many instances – for the financing of modern wars and an expansion of the state's economic activities that took place in this 19th century.

But for this new centralized fiscal machinery to operate smoothly, the transaction costs associated with extracting and deploying resources for the state in a heterogeneous national monetary system needed to be reduced. Different monetary standards that existed in different parts of the territory often greatly complicated tax collection and spending plans on a standardized basis. The motley collection of foreign coins that dominated many domestic monetary systems also greatly complicated the collection and assessment of taxes since these coins each had their own distinct and changing value *vis-à-vis* the official coin. Particularly troublesome was pervasive use among the poor of a variety of poor quality, sometimes privately-issued, low denomination forms of money. The transaction costs involved in assigning a value to, and even in physically collecting, these forms of money for revenue purposes were often enormous.

The creation of a more homogeneous and exclusive national currency was often driven by a desire to overcome these fiscal transaction costs. Indeed, monetary reforms frequently coincided with efforts to introduce modern fiscal administration into the state for this reason. In these instances, the objective of monetary reform was the same as Goodhart and the Chartalists suggest: to augment the extractive power of the state. But the specific goal was not to enhance the capacity for money creation but rather to increase the efficiency of taxation, budgeting and accountancy within the state.

For this reason, it may be wrong to contrast M theory and C theory so sharply. By drawing this contrast, Goodhart implies that only the private sector is concerned enough about transaction costs to consider reducing them through monetary reform. In fact, however, his own discussion highlights briefly how state authorities have often promoted monetary reforms in order to reduce the transaction costs associated with the fiscal administration of government. Many governments throughout history, for example, have encouraged the spread of money in order to enhance their ability to extract and mobilize revenue from the populations they governed.[10] These concerns with fiscal transaction costs played a particularly important role in encouraging state authorities to create modern territorially homogeneous and exclusive currencies during the 19th century.

THE IMPORTANCE OF PRIVATE TRANSACTION COSTS

In addition to calling attention to the importance of 'fiscal transaction costs', the creation of territorial currencies in the 19th century also highlights how M theory's focus on fiscal motivations is too limited an explanation for the evolution of money. Although state authorities were concerned with fiscal objectives, they were also driven to create territorial currencies by other goals.

One such goal was that predicted by M theory: the objective of reducing transaction costs for private economic actors. As noted above, states were prompted to reduce *fiscal* transaction costs as a result of their construction of modern centralized fiscal administrations. The catalyst for their interest in reducing transaction costs for *private economic actors* was a different one: the emergence of industrial capitalism. Industrial capitalism created larger economic spaces on a national scale which were no longer well served by traditional monetary systems. Commercial actors beginning to break out of the localized markets of the pre-industrial age by operating across the new national economic spaces became increasingly frustrated by the heterogeneous currency within the territory of the state. Their protests often played a key role in prompting monetary reforms that contributed to the creation of territorial currencies.

In addition to widening the spatial extension of markets, the emergence of industrial capitalism also incorporated the poor within a monetary economy in a much more extensive fashion than ever before. In this context, the poor began to protest against the often terrible quality and inadequate quantity of 'small change money' of the pre-industrial monetary order. In an age when the masses were recognized as 'national citizens', their protests had considerable influence, and they often acted as an important impetus for monetary reforms ranging from the monopolization of the paper money supply to the creation of a modern token coinage.

But state authorities were not just responding directly to the appeals and protests of these private actors, as M theory might suggest. Just as significant often were top-down initiatives by state authorities to construct a modern industrial economy for reasons of augmenting their nation state's power in global affairs. In many poor countries during the 19th and 20th centuries, the pursuit of 'latecomer' industrialization became a central objective of state policy since industrial economies were seen as synonymous with national power and the preservation of sovereignty in world politics. Policymakers in these countries usually saw the creation of a modern homogeneous currency as a key part of their project to promote industrialization, since it would reduce transaction costs in ways that encouraged private actors to participate in constructing the large-scale markets and more monetized society that were seen to be central to the industrial age. In this way, the 'political sovereignty' objectives of state authorities reinforced the 'transaction costs' objectives of private economic actors. Here, then, we have another reason why the distinction drawn by Goodhart between 'political/sovereignty' and 'economic/transaction costs' objectives may be too sharp.

OTHER OBJECTIVES NEGLECTED BY BOTH M AND C THEORY

In addition to the transaction cost and fiscal issues highlighted by C and M theory, there are two additional reasons why state authorities were interested in territorializing money during the 19th century. The first was their desire to gain a degree of national macroeconomic control. This goal became especially prominent as money came to permeate all levels of economic life in the industrial age and as token forms of money – especially subsidiary coinage, bank notes and bank deposits – proliferated. During the era of the gold standard, policymakers were most concerned with the macroeconomic goal of maintaining the external convertibility of their currency. The monopolization of the note issue and coin, for example, was frequently driven by the desire to control the supply of these forms of money in order to ensure that they conformed to the requirements of the gold standard. Indeed, it was not just domestic policymakers who had this objective. So too did external figures concerned with the maintenance of stable exchange rates and the smooth functioning of the international gold standard. For this reason, in the pre-1914 period and the 1920s, private economic actors and policymakers from leading commercial and financial powers strongly encouraged the establishment of modern central banks with a monopoly note issue and control of the supply of subsidiary coin in more peripheral regions.

Although the objective of macroeconomic control was thus an important one in driving monetary reform in the era of the gold standard, it was also a relatively limited objective in that period. Economic liberals who then dominated policymaking simply sought to ensure that the new token forms of money would be managed in a fashion that closely resembled the automatic market principles by which commodity money had been regulated. Many critics of this liberal approach during the 19th century, however, saw the broader potential of national currencies to serve 'popular sovereignty'. They envisioned a country in which token money was actively managed by the state with the more inward-looking objective of promoting domestic growth or reducing unemployment. This vision came to fruition on a large scale initially during the 1930s when industrial capitalism appeared close to collapse and then in a more systematic way after World War II with the triumph of Keynesian economics. And this goal became a central concern of the newly independent countries after World War II who sought to create national currencies. In these countries, money was to serve the national objectives of promoting rapid industrial growth and economic development, and for this to happen, a territorial currency was seen as a requirement.

In addition to these macroeconomic objectives, the creation of territorially homogeneous and exclusive national currencies in the 19th and 20th centuries has also been driven by the goal of bolstering national identities. Although money is rarely seen as a cultural object by economists (and many political economists), nationalist policymakers in the last two centuries have certainly seen it in this way. In a period when money increasingly penetrated across social relations at all levels of society, they recognized that a homogeneous national currency could act as an important carrier of nationalist imagery aimed at constructing a sense of collective tradition and memory. Being 'among the most mass-produced objects in the world',[11] national coins and notes had a communicative potential that was at least as extensive as literary or journalistic representations. Policymakers inspired by nationalist thinking took full advantage of advances in printing technology in this same period to provide detailed imagery of their vision of the nation on their coins and notes. These images, it was believed, would act as an everyday reminder to citizens that they were members of a larger community which nationalists tried to characterize as shared and homogeneous.

But the cultural movitation for creating homogeneous national currencies as a tool to strengthen national identities did not stop there. By reducing transaction costs within the nation, a common homogeneous national currency was seen by some nationalists policymakers to be similar to a national language; it would bring members of the nation together by facilitating 'communication' among them. As tools for national macroeconomic management, national currencies were also linked to the sense of 'popular sovereignty' that was crucial to the new nationalist sense of collective identity. Similarly, policymakers hoped that the feeling of being a member in a community of shared fate would be bolstered as citizens of the nation came to experience monetary events collectively through the use of common national currency. Because trust plays such a large role in the use and acceptance of modern forms of money, national currencies were also seen as something that might encourage identification with the nation state at a deeper psychological level. If the value of the national currency remained stable over time, trust might be fostered in the national community that issued and managed the money. Finally, the consolidation of money along national lines by the leading economic powers also came to be seen an important 'national model' to emulate. The creation of a central bank with monopoly note issue, or the exclusion of all foreign money from domestic circulation, emerged as symbols for formative nation states, regardless of their more concrete economic purposes.

RELEVANCE FOR UNDERSTANDING EMU

I have argued that a Chartalist perspective provides only a partial explanation of the important monetary revolution that created territorial currencies during the 19th century. Although states did play a central role in promoting this currency transformation, the reasons for their behavior are more complicated that Chartalist theory acknowledges. First, the fiscal motivations highlighted by C theory in fact are often closely linked to the kinds of transaction costs issues that M theory highlights. For this reason, it is important not to draw too sharp a contrast between these two theories. Second, concerns over private transaction costs also often drove state policy. The fact that these concerns were frequently linked to broader political goals of state power and national sovereignty provides another reason not to contrast 'political' explanations too sharply with 'economic/transaction cost' explanations. Finally, the focus in the debate between C and M theory on transaction costs and fiscal motivations blinds the analyst from seeing two other important reasons why state authorities created territorial currencies: the desire for macroeconomic control, and the goal of bolstering nascent national identities.

Recognizing these limitations of Chartalist theory is useful when we turn to address the question with which Goodhart begins his article: why are European countries replacing their national currencies with a supranational form of money? Goodhart is certainly correct to note that OCA theory, with its roots in M theory, provides a poor explanation of the creation of the euro. But his preferred Chartalist alternative with its focus on fiscal motivations does little better. As Goodhart notes, it is difficult to explain EMU on fiscal grounds since the project in fact breaks the link between fiscal authority (which remains primarily national) and monetary creation (which becomces supranational) in ways that will prevent national state authorities from creating money in the future to service their fiscal needs. Indeed, for this reason, Goodhart's endorsement of the Chartalist perspective leads him to a rather pessimistic conclusion about the sustainability of the EMU project.

But the fact that the EMU project has continued to move forward and has considerable political support throughout Europe can instead be seen to highlight the limitations of this Chartalist explanation of monetary change. EMU in fact is being driven forward politically by a mix of different motives, some of which have parallels in the politics which led to the creation of national currencies in the first place. On the fiscal side, for example, what may be more significant than seigniorage concerns are the kinds of fiscal transaction costs issues highlighted above. Just as national policymakers in the 19th century sought to lower transaction costs associated with administering emerging national-scale bureaucracies, their European counterparts today worry about the impact of intra-European exchange rate movements on the operations of the emerging Europe-wide fiscal arrangements. Particularly important are the operations of the Common Agricultural Policy (CAP) which still make up such a large portion of the European Union's budget. In an environment when national currencies have fluctuated dramatically against each other, the functioning of the CAP has been rendered very complicated. A desire to avoid these complications has played a significant role in encouraging European governments to consider ways to eliminate intra-regional exchange rates.[12]

European policymakers have also been driven partly by a desire to reduce transaction costs for private economic actors who are seeking to operate across the European economic space. Just as the industrial revolution encouraged the growth of national-scale markets, recent technological–economic changes have encouraged larger regional and global markets to come to the fore. In Europe, this transformation has led to a disenchantment among many policymakers with the constraints and limitations of national economic spaces, a sentiment that has extended to the national currencies that complement these spaces. By reducing transaction costs associated with region-wide economic activities, the euro has been supported partly because of its link to a broader project to construct a more coherent regional economic space designed to enable firms to become more competitive in the new economic environment. Not surprisingly, the euro has also been actively supported by transnational private interests across Europe for the same reason.[13]

The EMU project has also been driven by the two other objectives discussed above – macroeconomic and cultural – that are unrelated to the transaction cost and fiscal motivations highlighted by C and M theory. On the macroeconomic front, some support for the euro stems from the fact that it will make life more difficult for national policymakers who are committed to 'outdated' Keynesian macroeconomic policies. In some cases, enthusiasm for this objective has come from state officials who themselves became disillusioned with Keynesianism in the context of both the stagflationary experience of the 1970s and the rational expectations revolutions in the discipline of economics in recent years. Also encouraging the abandonment of this kind of monetary policy, however, have been the difficulties of pursuing it in the new environment of globalized financial markets.[14]

On the cultural front, the euro is supported by some people in Europe on the grounds that it may help erode national identities in Europe and foster a more pan-European identity. On the new euro notes and coins, for example, much of the nationalist imagery of the old national notes and coins has been replaced by 'Europeanized' images such as a map of the EU and the stars of the EU flag. They also include images of windows, gateways and bridges which are meant to be both 'symbolic for Europe's architecture heritage' and 'a metaphor for communication among the people of Europe and between Europe and the world' as well as 'symbols of the spirit of openness and cooperation in the EU'.[15] More generally, because of the historical link between national currencies and state sovereignty, the euro is seen by many as a symbol of the commitment of European governments to pooling sovereignty.

In sum, a Chartalist perspective on the evolution of money is certainly correct in identifying states as central agents of change in the monetary system. But *explaining* state behavior in the monetary realm requires much more than a focus on narrow fiscal objectives related to money creation. Territorial currencies were constructed in the 19th century because of a complex mix of motives related to fiscal needs, transaction costs in both the public and private sector, macroeconomic goals and identity formation. Political support for EMU today in Europe seems to stem from a similarly wide-ranging set of motives. This is not to suggest that the particular motives described above provide a complete explanation of contemporary developments in Europe. Nor am I implying that the EMU project will be a success. Rather, my argument is simply that the study of the evolution of money requires a broader perspective on the social significance of money than C theory provides. Indeed, given the limitations in M theory as well, it may be useful to identify more than just these *two* concepts of money. A broader debate on the social significance of money may help us to begin to analyse more fully why the relationship between nation states and currency areas seems to be breaking down in many different contexts in the contemporary period.[16]

NOTES

1. This short chapter is a comment on Charles Goodhart's 'The two concepts of money: Implications for the analysis of optimum currency areas', *European Journal of Political Economy*, 14(1998): 407–43

2. Viviana Zelizer, *The Social Meaning of Money* (New York: Basic Books, 1994), p. 205. The historical analysis in this article draws on my own work published elsewhere, such as 'Historicizing national currencies: Monetary space and the nation-state in North America', *Political Geography* 18(1999): 309–39; *One Nation, One Money: Territorial Currencies and the Nation-State* (ARENA Working Paper no. 17, University of Oslo, 1997); 'National currencies and national identities', *American Behavioral Scientist* 41(1998): 1409–36; co-editor (with Emily Gilbert), *Nation-States and Money: The Past, Present and Future of National Currencies* (London: Routledge, 1999); *The Making of National Money: Territorial Currencies in Historical Perspective* (Ithaca NY: Cornell University Press, 2003).

3. In most regions of Africa and Asia, the construction of territorial currencies was in fact begun during the colonial period. In many cases, however, colonial authorities constructed homogeneous currency zones that spanned several political jurisdictions. When these jurisdictions became independent nation states, the new governments almost always split up these currency unions and created modern territorial currencies. The most striking exception to this pattern involved most of the ex-colonies of France in Africa which maintained the common CFA franc zones of the colonial period.

4. The term 'infrastructural power' comes from Michael Mann, *The Sources of Social Power: Vol.1* (Cambridge: Cambridge University Press, 1986).

5. For these reasons, Chartalist theories, such as that offered by Knapp, which assert that the state is able to determine the money used within a national territory are best seen not as universally accurate but rather as relevant only to the period associated with the emergence of the nation state and its 'infrastructural' powers during the 19th and 20th centuries

6. Anthony Giddens, *The Consequences of Modernity* (Cambridge: Polity, 1990). Goodhart, 'Two Concepts', p. 418, also hints at this point.
7. As Goodhart (pp. 424–5) acknowledges, many supporters of C theory in fact accept this historical analysis, but argue on normative grounds that state intervention was neither necessary nor desirable.
8. The British government's resort to the large-scale use of paper currency to finance spending during the Napoleonic wars forced it to begin to develop mechanisms to prevent widescale counterfeiting of token forms of money. The same was true of the US federal government during the civil war.
9. Carolyn Webber and Aaron Wildavsky, *A History of Taxation and Expenditure in the Western World* (New York: Simon and Schuster, 1986).
10. As Goodhart (p. 416) puts it, 'money reduces the transaction costs of government'.
11. Virginia Hewitt, *Beauty and the Banknote* (London, British Museum Press, 1994), p. 11.
12. In the article being discussed, Goodhart downplays the growth of Europe-wide fiscal functions (Goodhart 1998: 424). Elsewhere, however, his analysis on this point has been more astute; 'The political economy of monetary union' in P. Kenen (ed.), *Understanding Interdependence* (Princeton: Princeton University Press, 1995).
13. See for example J.Frieden and B.Eichengreen (eds), *The Political Economy of European Monetary Integration* (Boulder: Westview, 1994).
14. See for example Kate McNamara, *The Currency of Ideas* (Ithaca: Cornell University Press, 1998).
15. Quotes from the official EU website: http://europa.cu.int/euro/html/rubrique-default5. html?lang=5&rubrique=100. Although the euro coins retain nationalist motifs on one side, the EU has made an effort to cultivate a more cosmopolitan outlook by allowing every coin to circulate across all member states. As the EU website puts it, this will create the possibility that 'a French citizen will be able to buy a hot dog in Berlin using a euro coin carrying the imprint of the King of Spain'.
16. See for example my 'The future of national currencies?', in E. Gilbert and E. Helleiner (eds), *Nation-States and Money* (London: Routledge, 1999).

5.   The neo-Chartalist approach to money

L. Randall Wray

In his interesting and important chapter, Charles Goodhart makes three main contributions. First, he argues that there are two competing approaches to the study of money, with one dominating most research and policy formation to the virtual exclusion of the other. Second, he examines and rejects Mundell's Optimal Currency Area approach, which is based on the dominant approach to money, leading to a criticism of the theoretical basis for European Monetary Union. Finally, he introduces some historical literature on the origins of coins and money that is not familiar to most economists, and that seems to conflict with the dominant approach to money. This chapter will focus primarily on what Goodhart identifies as the neglected 'Cartalist', or 'Chartalist' approach to money, with a brief analysis of the historical evidence and only a passing reference to the critique of Mundell's theory.

THE ORTHODOX, M-FORM, APPROACH

Goodhart calls the orthodox approach the M-form, for Metallist. This is so dominant that it scarcely needs any exposition, however it will be useful to briefly outline its main features in order to contrast them with the 'Chartalist' or C-form theory later. I still think the Metallist approach is best summarized in a quote from Samuelson I like to use.

> Inconvenient as barter obviously is, it represents a great step forward from a state of self-sufficiency in which every man had to be a jack-of-all-trades and master of none... If we were to construct history along hypothetical, logical lines, we should naturally follow the age of barter by the age of commodity money. Historically, a great variety of commodities has served at one time or another as a medium of exchange: ...tobacco, leather and hides, furs, olive oil, beer or spirits, slaves or wives...huge rocks and landmarks, and cigarette butts. The age of commodity money gives way to the age of paper money. ...Finally, along with the age of paper money, there is the age of bank money, or bank checking deposits. (Samuelson, 1973: 274–5)

According to M-form theory, money was invented to facilitate exchange, and that remains the most important thing about money. M-form economists argue that the value of money was initially determined by the value of the coined metal, or later by the backing held against paper money. It is only much later that evil governments came along and duped the public into accepting a fiat money with no backing. This would seem to be a hard thing to explain, thus, as we'll see, it isn't much explained. To economists, Samuelson's position seems obviously true; to anthropologists and historians, it should be hilariously wrong. Unfortunately, from what I've seen, if historians know any economic theory at all, they know M form. Thus, they would dismiss the Samuelson story as too simplistic, but every time I read accounts of money written by historians, it sure seems like they try to interpret the facts to make them loosely fit M-form theory.

In any case, the M-form approach begins with barter, which is replaced by transactions-cost-reducing exchange based on a commodity money. The next step in the orthodox story is to explain how the modern economy, which nowhere uses a precious metal as a medium of exchange, could have emerged. Indeed, all modern societies use as media of exchange items that have almost no value in alternative use. It is thus argued that at some point, the precious metal medium of exchange was deposited for safe-keeping, with evidence of the deposit provided to the depositor. The evidence might take the form of a note indicating the quantity of, say, gold left on deposit. So long as these notes were issued by trustworthy safe-keepers, and so long as the notes could not be easily counterfeited, they could circulate as a medium of exchange. This further reduced transactions costs, as it was much easier to carry notes than gold. (It was also possible to prepare the notes in such a way that they became worthless if they fell into the wrong hands – reducing risks associated with theft of one's gold.) Eventually, the safe-keepers discovered the 'deposit expansion process'. At first they might have occasionally lent gold, holding the IOUs of borrowers and hoping that depositors would not try to redeem their notes for gold until the gold loans were repaid. This could increase the money supply up to a factor of two – all of the notes could be circulating as media of exchange, as well as all the gold borrowed (lent by the safe-keepers). Soon, however, the safe-keepers would have recognized that they could simply lend notes, creating them for use by borrowers while holding IOUs. In this case, the gold could remain within the safe, with a multiple number of notes circulating – both those initially created when depositors stored their gold but also all those created in loans. At this point, we essentially have the characteristics of a modern bank, which recognizes that it is safe to issue deposits to an amount that is, say, ten times its reserves on the expectation that only a small fraction of depositors will try to 'cash-out' deposits, redeeming them for reserves.

Given a relatively stable 'deposit multiplier' (itself a function of the ratio of reserves held against deposits), the supply of deposits will then be determined by the quantity of loans demanded and the quantity of reserves supplied. It is often presumed that governments exert substantial control over this, first by dictating what will be held as reserves, and second by establishing a legally required reserve ratio. While in the distant past, bank reserves consisted of gold, today in virtually all nations, government fiat money (or, base money, or, 'high powered money', HPM) is required as the banking system reserve. This allows the government to obtain seigniorage by issuing fiat money, desired by banks since their own ability to make loans is constrained by the quantity of reserves they can obtain. Thus, in the modern economy, the money supply consists of bank deposits (created as banks make loans) plus the portion of HPM created by government that is not held by banks as reserves. Banks have some influence over the portion of fiat money held by the non-banking public as they can offer to pay interest to induce the public to hold deposits rather than fiat money. However, given preferences of the public, deposit interest rates, and required reserve ratios, the government 'exogenously' controls the money supply through its supply of fiat money to be held as banking system reserves. Thus, most orthodox monetary theory simply begins with the presumption that the money supply is determined by government policy; Friedman's (1969, p. 4) famous declaration that we might as well assume that money is dropped from central bank helicopters is a good, albeit extreme, example.

In 1999, Mundell was awarded the Nobel Prize, largely for his extension of orthodox monetary theory to the international sphere. Several contributions were mentioned in justification for the award, including his contributions to the Mundell–Fleming model, some less important work on dynamic stability, and most importantly for our purposes, his Optimal Currency Area (OCA) theory. (See Royal Swedish Acadamy of Sciences Press Release, 13 October 1999.) This latter work was cited due to its supposed real-world relevance for the development of the European Monetary Union. Briefly, Mundell had recognized that if money developed primarily as a medium of exchange, then there is no reason to suppose that the optimal region within which a particular currency ought to be adopted should coincide with nation states. Instead, an optimal region should be defined as one within which labor is mobile (and several other less important conditions would also hold). If capital were mobile between two regions, but labor were not mobile, then it would be 'optimal' for each region to adopt its own currency. Thus, he provided an example in which it was presumed that the eastern US and eastern Canada formed an 'optimal' region, with highly mobile labor and similar (manufacturing) production characteristics, while the western US and western Canada formed another 'optimal' region with production based on natural resource exploitation. He explained that it is not optimal to have a US dollar and a Canadian dollar, rather, there should be an eastern dollar and a western dollar. When applied to Europe, it was argued that the individual nation states within Europe did not represent Optimal Currency Areas but rather had issued currencies based on arbitrary political boundaries. Hence, formation of the EMU based on a euro could be promoted as an application of Mundell's OCA theory. Certainly, not all orthodox theorists would agree that the EMU is the appropriate OCA; however, what is important for our purposes is the belief that it is not necessary to link a currency with a nation state. In a similar vein, many orthodox economists have applauded the creation of currency boards in (mainly) less developed countries on the argument that abandonment of monetary sovereignty by explicitly tying a nation's (weak) currency to another nation's (strong) currency helps to discipline profligate governments. Again, what is important for our purposes is the orthodox belief that nations are not benefited by monetary sovereignty.

THE NEO-CHARTALIST APPROACH

In this section, we will first examine what Goodhart calls the C-form or Chartalist approach before turning to recent extensions made by Post Keynesians – what might be termed a neo-Chartalist (or nC) approach.

The central idea of the alternative view is that the value of money is based on the power of the issuing authority, and not by any embodied or backing precious metal. Hence, Chartalists give a central role to the state in the evolution and use of money. For the most part, this evolution is not linked to reduction of transactions costs of exchange. Rather, the evolution of money is linked to the needs of the state to increase its power to command resources through monetization of its spending and taxing power. Thus, money and monetary policy are intricately linked to political sovereignty and fiscal authority – a point to which we shall return below when we examine the origins of the first coins in classical Greece.

Unfortunately, Schumpeter has misled generations of economists by equating Chartalism with legal tender laws. Rather, as I'll show below, early Chartalists argued that all that is required is that the state impose a tax payable in the state's own currency. In what follows, I am not arguing that legal tender laws ought to be thrown out, along with the civil law of contracts, trust in our government and democratic election procedures. All of those things are also important in the evolution of money, monetary institutions and monetary contracts, but the critical point is that governments impose fees, fines and taxes to move resources to the government sector, and that for many thousands of years, governments have imposed these liabilities in the form of a monetary liability. Originally, the money liability was always in terms of a unit of account as represented by a certain number of grains of wheat or barley. In fact, all the early money units were weight units for grain – the mina, the shekel, the lira, the pound. Once the state has imposed the tax liability, the taxed population has got to get hold of something the state will accept in payment of taxes. This can be anything the state wishes: it can be clay tablets, hazelwood tallies, iron bars, or precious metal coins. This, in turn, means the state can buy whatever is offered for sale merely by issuing that thing it accepts in payment of taxes. If the state issues a hazelwood tally, with a notch to indicate it is worth 20 pounds, then it will be worth 20 pounds in purchases made by the state so long as the state accepts that same hazelwood stick in payment of taxes at a value of 20 pounds. And that stick will circulate as a medium of exchange at a value of 20 pounds even among those with no tax liability so long as others need it to pay taxes. The matching of those with tallies but no taxes with those who have tax liabilities but no tallies is accomplished by bankers – who have always been the agents of government precisely to accomplish such matching.

The modern post-Keynesian view of money is based on a neo-Chartalist, or state money, approach. The most important early contributor to this approach was Knapp (1924), whose work heavily influenced Keynes. However, a relatively unknown 1913 article by Innes lays out the approach in a clear and concise manner. The most recent precursor to the revival of this approach was Lerner, whose 1947 AER article was titled 'Money as a creature of the state'. This approach leads to very different conclusions regarding the origins and functions of money, the relation between national sovereignty and currency, appropriate monetary policy, and the relations between money and prices. In the remainder of this section we will examine the neo-Chartalist (nC) approach, while in the final section we will conclude with policy implications.

The nC approach begins with the recognition that no matter what might have been the case in the long distant past, the nearly universal situation today is one in which the nation state establishes the unit of account to be used within its boundaries (Lerner, 1947). As Goodhart has persuasively argued, if it were true that money originated as a cost-minimizing medium of exchange it would be difficult to explain why the one nation–one currency rule is so rarely violated today or in the past. The first task of every newly independent nation state has been the creation of its own new currency. When the American Confederacy seceded from the Union, it adopted its own currency; when America revolted, it adopted a new currency loosely based on the Spanish currency; and more recently, as the USSR disintegrated, each new independent state adopted a new currency. The examples are endless. Obviously, this does not in itself demonstrate that each nation must have its own currency (and there are examples, albeit very few, of nations that choose to adopt foreign currencies as their own), nor does it necessarily tell us anything about the origins of money. However, it does tend to focus attention away from money as a medium of exchange and toward money as a unit of account, for it is difficult to see why transactions costs of exchange are nearly uniformly reduced by adoption of a new currency. If anything, one would suppose that a new nation would face increased transactions costs by creating a new currency that markets would have to become accustomed to using. Thus, we are faced with one of two possibilities: either a) nation states are almost universally irrational in choosing a transactions cost increasing sovereign currency, or b) transactions costs of exchange are not a primary consideration in adoption of a money of account.

The nC-based post-Keynesian approach is, rather obviously, largely based on Keynes's beliefs. In the Treatise, Keynes argued 'Money proper in the full sense of the term can only exist in relation to a money of account' (Keynes, 1930, p. 3), hinting that the unit of account must pre-exist use of a medium of exchange (or, at the very least, be created simultaneously). Elsewhere, he went further in arguing 'Now for most important social and economic purposes what matters is the money of account; for it is the money of account which is the subject' (Keynes, 1982, p. 253). According to Keynes, the money of account 'comes into existence along with Debts, which are contracts for deferred payment, and Price-Lists, which are offers of contracts for sale or purchase. Money itself derives its character from its relationship to the Money-of-Account, since the debts and prices must first have been expressed in terms of the latter' (Keynes, 1930, p. 3).

It is difficult for orthodoxy to explain how 'spontaneous consensus' could have emerged to choose some commodity or other for use as a medium of exchange, necessarily prior to its use as unit of account in which prices are denominated. Keynes, following the Chartalists, reversed things and emphasized the role played by the state in first establishing a money of account – or what Ingham (2000) has called 'value in the abstract'. Keynes argued 'Chartalism begins when the State designates the objective standard which shall correspond to the money-of-account' (Keynes, 1930, p. 11). The 'right' to designate the money of account 'is claimed by all modern states and has been so claimed for some four thousand years at least' (Keynes, 1930, p. 4). While Keynes did not go so far as to claim that money originated as a state-designated unit of account, he did emphasize that for 'at least' the past 4000 years, the state has claimed 'the right to determine and declare what thing [money] corresponds to the name [unit of account], and to vary its declaration from time to time' (ibid., p. 4). Thus, it is no coincidence to find that the one nation–one money phenomenon is so ubiquitous around the world today and throughout recorded history.

Just how does a state adopt a unit of account, or 'write the dictionary' as Keynes put it? Some, including Schumpeter (1954) and Davidson (1978), have emphasized legal tender laws – the state issues a currency in terms of a unit of account, then passes laws that require 'acceptation' of that currency in designated (public and private) payments. Knapp, however, doubted that this would be sufficient, arguing that such laws 'merely express a pious hope' (Knapp, 1924, p. 111). In Knapp's view, the state does play a critical role in determining what will serve as the unit of account, for trying to 'deduce' the monetary system 'without the idea of a State' is 'absurd', but the state establishes the money of account when it determines what will be 'accepted at public pay offices', rather than through 'jurisprudence' (Knapp, 1924, pp. vii–viii; 40). Keynes endorsed this view, arguing 'Knapp accepts as "Money" – rightly I think – anything which the State undertakes to accept at its pay-offices, whether or not it is declared legal-tender between its citizens' (Keynes, 1930, pp. 6–7). Later, Abba Lerner explained

> The modern state can make anything it chooses generally acceptable as money. It is true that a simple declaration that such and such is money will not do, even if backed by the most convincing constitutional evidence of the state's absolute sovereignty. But if the state is willing to accept the proposed money in payment of taxes and other obligations to itself the trick is done. Everyone who has obligations to the state will be willing to accept the pieces of paper with which he can settle the obligations, and all other people will be willing to accept these pieces of paper because they know that the taxpayers, etc., will accept them in turn. (Lerner, 1947, p. 313)

Recall that in the orthodox story, market participants 'spontaneously' decide to use some relatively scarce, hence valuable, commodity as a medium of exchange (Dowd, 2000). A few orthodox economists still argue that if only we returned to a gold standard that required full gold backing against paper money, this would provide for a money with stable value. The nC approach insists that money does not derive its value from the commodity from which it is manu-factured (nor from reserves of a commodity held against its issue in the case of a paper money), but rather from the willingness of the state to accept it to retire obligations to the state. As Keynes argued, 'money is the measure of value, but to regard it as having value itself is a relic of the view that the value of money is regulated by the value of the substance of which it is made, and is like confusing a theatre ticket with the performance' (Keynes, 1983, p. 402). A theater ticket has value not because it is manufactured from precious paper but rather because it is accepted as payment for entry to the performance. Adam Smith had long ago recognized that

> A prince, who should enact that a certain proportion of his taxes should be paid in a paper money of a certain kind, might thereby give a certain value to this paper money; even though the term of its final discharge and redemption should depend altogether upon the will of the prince. (Smith, 1937, p. 312)

Echoing Smith, Minsky argued 'the fact that taxes need to be paid gives value to the money of the economy. [T]he need to pay taxes means that people work and produce in order to get that in which taxes can be paid' (Minsky, 1986, p. 231). Goodhart argued that 'the state levies taxes and can insist that these be paid in state-issued money. This ensures that such fiat currency will have some value' (Goodhart, 1989, p. 36). Even the 'Keynesian' Tobin has lately recognized that 'By its willingness to accept a designated asset in settlement of taxes and other obligations, the government makes that asset acceptable to any who have such obligations, and in turn to others who have obligations to them, and so on' (Tobin, 1998, p. 27).

However, perhaps the clearest and fullest expression of the Chartalism that underlies the modern nC approach to money is in the aforementioned, and rather obscure, article by Innes. In contrast to the orthodox preoccupation with precious metal coins, Innes recognized that coins were a very late development and that they remained relatively unimportant even after their invention. Instead, he focused on hazelwood tallies, although the main principle advanced was simply that money is a token of indebtedness, issued by the 'spender' who automatically becomes a 'debtor', and accepted by the 'seller' who automatically becomes a 'creditor'. A tally was simply 'a stick of squared hazel-wood, notched in a certain manner to indicate the amount of the purchase or debt', with the name of the debtor and the date of the transaction written on two opposite sides of the stick (Innes, 1913, p. 394). After notching, the stick was split down the middle in such a way that the notches were cut in half. The split was stopped about an inch from the base, with the longer piece (called the stock, from which our term 'capital stock' derives) retained by the creditor, with the 'stub' (a term still used as in 'ticket stub') held by the debtor. The two pieces of the tally would be matched later (most significantly at the time of settlement) to verify the amount of the debt. Importantly, governments spent by raising a 'tallia divenda' on the exchequer, issuing tallies for payment for goods and services delivered to the court (after 1670, wooden tallies were supplemented by paper 'orders of the exchequer', although tallies were still held in the English House of Commons until 1834) (Davies, 1996). But why on earth would the crown's subjects accept essentially worthless sticks, and later, paper?

> The government by law obliges certain selected persons to become its debtors. This procedure is called levying a tax, and the persons thus forced into the position of debtors to the government must in theory seek out the holders of the tallies or other instrument acknowledging a debt due by the government, and acquire from them the tallies by selling to them some commodity or in doing them some service, in exchange for which they may be induced to part with their tallies. When these are returned to the government Treasury, the taxes are paid. (Innes, 1913, p. 398)

Note that the key is the ability of the crown to impose a debt on its subjects. More generally, Minsky had later recognized that 'bank money', which today takes the form of demand deposits (although for most of bank history, bank money took the form of paper notes) has 'exchange value because a multitude of debtors to banks have outstanding debts that call for the payment of demand deposits to banks. These debtors will work and sell goods or financial instruments to get demand deposits' (Minsky, 1986, p. 231). This focus on debt turns the barter paradigm on its head, for market activity derives from monetary debts as debtors work to obtain the means of debt settlement that is accepted by their creditors.

Exactly how debts became denominated in a generalized money of account will probably never be known with certainty. As Grierson argues,

> Units of value, like units of area, volume, and weight, could only be arrived at with great difficulty, in part because natural units are absent, in part because of the much greater diversity of commodities that had to be measured and the consequent difficulty of finding common standards in terms of which they could reasonably be compared. (Grierson, 1977, p. 18)

However, he insists that 'monetary evaluations were already in existence in what Sir John Hicks has felicitously christened "customary" and "command" pre-market societies' (Grierson, 1977, p. 19). We do know that many of the early monetary units were based on weight units, specifically, on the weight of a specific number of grains of wheat, barley or rice. It is possible that the practice of valuation came out of the elaborate compensation schedules established in tribal society – the wergeld, Cumhal, and Brehon codes. 'The general object of these laws was simple, that of the provision of a tariff of compensations which in any circumstances their compilers liked to envisage would prevent resort to the bloodfeud' (Grierson, 1977, p. 19). (And note that the verb 'to pay' derives from the verb 'to pacify' – indicating the original purpose of the payment of wergeld fines or bridewealth.) These 'tariffs' were 'established in public assemblies, and the common standards were based on objects of some value which a householder might be expected to possess or which he could obtain from his kinsfolk' (ibid.). Note, however, that these schedules did not use, nor did they require, a unit of account since specific payments were required for each type of inflicted injury – and as they were established in public assembly, the required payment would have been widely known.

It is probable that with the development of class society, an upper class or authority attempted to impose (or at least, to share in) fines, fees, tithes, and tribute – essentially 'socializing' the wergeld compensation. It may not be too far from the truth to argue that our monetary system developed out of the criminal justice system, rather than to replace inefficient barter in markets. While we view justice today as the process that forces criminals to 'pay their debt to society', in tribal society, justice meant compensation of victims in order to prevent bloodfeuds from developing. In a very interesting book, Innes (1932) argued that tribal justice was gradually replaced by the modern justice system that was designed to maximize payments to 'pacify' the elite. If correct, standardization of fines, fees, tithes, tribute, and, later, taxes, in terms of a monetary unit of account was accomplished to reduce the transactions costs of enforcement of 'justice' and centralization of collection rather than to replace inefficient barter. Note that even after the development of capitalism, the crown still relied on fines (levied on almost every conceivable activity) for a substantial portion of state revenues (see Madox, 1769). Above we noted the importance of the imposition of a tax debt in generating a demand for the money issued by the state; taxes are of course just a set of specific fines – a 'fine' for owning property, a 'fine' for earning income, or a 'fine' for importing commodities – although no one today thinks of these activities as 'crimes'. While the modern economy has largely separated the state's fiscal system from its criminal justice system, they were closely intertwined until very recently.

The origins of the modern, Chartalist, money (used for the last 4000 years, according to Keynes) might be traced to the levies of the palaces of the great granary empires, eventually standardized in the wheat, or barley, weight units of account to lower 'tax' (or more generally, fee, fine, rent, tithe, tribute and tax) collection costs. It also seems likely that the authority played a role in development of 'private' debts denominated in the unit of account. Apparently temples and palaces acted as neutral witnesses, recorders, and enforcers of debts and transactions between third parties. Indeed, it is often surmised that writing was invented in the temples to keep accounting records of debts and credits, inscribed on clay tablets held in the temples for safe-keeping. Later, 'encased' tablets were developed that could circulate without danger of tampering since the information regarding the debt was inscribed on both the case and on the tablet enclosed. When the debt was paid, the case would be broken to examine the tablet, verifying the terms. In this way, one could retire one's own debt by delivering a third party debt recorded on an encased tablet. These clay tablets were essentially the same as the hazelwood tallies discussed above, with encasement serving the same purpose as the division of the tally into stock and stub.

Why is this important? Recall that the orthodox story begins with barter, which is replaced by market exchanges using some valuable commodity. The nC story begins with debts denominated in a unit of account. The physical representation of these (encased tablets, wooden sticks, paper notes) can circulate among third parties for the purposes of retiring debt. Indeed, the great medieval fairs appear to have begun as a convenient way to bring creditors and debtors together to match tally stock and stub (and to clear bills of exchange – the principal 'private' debt instruments used in 'international' trade within Europe at the time). To sum up: money derives from obligations (fines, fees, tribute, taxes) imposed by authority; this authority then 'spends' by issuing physical representations of its own debts (tallies, notes), demanded by those who are indebted to the authority. Once one is indebted to the crown, one must obtain the means of payment accepted by the crown. One can go directly to the crown, offering goods or services to obtain the crown's tallies – or one can turn to others who have obtained the crown's tallies, by engaging in 'market activity' or by becoming indebted to them. Indeed, 'market activity' follows (and follows from) imposition of obligations to pay fees, fines and taxes in money.

In this view, banks developed not as 'intermediaries' between depositors of gold and borrowers of gold, but rather as intermediaries between the crown and his indebted subjects. Furthermore, as Innes argued, the 'market' is not a place for obtaining desired commodities, but rather the place one earns the means of settling debts. For this reason, money can never be a neutral 'veil' obscuring the real exchanges that are of primary importance, for what is truly important is the money-denominated obligations one must retire. As Ingham (2000) suggests, this leads to the conclusion that a medium of exchange is not at all necessary for operation of a monetary economy. What is needed is a unit of account in which debts are denominated, some means of recording debts (including an oral history, a system of notching sticks, or, after writing was developed, a written record), and an agreed upon means of payment for final settlement. While circulating evidences of debt might be used as media of exchange, they certainly are not necessary to enable an elaborate market system to develop, and it is clear that such evidences of debt can become media of exchange only *after* a money of account is adopted.

How, then, do we explain the apparent use of gold and silver 'commodity money'. First, it must be recognized that development of precious metal coins comes several thousand years after the development of a money of account, clay tablets and other debt instruments, and, indeed, after the development of quite complex domestic and international trade. Even after their invention, coins played a rather minor role – both in terms of the finance of 'government' spending (which, as discussed above took place mainly on the basis of tallies and, later, exchequer notes) and in terms of 'private' spending. We have already mentioned bills of exchange, which sufficed for most long-distance wholesale trade. However, even the smallest retail transactions took place on the basis of credits and debits with, for example, the merchant keeping a running 'tally' of his customers' purchases, with clearing occurring only after several years (McIntosh, 1988). Further, the earliest known coins are thought to have been too valuable for use in retail trade. For example, the earliest electrum (an alloy of silver and gold) coin had a value of about ten sheep. Nor is it likely that precious metal coins would have reduced transactions costs in trade – the typical case until recently was a wide variety of coins issued by kings, feudal lords, barons, ecclesiastics and others. Until recently, these never had a nominal value stamped on them, but, rather, nominal value was announced by proclamation. Given that trade had occurred for many hundreds of years on the basis of highly efficient, cheap, and abundant hazelwood, clay tablets, papyrus and other papers, it seems implausible that coins would have represented any transactions-cost-minimizing advance for retail or wholesale trade.

Indeed, using a precious metal coin whose non-money use is supposed to govern its value as money would have to be a very high cost way to conduct transactions. (And recall that the orthodox story recognizes that paper money replaced precious metal money precisely to reduce such costs – which indicates that introduction of precious metal coins would have been a backward step if wood, paper or clay were already in use.) Instead, it seems probable, as argued by Goodhart, that 'coinage was invented to make a large number of uniform payments of considerable value', and probably 'the purpose of coinage was the payment of mercenaries' (Cook, 1958, p. 257). More specifically, Kraay (1964) argued that coins were minted by government to provide a simple means of paying taxes, issued as the crown paid mercenaries. Previously, Innes had argued that the coins issued by the crown were nothing more than 'tokens of indebtedness with which they made small payments, such as the daily wages of their soldiers and sailors' (Innes, 1913, p. 399). This explains a) the relatively large denomination of the coins, b) why the invention of coinage was at the hands of government rather than of markets, and c) why coins did not have nominal value stamped on them. As tokens, the coins were worth whatever the crown declared them to be worth at government pay offices. Use of precious metal in the coinage made it more difficult to counterfeit them (as metal was scarce and the mines were usually controlled by the crown). This does not mean that the embodied silver or gold determined the value of the coins, for it would make little sense for the crown to issue full-bodied coins. Indeed, we know that kings 'cried down' the coinage from time-to-time, which was a sort of 'debasement' in which the king would simply announce that the nominal value of previously issued coins would henceforth be lower when accepted in payment of taxes. This was a well-recognized form of raising taxes, for instead of delivering one of the king's coins to pay the tax, one might now have to deliver two coins – by offering twice as much labor services or commodities to earn the means of paying the tax.

Kurke has offered a detailed analysis of the invention of coinage, somewhat modifying the views of Cook, Kraay and Grierson. She notes that coins seem to have originated in seventh century (BC) Greece, at a time when the economy was largely embedded, and argues 'the fact of an embedded economy must make a difference to the causes for the invention of coinage' (Kurke, 1999, p. 5). While Kurke notes that Kraay (1964) revolutionized numismatics when he argued that coins were invented to standardize payments made by and to the state, she recognizes that some of Kraay's evidence has since been disputed. However, her primary objection is that Kraay had not paid sufficient attention to culture, institutions, and other social and political motivations. In her view,

the minting of coin would represent the state's assertion of its ultimate authority to constitute and regulate value in all the spheres in which general-purpose money operated simultaneously – economic, social, political, and religious. Thus, state-issued coinage as a universal equivalent, like the civic *agora* in which it circulated, symbolized the merger in a single token or site of many different domains of value, all under the final authority of the city. (Kurke, 1999, pp. 12–13)

In a sense, the choice of precious metals for coinage was a historical accident, a pointed challenge to elite monopoly over precious metal (the elite valued precious metal for use in complex hierarchical gift exchange). By coining precious metal, the *polis* appropriated the highest sphere of gift exchange, and with its stamp it asserted its ultimate authority – both inwardly (or domestically) but also outwardly (in long-distance trade): 'For every Greek *polis* that issued its own coin asserted its autonomy and independence from every other Greek city, while coinage also functions as one institution among many through which the city constituted itself as the final instance against the claims of an internal elite' (Kurke, 1999, p. 13). As the *polis* used coins for its own payments and insisted on payment in coin, it inserted its sovereignty into retail trade in the *agora*. By tying the invention of coinage to the special circumstances of Greece, Kurke's analysis makes it clear why coins have been so unimportant to other economies before and since.

Of course, from the perspective of Greece, coinage was no historical accident. As Kurke argues, introduction of coins arose out of a 'seventh/sixth century crisis of justice and unfair distribution of property' (Kurke, 1999, p. 13). Coins appeared at this particular time because the *polis* had gained sufficient strength to rival the *symposia*, *hetaireiai* (private drinking clubs) and other institutions and *xenia* (elite networking) that maintained elite dominance. At the same time, the *agora* and its use of coined money subverted hierarchies of gift exchange, just as a shift to taxes and regular payments to city officials (as well as severe penalties levied on officials who accepted gifts) challenged the 'natural' order that traditionally had relied on gifts and favors. As Kurke argues, as coins are nothing more than tokens of the city's authority, they could have been produced from any material. However, because the aristocrats measured a man's worth by the quantity and quality of the precious metal he had accumulated, the *polis* was required to mint high quality coins, unvarying in fineness. The citizens of the *polis* by their association with high quality, uniform, coin (and in the texts the citizen's 'mettle' was tested by the quality of the coin) gained equal status; by providing a standard measure of value, coinage rendered labor comparable and in this sense coinage was an egalitarian innovation. As Kurke argues, the 'mystification' of the origins of money that ties it to markets (rather than to the *polis* or state) is ideological – as it remains today – a purposeful rejection of the legitimacy of democratic government.

Hence, while Kurke modifies to some extent the argument above, she similarly maintains that coinage was not a transactions-cost-minimizing invention but rather emerged from a spatially and temporally specific contest between an elite that wished to preserve the embedded hierarchy of gift exchange and a democratic *polis* moving to assert its sovereignty. Precious metals were not chosen for coinage to ensure that nominal value would be maintained by high embodied value, but rather because of the particular role played by precious metals in the hierarchy. Always above all a means of providing for state finance, coins were mystified by an elite that associated their creation with petty, debasing and contaminating retail trade. While both the elite and the supporters of the *polis* claimed legitimacy for their positions through reference to the natural, embedded order, coinage, development of sovereign government, and evolution of retail trade all contributed to the gradual disembedding of the economy. It is ironic that today's M-form approach views the completely disembedded economy as the natural case, emerging from rational, individualistic, pursuits, and even sees the 'pure' case as one in which only precious metals are used as media of exchange. The evil government only corrupts the natural, disembedded economy by debasing the currency and by substituting its own tokens. As Kurke's analysis makes clear, through their ignorance of history these economists have wholly misinterpreted the nature of money and the importance of government to the formation of democratizing market exchange.

Kurke's arguments are largely consistent with the Chartalist or state money approach outlined above. Money is, and always has been, a 'creature of the state' (in Lerner's felicitous phrase), and currency has always been a state token. Precious metal coins merely represent one kind of state token, and their origins can be traced to the specific social upheaval that took place at the end of the seventh century BC. Except in rare circumstances, the value of a coin was never determined by, or governed by, the quantity of embodied precious metal. Use of such coins could not have originated 'spontaneously' in market exchange. This is not to say that the value of coins would never be determined by precious metal content. The nominal value of a coin would be determined initially by the value placed on it by the issuing government's pay offices – and this would normally be far higher than the coin's value as metal. However, if that government were overthrown, the new government might not accept it at all, or, more likely, only at its bullion value. Furthermore, the coin might leave the jurisdiction over which the government could enforce tax obligations. For example, a French coin might migrate to Italy. In Italy, the coin could still have a nominal value in excess of its bullion value if there were money changers willing to send it home to France, or if there were individuals in Italy who desired the coin because they might directly or indirectly use it to retire obligations to the French government. While distance from the issuer would not be the sole determinant of a coin's value in excess of its bullion value, it is easy to see why a coin could fall in value as it became increasingly difficult to reflux the coin back to its issuer. At the limit, coins would fall to their bullion value, and would be weighed like so much gold or silver. These would not be 'Chartal' (or token) monies, and any market exchanges based on full-bodied coin would be closer in character to barter than to monetary exchange.

Of course, it is difficult for a government to impose obligations on the subjects of another sovereign nation – that is, France cannot easily tax Italians. International trade between the French and Italians took place on the basis of bills of exchange, which provided a complicated way to trade goods using the exchange of liabilities denominated in two (or more) different monies of account. This, however, leaves us with two problems. Within a sovereign nation, ultimate clearing is accomplished using high powered money (HPM) – the money issued by government and accepted at government pay offices. This is necessary when one economic unit has a net claim on another – after canceling debits and credits, if there is still a net claim, the debtor delivers to the creditor some HPM. In the case of international trade, however, there is no ultimate HPM because there is no international government that stands above all sovereign nations. While an ultimate, world, HPM could be created (as Keynes had advocated – see Davidson, 1994), for most of world history nations had to rely on a second (or third) best solution. In recent centuries, the currency of the dominant nation (the USA after World War II, or the UK previously) was used as the HPM in much of the rest of the world. The 'third best' solution was to use gold for net clearing. In practice, most of the clearing was actually accomplished through movement of sterling-denominated UK liabilities; however, the UK had pegged the pound to gold. We needn't go into this in more detail, except to note that choice of gold as the 'ultimate' clearing unit also provided a solution to the second problem associated with absence of an international money. It was rather difficult for the King of England to directly purchase the goods and services of the subjects of the King of France, for he could not directly impose tax obligations on them, thus, they would be reluctant to accept his token coins. This would become a serious problem whenever England invaded France – how could England purchase French mercenaries and supplies to wage the war against France within its own borders? (Today, of course, we generally expect an invading army to carry with it the soldiers and supplies needed, but that was impractical several centuries ago.) Thus, the King of England needed something of high and easily recognized value to conduct foreign wars, and precious metals fit the bill. As discussed above, use of full bodied coin in this instance would be more akin to bartering gold for military provisions than to use of money to purchase them. It is not surprising, we believe, that Mercantilism, the international gold standard, and large-scale foreign wars all developed at about the same time.

Unfortunately, these developments misled economists for hundreds of years, hiding the true nature of money behind a veil of gold. The value of a Chartal money is not determined by the substance of which it happens to be made. First, of course, there must be a demand for the money. It is not enough to argue that money can be used in markets – for this simply returns us to the question as to why anyone ever traded goods and services for money in the first place. Rather, there must have been an involuntary payment required – such as a fee, fine, tribute, tithe, or tax obligation – in terms of money. This generates the underlying demand for money. The *value* of a Chartal money (that is, its value in terms of what it can buy) depends on the difficulty of obtaining it. If the state simply handed out HPM on request, its value would be close to zero, as anyone could meet her tax liability simply by requesting HPM. On the other hand, if the state required an hour of hard labor to obtain a unit of HPM, then that unit would be 'worth' an hour of hard labor. As the monopoly issuer, the state can determine what must be done to obtain its HPM, thus, can set the value of HPM far above the value of the material from which it is manufactured. This is why precious metal coins issued by the state normally carried a nominal value far above the value of the embodied precious metal.

POLICY IMPLICATIONS

Above we had discussed the orthodox belief that the government controls the money supply through control over bank reserves. This position is rejected by post-Keynesians, who argue that banks expand the money supply endogenously. How is this possible in nations with a legally required reserve ratio? Banks, like other firms, take positions in assets by issuing liabilities on the expectation of making profits. Much bank activity can be analysed as a 'leveraging' of HPM – because banks issue liabilities that can be exchanged on demand for HPM on the expectation that they can obtain HPM as necessary to meet with-drawals – but many other firms engage in similar activity. For our purposes, however, the main difference between banks and other types of firms involves the nature of the liabilities. Banks 'make loans' by purchasing IOUs of 'borrowers'; this results in a bank liability – usually a demand deposit, at least initially – that shows up as an asset ('money') of the borrower. Thus, the 'creditors' of a bank are created simultaneously with the 'debtors' to the bank. The creditors will almost immediately exercise their right to use the created demand deposit as a medium of exchange.

Indeed, bank liabilities are the primary 'money' used by non-banks. The government accepts some bank liabilities in payment of taxes, and it guarantees that many bank liabilities are redeemable at par against HPM. In turn, reserves are the 'money' used as means of payment (or inter-bank settlement) among banks and for payments made to the central bank; as bank 'creditors' draw down demand deposits, this causes a clearing drain for the individual bank.

The bank may then operate either on its asset side (selling an asset) or on its liability side (borrowing reserves) to cover the loss of reserves. In the aggregate, however, such activities only shift reserves from bank to bank. Aggregate excesses or deficiencies of reserves have to be rectified by the central bank. Ultimately, then, reserves are not discretionary in the short run; the central bank can determine the price of reserves – admittedly, within some constraints – but then must provide reserves more-or-less on demand to hit its 'price' target (the fed funds rate in the US, or the bank rate in the UK). This is because excess or deficient reserves would cause the fed funds rate (or bank rate) to move away from the target immediately.

This means that central banks cannot control the money supply. Indeed, rather than viewing monetary policy as the source of 'money', the nC approach recognizes that most HPM enters the economy as a result of fiscal policy. Whenever the government spends, it 'emits' HPM (usually in the first instance, it issues a check drawn on the treasury, but this is normally deposited into a private bank whose account is then credited by the central bank with HPM). On the other hand, payment of taxes drains HPM from the economy (usually, taxpayers write checks on their bank accounts; bank reserves are then debited by the central bank). Thus, government budget deficits mean that there has been a net creation of HPM, while surpluses drain HPM from the economy. While it is true that the central bank can also intervene to inject or drain HPM from the economy, this is done – as described above – only to accommodate bank demands for HPM. When banks are deficient the central bank injects HPM; when banks have excess reserves, the central bank removes them. Interventions by the central bank are made on a day-to-day basis as necessary, and are required to keep the overnight interest rate on target.

Thus, while fiscal policy consists of spending and taxing, and has a direct impact on the supply of HPM to the economy, monetary policy consists of accommodative behavior required to target the shortest of interest rates. Furthermore, while orthodoxy views inflation-fighting as a primary role of monetary policy, the nC approach again stands that on its head and assigns responsibility over inflation primarily to fiscal policy. As we noted above, Chartalism insists that the value of money is determined by what must be done to obtain it. Placing an onerous tax liability on the population creates a residual demand for money – the population must obtain HPM to pay taxes. The government then provides the money necessary to pay taxes when it spends. If it spends 'too much', it can reduce the value of the currency. This could be because the total volume of spending is too high as the government tries to move too many resources to the public sector, or because the government places too high a price on the things it buys. Indexing the prices of things the government buys (for example, to the CPI) is common and can devalue the currency.

Modern governments typically use unemployment to try to fight inflation. While it is commonly believed that this is accomplished through tight monetary policy (which raises interest rates), tight fiscal policy is much more effective at raising unemployment. However, as some working within the nC approach have recognized, it is not necessary to use unemployment in order to enhance price stability, indeed, full employment can be more effective at reducing inflation – if it is properly implemented. While we cannot go into the details here, it has been proposed that the government develop a labor 'buffer stock' program (Mitchell, 1997; Mitchell and Watts, 1997; Gordon, 1997; Harvey, 1989; Minsky, 1986; Wray, 1998). While there are alternative formulations, the employment buffer stock program would have the government offer a job to anyone ready, willing and able to work. The wage and benefit package would be fixed at some level, which would become the base compensation package for the economy. The government would essentially stand ready to 'buy' or 'sell' labor, offering jobs to any workers who showed up, or offering workers to any employers willing to hire workers out of the buffer stock. Of course, employers would have to offer a more attractive job, or a better wage and benefit package, to induce workers out of the buffer stock pool.

In economic booms, the buffer stock would be 'selling' labor and helping to dampen wage pressures (since wages in the buffer stock program would be held constant); in recessions, buffer stock employment would grow and would prevent wages from falling below the base rate (since workers could always choose to leave the private sector and take buffer stock jobs). Employment in the buffer stock program would be superior to unemployment because it would prevent deterioration of labor skills, would maintain income at a base level, and could actually be geared toward enhancing education and skills of its employees to make them more productive. Recall that the nC approach emphasizes that government is the monopoly supplier of HPM. As such, it can always 'emit' HPM to buy anything for sale in the domestic currency. This means it is always financially able to run a buffer stock program, without fear that it will 'run out' of the money to buy the commodity (in this case, labor) that is for sale when the government's bid price is hit.

If HPM grew on trees it would be worth very little. However, if one must work to obtain HPM to pay taxes, that gives HPM value. By operating a labor buffer stock program the government is essentially offering to provide HPM in exchange for labor. So long as the wage and benefit package is not increased, HPM will maintain a stable value in terms of the buffer stock labor it can purchase. This is not to say that all wages in society will remain constant – in an economic boom, it is likely that demand for some specialized skills will cause wages for specific types of workers to rise relative to the buffer stock wage. This will then induce two processes – it will encourage more individuals to pursue education and training to obtain the specific skills demanded by markets, and it will encourage firms to attempt to find ways to substitute less-skilled workers for those types of workers in shortage (for example, by changing production processes, using more capital plus lower skilled workers). In this way, the buffer stock program complements 'market processes' to reduce, but not necessarily eliminate, inflationary pressures even as it maintains full employment and enhances economic stability by causing the government's budget to move countercyclically.

Finally, something should be said about the policy implications of the nC view for operation of the international monetary system. Above we briefly examined Mundell's Optimal Currency Area approach, which is credited for spurring creation of the monetary union of Europe. Perhaps this can be taken as the future direction in the international sphere, a direction based on M-form analysis. Alternatively, some C-form economists have advocated that other nations should simply adopt the US dollar for use as their domestic currency – a policy actually adopted by several nations. Again, this appears to be consistent with C-form theory in which money is simply a transactions-cost-reducing medium of exchange.

As Goodhart rightly emphasizes, the real world observations that we use fiat money and that there is a nearly perfect one-to-one correlation between each fiat money and each fiscal authority are easy to explain from the point of view of C-form theory – although they are quite difficult to explain from the vantage point of M-form theory. I would underline Goodhart's point that the European Monetary Union is a unique and scary experiment, and one that comes at a particularly bad time – just as Europe, the USA and the rest of the world prepare to spiral down into deep recession, if not depression. By divorcing money from fiscal authority, the individual European nations will probably have to retrench, precisely when they should adopt expansionary policy. (However, I'm not sure things will be a whole lot better in the US, since the President and Congress are committed to running fiscal surpluses for the next 15 years in order to save Social Security. Such a policy represents a fundamental misunderstanding of the pressures placed on the private economy as the government drains HPM and income from the system.) Kregel (1999) has provided a proposal that would actually reconnect money and fiscal policy in Europe – by having the European Central Bank (ECB) finance an Employer-of-Last-Resort (ELR) program much like the one described above. In this way, deficit spending would automatically increase, in the form of euros, whenever the private sector shed workers. Under the euro, individual nations would not be able to operate an ELR program precisely because monetary integration has divorced fiscal policy from the currency. However, Kregel's plan would have the funding come from the ECB – operating much like a European Treasury – for national ELR programs. Without some sort of reconciliation of monetary and fiscal policy, the European

Union will be unnecessarily hampered in its attempts to fight recessionary pressures as they arise.

According to the nC approach, then, sovereign countries ought to operate with their own, sovereign, currencies. If they do so, they can always obtain full employment through an ELR program. However, the Chartalist 'rules' operate only within a nation – it is difficult to tax foreigners and difficult to control the foreign value of a currency (in other words, the exchange rate). Most domestic currencies will have some value outside the borders of the issuing nation – because, ultimately, citizens of the issuing nation will demand the currency so they can pay taxes. This means that a foreigner can accept the currency, safe in the belief that at the very least, citizens of the issuing nation will provide goods, services and assets to obtain that currency. However, the forces that determine the day-to-day (or hour-to-hour) exchange rates are complex and probably impossible to predict. To avoid uncertainties over exchange rates, countries are frequently tempted to attempt to maintain fixed exchange rates. This gives rise to two primary problems: first, it is really impossible to prevent a depreciation of the currency if international markets are determined to push it down; more fundamentally, a nation that attempts to fix the foreign exchange value of its currency must relinquish fiscal policy independence. This is because a country facing downward pressure on its currency must try to slow emission of the currency by tightening fiscal policy (reducing spending or raising taxes). It would be dangerous to adopt an ELR program in a nation that is attempting to fix its exchange rate because a growing ELR pool automatically increases government spending and thus emission of HPM. This may make it impossible to maintain a fixed exchange rate.

Thus, while it is difficult to say exactly what the international monetary system should look like (should nations use the US dollar as the international reserve, or should a new international reserve currency be created along the lines suggested by Keynes?), it is clear that the principles of Chartalism point toward a system of flexible exchange rates for the international sphere, and toward sovereign currencies with full employment programs (such as ELR) at the domestic level.

REFERENCES

Balbach, Anatol B. (1981), 'How controllable is money growth?', *Federal Reserve Bank of St. Louis Review*, **63**(4), April, 5.

Brunner, Karl (1968), 'The role of money and monetary policy', *Federal Reserve Bank of St. Louis Review*, **50**(7), July, 9.

Cook, R.M. (1958), 'Speculation on the origins of coinage', *Historia*, 7, 257–62.

Dalziel, Paul (1996), 'The Keynesian multiplier, liquidity preference and endogenous money', *Journal of Post Keynesian Economics*, 18, 311–31.

Davidson, Paul (1978), *Money and the Real World*, London: Macmillan.

Davidson, Paul (1994), *Post Keynesian Macroeconomic Theory*, Aldershot, UK and Brookfield, US: Edward Elgar.

Davies, G. (1994), *A History of Money from Ancient Times to the Present Day*, Cardiff: University of Wales Press.

Dowd, Kevin (2000), 'The Invisible Hand and the evolution of the monetary system', in John Smithin (ed.), *What is Money?*, London and New York: Routledge, pp. 139–56.

Friedman, Milton (1969), *The Optimal Quantity of Money and Other Essays*, Chicago: Aldine.

Goodhart, Charles A.E. (1989), *Money, Information and Uncertainty*, Cambridge, MA: MIT Press.

Goodhart, Charles A.E. (1998), 'The two concepts of money: implications for the analysis of optimal currency areas', *European Journal of Political Economy*, 14, 407–32.

Gordon, Wendell (1997), 'Job assurance – the job guarantee revisited', *Journal of Economic Issues*, **31**, September, 826–34.

Grierson, Philip (1977), *The Origins of Money*, London: Athlone Press.

Grierson, Philip (1979), *Dark Age Numismatics*, London: Variorum Reprints.

Hahn, F. (1983), *Money and Inflation*, Cambridge, MA: MIT Press.

Harvey, Philip (1989), *Securing the Right to Employment*, Princeton: Princeton University Press.

Ingham, Geoffrey (2000), '"Babylonian madness": On the historical and sociological origins of money', in John Smithin (ed.), *What is Money?*, London and New York: Routledge.

Ingrao, B. and Israel, G. (1990), *The Invisible Hand: Economic Equilibrium in the History of Science*, Cambridge, MA: MIT Press.

Innes, A.M. (1913), 'What is money?', *Banking Law Journal*, May, 377–408.

Innes, A.M. (1932), *Martyrdom in Our times: Two Essays on Prisons and Punishments*, London: Williams & Norgate.

Keynes, John Maynard (1964), *The General Theory*, New York, Harcourt-Brace-Jovanovich.

Keynes, John Maynard (1976 [1930]), *A Treatise on Money: Volume 1: The Pure Theory of Money*, New York: Harcourt-Brace-Jovanovich.

Keynes, John Maynard (1982), *The Collected Writings of John Maynard Keynes, Vol. XXVIII Social, Political and Literary Writings*, edited by Donald Moggridge, London and Basingstoke: Macmillan.

Knapp, Georg Friedrich (1973 [1924]), *The State Theory of Money*, Clifton: Augustus M. Kelley.

Kraay, C.M. (1964), 'Hoards, small change and the origin of coinage', *Journal of Hellenic Studies*, 84, 76–91.

Kregel, J.A. (1999), 'Price stability and employment: a proposal', in *The Launching of the Euro*, Annandale-on-Hudson: The Bard Center, Bard College.

Kurke, Leslie (1999), *Coins, Bodies, Games, and Gold: The Politics of Meaning in Archaic Greece*, Princeton, NJ: Princeton University Press.

Lerner, Abba P. (1943), 'Functional finance and the federal debt', *Social Research*, **10**, 38–51.

Lerner, Abba P. (1947), 'Money as a creature of the state', *American Economic Review*, **37**(2), May, 312–17.

Maddox, Thomas, Esq. (1969 [1769]), *The History and Antiquities of the Exchequer of the Kings of England, in Two Periods*, vols I&II, 2nd edn, NY: Greenwood Press.

McIntosh, Marjorie (1988), 'Money lending on the periphery of London, 1300–1600', *Albion*, **20**(4), 557.

Minsky, H.P. (1986), *Stabilizing an Unstable Economy*, New Haven: Yale University Press.

Mitchell, William F. (1997), 'Unemployment and inflation: a demand side focus', paper presented at the PKT seminar, an on-line seminar (http:csf.colorado.edn/pkt), January.

Mitchell, William F. and Martin J. Watts (1997), 'The path to full employment', manuscript, University of Newcastle.

Moore, Basil (1988), *Horizontalists and Verticalists: The Macroeconomics of Credit Money*, Cambridge: Cambridge University Press.

Mosler, Warren (1995), *Soft Currency Economics*, 3rd edn (http://www.warren-mosler.com/docs/docs/soft0004.htm).

Royal Swedish Academy of Sciences, Press Release (1999), 'The Bank of Sweden Prize in Economic Sciences in Memory of Alfred Nobel 1999', 13 October, www.nobel.se/announcement-99/economics99.html.

Samuelson, Paul (1973), *Economics*, 9th edn, New York: McGraw-Hill.

Schumpeter, J.A. (1954), *History of Economic Analysis*, New York: Oxford University Press.

Smith, Adam (1937), *The Wealth of Nations*, The Cannan Edition, New York: The Modern Library.

Tobin, James (1998), *Money, Credit and Capital*, Boston, MA: Irwin McGraw-Hill.

Wray, L. Randall (1998), *Understanding Modern Money: The Key to Full Employment and Price Stability*, Cheltenham, UK and Lyme, US: Edward Elgar.

Wray, L. Randall (1990), *Money and Credit in Capitalist Economies: The Endogenous Money Approach*, Aldershot, UK and Brookfield, US: Edward Elgar.

6. Nominal money, real money and stabilization*

Edward J. Nell

Throughout the whole time – back before Ricardo, forward after Keynes – money itself has been evolving. ... metallic money has given place to credit money, ... [but] ... credit money is just a part of a whole credit structure that extends outside money; ... The obvious change in the money medium, from 'full-bodied' coins to notes and bank deposits, is just part of a wider development, the development of a financial system. This has taken the form of the growth of financial institutions, not just banks but other 'financial intermediaries' as well; it has carried with it a fundamental change in the financial activities of governments. ... In a world of banks and insurance companies, money markets and stock exchanges, money is quite a different thing from what it was before....

This evolution ... clearly called, as it proceeded, for a radical revision of monetary theory. As the actual system changed, the [theory] ought to have changed with it. We can now see that it did not ... (Sir John Hicks, *Critical Essays in Monetary Theory*, 1967, pp. 257–8)

Goodhart argues that M theory is wrong, and that policies based on it must come to disaster. However, his account of M theory focuses on efficiency questions, and while he shows that the M approach is misleading in these matters, he neglects stabilization. Yet it is surely more to the point than efficiency. M theory holds that, in principle, the market is self-adjusting through the rate of interest. So if practical considerations call for policy to supplement or replace the market, policymakers therefore should be able to draw on interest rates to adjust the system in desired directions. But a nominal C system is not self-adjusting, and the nominal interest rate is not an adequate policy tool for stabilization. A supporting fiscal policy is required, and without it the euro is likely to face problems. But a self-adjusting fiscal policy could be designed.

GOODHART'S DICHOTOMY: M SYSTEMS VS. C SYSTEMS

Charles Goodhart begins his discussion with an account of the role of 'efficiency' in the establishment of money, according to what he calls the 'Metallist' perspective. According to this line of thinking, metal-based money is established because markets consider it more efficient than barter. Metallism, then, is the doctrine that money is established spontaneously, without regard to the state, because trading using stamped metals is efficient in reducing trans-actions costs. (Paper backed by metal is even more efficient.) This Goodhart calls 'M theory', in contrast to Chartalism, or C theory, which holds that money depends on the power and backing of state authority. C theory regards currencies as national, holding sway within borders.

1. Goodhart argues that M theory's account of the way money came to be used is not well grounded in history. Metal money did not emerge spontaneously and was not adopted for efficiency reasons; it came into use in relation to paying off debts, including especially taxes and debts of the state. From the first it was a public good. Metal was normally minted and coined by the state.
2. Moreover, it was not necessarily more efficient, and did not come into use to improve the efficiency or reduce the costs of trade.
    • For example, most early coins were too large to be useful in retail trade. Token money was often used for small transactions, and manors kept accounts that were settled at the year's end.
    • Trade, in fact, was largely based on credit, which depended on courts and police powers of enforcement. 'Trade follows the flag'.
    • A closer look shows that money was always tied closely to credit and based at least in part on the power of the state.

Surely these points are correct. Their relevance is that they cast doubt on M theory's neglect of the role of the state. Goodhart builds on them by going on to argue that Metallism underlies the idea of an Optimal Currency Area, that is, the area in which a single currency holds sway. By shifting to a common currency, countries that trade extensively with each other will save enough on transaction costs to justify the costs of making the change. The OCA in turn is the presumed basis of the euro; that is, the states of the European Union are supposed to form an Optimal Currency Area – although not much evidence has ever been presented on this. Moreover, this approach explains why there is (felt to be) no need for fiscal policy to support the euro; the state plays no necessary role in establishing a currency. As for stabilization, Metallism argues that it will be accomplished through monetary policy. Indeed, M theory supporters tend to argue that fiscal policy is ineffective; markets will anticipate it and adjust so as to offset its impact. Further, they contend that monetary policy can be adjusted quickly, by experts. Fiscal policy, by contrast, could not generally be brought to bear in a timely way, since it depends on political decisions.

This efficiency-based account of Metallism, however, is not the only way to approach the issues. Certainly Goodhart is right to contrast the broadly

'Monetarist' and free-market /limited government support for the organization of the euro with a more Keynesian or interventionist approach. But efficiency and optimality of the currency area are not, by themselves, central. They have to be linked to stabilization.

And the celebrated efficiency of markets includes the claim that markets adjust on their own. The central storyline is that markets have always worked their magic because they adjusted on their own; by intervening, the state could only upset the apple cart. Markets, it is claimed, tend to adjust towards *optimal* positions. So intervention would be likely to result in suboptimal ones. In addition, certain kinds of intervention are difficult both technically and politically – stopping an asset-price inflation, for example. It is for these reasons, surely, that the proponents of the euro have sought to restrain the activities of the states.[1]

Real-world metal-based currency systems certainly did have a built-in and partially automatic stabilizer, which complemented the craft economy's price mechanism. But it was not fully automatic, nor was it always reliable. Hicks, for example, has repeatedly stressed that monetary systems could always react in *unstable* ways (Hicks, 1967; Nell, 2000). And indeed, actual M systems were *managed* by the state – and had to be; the market could not establish a uniform currency, and could not guarantee stability. The automatic stabilizers were institutionalized policy.

But real money, based on metal, curiously, is not 'efficient' or at least not appropriate for a modern economy operating large-scale industrial processes, employing a large and adjustable labor force. Its supply is not sufficiently flexible. But it does have one important property, which the later and more flexible C systems lack. Rather than efficiency, its important property is its capacity for stabilizing self-adjustment. A real money system tends to adjust itself, to determine the rate of interest in the market, and to cause that rate to move in a stabilizing manner. It also leads to changes in the value of money that are stabilizing. All these, however, are conditional on the Mint preventing destabilizing movements from developing.

A modern industrial economy, in which short-run levels of employment and output may vary over a wide range, needs bank money, supplied as credit and accepted in payment of taxes. The monetary system must be able to supply varying quantities of universally acceptable credit-based means of payment at short notice. But we shall see that such a system is no longer self-adjusting.

For all practical purposes nominal money *has* to be based on the state, that is, on an exogenous, non-economic source of power. Since it is intrinsically worthless, there must be a powerful reason to accept it; this is provided by the need to pay taxes. For *prima facie*, it does not make sense to accept bank liabilities that have no backing. Why should anyone accept the promise of a bank to pay, if the means with which it proposes to pay is nothing but more of its own liabilities? Or those of banks in a similar position? Bank A can pay with liabilities of Bank B, and Bank B with those of Bank C, ... but why should the public accept any of them? The fact that they can pay their taxes with such liabilities provides a good and sufficient reason.

Purely nominal money could not exist in the past. Real money was required precisely because of the weakness and unreliability of the state.[2] Governments might be overthrown or conquered and restructured, on the one hand, or, on the other, a state might choose to repudiate its debts, and direct its power against its creditors. The paper liabilities of the state could not be trusted.

> Ah, take the cash and let the credit go
> Nor heed the rumble of a distant drum (The Rubáiyát of Omar Khayyám)

Gold, silver, etc. had intrinsic value. The precious metals might fluctuate in value to some extent, but usually not very dramatically, and they were always in demand. As the institutions of the state and the banking system developed, convertibility into gold and silver provided a kind of *insurance*. Paper money or bank deposits could always be converted into gold or silver, which had traditional value, grounded in their cost of production and supported by 'supply and demand'. Gold and silver could fluctuate in value, but they could not collapse altogether. Credit instruments, paper money and bank deposits, however, could literally become worthless in a matter of days or hours, if in a crisis, the issuer were forced to close its doors.

State money, also, could become worthless if the state chose to repudiate its debts. For state money backed by the power to tax to become generally accepted, the market and the public must have confidence that the state will play by the rules, and will not repudiate its debts. Wealthy merchants and bankers in the late Middle Ages and Renaissance were often reluctant to lend to monarchies out of fear that debts would be repudiated, or that an indebted monarch would find an excuse to seize the assets of his creditors. (Jacques Coeur, in the time of Joan of Arc, suffered this fate, as did others.)

There must likewise be confidence in the strength and stability of the state; it must be felt that it will not collapse or be overthrown. Confederate money lost value, as the Confederate forces began to lose the Civil War. Prices rose as confidence fell; to purchase supplies the Confederate Government had to increase the issue. In the end the price level in the Confederacy rose by a factor of 28. The North issued 'greenbacks' but was able to control profiteering and keep prices from rising excessively. Prices in the North only doubled. 'Assignats', issued by the Directory during the later stages of the French Revolution, and supposedly 'backed' by the confiscated lands of the Church, were initially successful, and were retired by being used to purchase such lands. But as the government became unstable, they fell to 1/300th of their initial value – and then became unacceptable altogether. The British suspended convertibility during the Napoleonic Wars but controlled the issue. Prices no more than doubled and fell back when convertibility was restored.

But as we shall see, such a C-based monetary system has no built-in stabilizing propensities, and so provides no check against inflation either. Moreover, in a modern industrial economy the corresponding aggregate markets are based on the multiplier-accelerator, are highly volatile, and the credit-based monetary system provides no constraining forces.

TRANSFORMATIONAL GROWTH AND MONEY: PREDOMINANTLY M SYSTEMS TURN INTO C SYSTEMS

Today's monetary systems have no metallic anchor and provide no automatic stabilization. They are pure C systems, in Goodhart's terms – nominal money rather than real. They are therefore prone to generate inflation, and the inflations will normally not be uniform. Interest rates must be pegged, but monetary policy cannot stabilize the economy because there is only one policy variable, the nominal interest rate, which must be used to control inflation, unemployment and the exchange rate – as well as maintain orderly markets, especially the Stock Market.

The problem has roots in both the private and public sectors. The modern private sector needs to be able to adjust its working capital rapidly; this is necessary if output and employment are to be adjusted quickly to demand. In the same way, the public sector that developed after World War II also required a flexible monetary system, one in which money could be created at will when the government wished to spend. For if government spending were to meet the needs of the modern economy it could not wait until taxes have been collected, or funds raised through a treasury auction. Moreover, policy considerations also demanded this: if a deficit is called for, the government must spend at once – otherwise the counter-cyclical force would not appear when it is needed. But in early small-scale capitalism government deficits would tend to add to the demand for reserves and so drive up interest rates. On the other hand, later, when money creation adjusts flexibly to demand, the system provides no protection against inflation.

Real Money and Stabilization

The monetary system has changed from one in which there were automatic stabilizing mechanisms to one with no such mechanisms.[3] To begin from the beginning: in one sense money is always a token; it has very little use in itself.[4]

And the unit of account is always 'imaginary' – it is the basis for an accounting system. But the unit of account may be attached to valuable metal in a process that results in a coin with an 'intrinsic value'.[5] Alternatively the unit of account may be stamped on paper, or recorded in depository records, which have no value in themselves, resulting in money with a mere conventional value. In the first case, there are market adjustment processes that tend to fix and maintain the value of the circulating medium; in the second there are no such processes. That is, in the cases of intrinsic value and fiduciary money, the money medium acquires value through market processes, although these may be mediated or managed by the state. But market processes are not involved in the valuation of either fiat money or bookkeeping money. They can't be: an economic process involves balancing supply and demand, but neither of these forms of money is *supplied* in an economic sense.

a) Stabilizing the value of money

In the economy of early capitalism money is based on the value of metal – gold or silver. In the early stages coin is the principal medium of circulation, assisted by trade credit. Later on, paper money and bank deposits take over the bulk of circulation. Paper money and bank deposits, however, are understood to be tokens; they stand in for 'real' money, which is metal. They are therefore convertible on demand into a medium possessing intrinsic value. This means that the quantity of money flowing through the system adjusts through the price mechanism. When prices change, the value of money in circulation changes inversely – when prices rise, money is worth less than before, when prices fall, money is worth more. The money in circulation may be thought of as money demanded for use. But money (metal) has a real value which derives from production; this may be considered its supply price. If the value in circulation is out of line with this real value, then money must be withdrawn from, or added to, the circulation. (Alternatively we can think of money being added to or released from hoarding.) Supply and demand determine the amount of money in circulation, through the price mechanism. This process brings about adjustments in the quantity of money in circulation, and – much less reliably – in the amount of credit offered.

Money of intrinsic value acquires its value in production, and this is maintained and stabilized through the working of the Mint. The supply function relates the value of a unit of money to the amount mined and minted in the current period. This curve will tend to be flat or possibly rising. The demand function shows the number of units required at various levels of unit value to circulate the currently produced volume of goods and services. Such a curve would be falling from left to right, and in the simplest case, would have unitary elasticity.[6]

Suppose the circulation curve shifts out and up. There are now more goods to be circulated, but these goods face the same amount of money. So prices

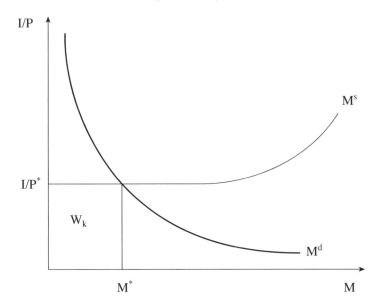

Figure 6.1 Determination of price level and quantity of money

fall; the value of money rises. Goods and services are at bargain prices. More money will therefore be released from hoards to be thrown into circulation. Similarly if the curve shifts down and in, prices will rise – the value of money will fall – and money will be withdrawn from circulation and hoarded. In each case the responses are stabilizing.

Yet destabilizing responses are always possible. Suppose prices begin to fall, but come to be expected to *continue falling*. Money will then be progressively *withdrawn* from circulation, rather than being added. This withdrawal will then drive prices down further, justifying the belief that prices will continue falling. The beliefs are self-justifying and the pattern of behavior will be self-sustaining. The same will hold in reverse for the case of rising prices that are expected to continue rising. (The Mint then stabilizes prices by setting 'gold points', levels of the value of money at which it will buy or sell gold. This blocks the formation of destabilizing expectations since a movement of prices will tend to be blocked at these points.)

Fiduciary money acquires value because it is 'backed' by a stock of goods, for which it can always be exchanged at a stable price. So it also has intrinsic value though it acquires such value 'second-hand'. (For example, the lord of the manor issues tokens – in pay for labor or for goods – which can be turned in for grain at his warehouse; a merchant issues a bill which can be redeemed for goods. The value is guaranteed by the promise of redemption at a fixed rate.)

In a more advanced case, money of some kind is backed by a 'buffer stock' of goods, whose prices are stabilized by the managers of the stock, who buy when prices are falling and sell when they are rising.

b) Stabilizing the interest rate

In a boom, banks will lend more and will seek to create new deposits or issue additional notes; to support these activities they will have to attract additional reserves. This will lead them to bid up interest rates, as they seek to attract idle reserves from each other and from hoards. In a slump, they will issue less and lend less, and will seek to shed reserves, lowering interest rates. In other words, while long-term average rates are determined by costs and competition, current interest rates reflect the balance of supply and demand in the market. They move pro-cyclically. Let's look more closely.

A simple model may be suggested. On the one hand, the rate of interest (in relation to the rate of profit) is likely to affect investment inversely, and investment, in turn, will have an impact on prices and employment. Changes in prices and employment will call for changes in reserves. (Even in the conditions of early capitalism, the monetary system and the real economy cannot be separated – the classical dichotomy does not hold.) On the other hand, shortages or surpluses of reserves will lead to market pressures driving interest rates up or down. Monetary adjustments do complement and reinforce the stabilizing effects of the price mechanism.

Interest Rates, Investment and the Demand for Reserves

To see these relationships clearly, we can plot them on a diagram. The origin will represent the normal position – assumed to be the average over the cycle. Here the rate of profit will be at its normal level, and the rate of interest will be just sufficient to cover the expenses of the banking system, allowing it just enough profit to grow at the same rate as the rest of the economy (Nell, 1998a, 2000). The vertical axis will represent increases of the interest rate above and below the normal level. The horizontal axis will show the level of reserves, similarly above and below the normal level.

First we have the relationship between above- or below-normal interest rates and investment, which translates into demand for reserves.

- investment depends inversely on the interest rate – the more expensive it is to borrow in relation to normal profits, the lower will be investment spending, and the less expensive, the higher it will be.
- savings depends positively on prices (in relation to wages) and on employment – when prices are bid up, profits increase and profits are saved.

- prices in relation to wages, and employment and output, all depend positively on investment
- for equilibrium, savings has to equal investment

Taken together, these propositions tell us that if interest is low, for example, investment will be high, and the resulting demand pressure will drive up prices in relation to money wages, lowering the real wage and increasing employment (and output), raising profits and thus savings; this will go on until savings has risen to match the high level of investment. The process works in reverse; if interest rates are high, investment will be low, prices will fall relative to money wages, so with real wages high employment will fall, and profits and savings will be down. So savings *adapts* to investment, in a Keynesian fashion. But savings depends on profitability and employment, and not on the interest rate, so the latter cannot be determined here.[7]

The preceding implies that the level of reserves required depends on the money value of output, so on prices and employment. Thus required reserves will be large when interest rates are low, and smaller when they are high. Banks start out with a 'normal' level of reserves; this will have to be adjusted as the interest rate changes. So the curve passes through the origin, falling from the left to the origin and continuing through it. Higher than normal interest rates mean low investment, output and employment, so lower than normal demand for reserves. Lower than normal interest means higher activity, and higher required reserves.

Interest Rates and the Supply of Reserves

To complete the simple diagram, we must explain how reserves will be increased when interest rates are raised; and when interest rates are lowered, reserves will be reduced. That is, the supply of reserves varies positively with interest rates. This needs careful explanation.

A boom implies a higher rate of growth of output, so it might seem that gold output would rise *pari passu*. If so, things would be simple. Gold producers would expand mining and processing, and so increase their purchases of capital inputs by an amount necessary to raise gold output to the higher level necessary to ensure that new gold/existing gold stock will equal the new higher growth rate. But the increased purchase of capital inputs would mean an increase in the supply of gold; reserves would therefore increase. The increased purchase of capital inputs/normal purchase of capital inputs would equal the new growth rate, assuming equilibrium ratios. Hence gold reserves would expand in the necessary ratio. But what *incentives* would lead gold producers to this?

Consider: the pressure of the boom will tend to bid up prices (relative to money wages), which would seem to *reduce* the value of money, whereas a *rise* in the value of money is needed to induce mining. That is, there should be a shortage of money relative to goods, as would be expected with a rise in employment and output in a boom; this would call for more output from the mines. But the rise in prices suggests an increase in money relative to goods!

This would mean a lower value of money (monetary gold), which would hardly be an inducement to produce/supply gold.

However, gold producers do not necessarily have to sell gold. They could hold it and deposit it with the banks, in return for interest. In equilibrium, the rate of interest should equal the rate of profit. So gold producers should be indifferent between *investing* new gold, for example, plowing it back into the business (selling gold to buy capital inputs), to earn the rate of profit, or *lending* it to earn the rate of interest. They will sell enough to keep the supply of gold in circulation at the level required, and will lend enough to keep the rate of interest at the equilibrium level.

So when a boom develops, the growth rate will rise, and prices will be driven up relative to money wages, raising profits. That is, goods prices measured in the *actual circulating medium* – paper and credit – will rise, relative to wages in that medium. By itself, this would appear to lower profits in gold, since gold's command over goods would be less; but the boom is fueled by an *excessive* issue of paper and credit. So paper and credit will fall in relation to gold. Thus new gold can be exchanged for more paper than the invested gold commanded earlier. In current terms the rate of profit will be unchanged.

The banking system will be pressed to find reserves to back the new issues of paper and credit. Their efforts will drive up the interest rate. When the growth rate rises (a boom develops) as new paper and credit are issued, existing reserves come to be inadequate; so to back their issues, banks will compete to borrow reserves from one another. (There will always, normally, be periods in which a given bank's reserves will temporarily be excessive, making them willing to lend.) This will engender a widespread increase in borrowing pressure, driving up interest rates. This may increase reserves somewhat, as it will attract 'hoarded' gold, from inventories. But why would a rise in interest rates lead directly to a rise in mining?

Mining will increase because the higher rate provides gold producers an opportunity to increase earnings. Their normal output will continue to be sold as before. But if they increase their output they can now deposit the additional gold with the banks, and collect interest at the higher rate. (This is equivalent to selling the gold for goods. That is, the interest rate must mirror the relation between the spot price of gold, and its price for delivery at a later date. A rise in the interest rate must be reflected in a rise in the discount applied to the delivery price of gold).

Thus adjustments in the interest rate will tend to attract or release reserves so that the actual level on hand will be brought into line with that required by the level of activity. Higher prices and output call for higher reserves; to attract more reserves a higher interest rate will be needed, but this will also tend to reduce investment and so bring about lower levels of output and employment. A lower interest rate, in turn, would tend to release reserves, but it would also tend to stimulate investment, and so increase activity and thus raise the demand for reserves. At some intermediate level of the interest rate the level of reserves attracted should just match the level required. This will be the temporary equilibrium level, as determined by market forces.[8]

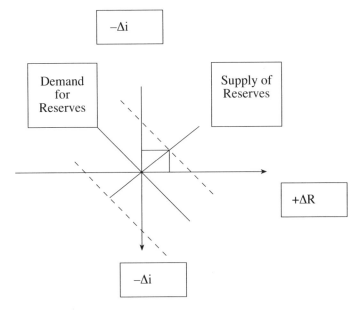

Figure 6.2   Interest rates and reserves

Putting the two functions together in Figure 6.2, with the normal equilibrium at the origin, we see that a shift upward in investment – due, perhaps, to boom psychology or to government borrowing and spending – will raise the demand for reserves (upper dotted line). This will now intersect with the supply at a higher rate of interest, and higher than normal level of reserves. A slump would lead to just the reverse (cf. lower dotted line).

As in the case of supply and demand for circulating funds, this should be a stable market – by the conventional account. If actual reserves are inadequate, those demanding reserves will be willing to pay higher interest charges, and the higher interest will attract more reserves. But note that if there are delays or time lags, the reactions could take the form of a 'cobweb'. In this case, with a steep demand function and a moderate supply function, the cobweb might well be divergent. In that case, government would be needed to maintain stability by adjusting the interest rate. The policy of the central bank would be 'to lean against the wind' – so the interest rate will move in the right direction – but the bank can also ensure that the changes will be large enough to have the desired impact.[9]

In a modern system, however, things work differently. The rate of interest is not determined by demand and supply for reserves – for the good reason that reserves are not what they used to be. They are no longer a special kind of money, like gold. They are arbitrary and can be manipulated, so that reserve ratios can be evaded and do not function as effective constraints. Reserves are just accounts at the central bank – which can be created by the central bank. As a result, there is no independent supply function.[10]

The chief reason for shifting from gold and convertible paper to modern bank money was that gold and real reserves could not be quickly adjusted. The quantity in circulation adjusted through the price mechanism; but as the economy shifted to mass production, employment became highly variable; the wage bill would fluctuate with layoffs and re-hiring. The wage bill, however (together with spending on investment), provided the chief market for bank lending, which would now have to adjust quickly to changing demand. But a gold-based system could not expand without first increasing reserves, which had to be attracted by higher interest rates. In a slump leading to extensive layoffs and reduced demand for loans, reduced lending would leave banks with excess reserves – an unnecessary expense – leading to reductions in rates and efforts to shed reserves. The countercyclical movement of the interest rate certainly helped to stabilize the economy, but it put a great strain on the banking system.

Fiat and Bookkeeping Money: Flexibility without Stabilization

Now let's look at modern money, which is not anchored in gold or precious metals, and consider how money that is purely a matter of convention or fiat obtains and keeps its value. In the older economy money was anchored to metal that had 'intrinsic value'. Such money is an asset to its possessor, but it is no one's liability.[11] This connection is broken in modern systems; money has no intrinsic value. It is an asset to its possessor, and a liability to its issuer. In between we have a system in which paper money and bank deposits are *loosely tied* to intrinsic value by being *convertible* into bullion, plate or coins. Such convertible money is also a liability to its issuer. 'Modern money, however, is not convertible; it is issued by banks, supported by the Central Bank, which is backed by the taxing power of the Government. What are called "reserves" are really more like clearing balances. They are accounts at the Central Bank, which can be created by the Central Bank. Moreover, "reserve ratios" can be evaded in various ways and do not provide an effective constraint.'

The implications of this change are striking, as we shall see. Market forces no longer determine the value of money, nor do such forces set the interest rate. The value of money now becomes a matter of 'exogenous pricing', as we will explain shortly. And the interest rate has to be pegged. The basic reason is *that there is no supply function*; there is no anchor tying nominal money to market-determined values, so there is no market-enforced connection to real reserves or backing. Gold, for example, was supplied in the sense of being produced and so having a unit cost. In modern systems there is nothing comparable. Of course banks produce a service, for which they are compensated by earnings from interest charges. But the service does not have a unit cost, nor is the cost of the service in any way tied to the number of units of money issued. So bank activites and bank costs contribute nothing to determining the value of money. In short, there are now no market processes to determine money's value. It is set by history – in particular the history of money wages – and by accident.

Fiat money is just paper or some other token that becomes generally accepted because it may be used or even required in payment of taxes. The tokens have no value in themselves; they are given value by fiat, and the particular rate at which they exchange is arbitrary. It will be chosen for convenience and accepted – if it is accepted – by convention.[12] We can call this *conventional value*.

However, even if paper can be given a value arbitrarily, that value must be maintained, and here supply and demand come into play again. When government is small, and the banking system is privately managed, the *conventional value* of money in exchange for privately produced goods depends on the quantity that has been issued in relation to those goods, and must be supported by limiting that quantity. Limiting the issue, however, may be undermined by the ability of markets to leverage the money issued, creating credit and near-monies. Moreover, if the government issues fiat money to cover its purchases, requiring that money back in taxes, a deficit will create an excess supply. Once this supply has become greater than what the public wishes to hold for precautionary reasons, the excess will tend to drive down the value.

When government is large and manages or oversees the banking system,[13] however, it may be able to set or at least to influence prices through its budget. It may have enough market power to force businesses to sell to it at prices of its choosing. Or it may use its own production to set 'yardstick' prices, as TVA did, for example (Nell, 1996).

Modern bank money is created on the basis of a given unit of account and given set of prices, and so on, expressed in that unit. Banks create deposits by making loans, generally as the result of firms activating pre-negotiated lines of credit – analogous to the credit cards that households use. These advances are paid to workers, who spend them on consumer goods; they reappear as receipts, and are used as profits to fund investment spending, and so on. Imagine that the economy can be neatly divided into two sectors – one producing capital goods, the other consumer goods. Workers in the capital goods sector are paid wages and buy consumer goods; consumer goods firms receive revenue and pay wages to their workers, who buy consumer goods, returning the funds to consumer goods firms. These funds now figure as profits, and can be used to buy capital goods from the capital goods sector; they then circulate in that sector, monetizing profits, and repaying advances (Deleplace and Nell, 1996; Nell, 1998a; 2000, 2001). In other words, bank advances for working capital circulate – and it can be shown that such circulation effectively monetizes all the transactions of the economy[14] (Deleplace and Nell, 1996; Nell, 1998a, Ch. 5; Nell, 2001).

Bank money is created *ex nihilo*, but the circumstances have to provide appropriate institutional support. Like inconvertible paper, this kind of money will also have value only by convention. That is, it has no intrinsic value and it is not backed by anything. It cannot be converted into gold, for example. Why then should anyone accept it, if, say, they could obtain gold-backed money? Suppose some banks offered convertible money, and others offered inconvertible money. The inconvertible money, but not the gold-based money, can be used to pay taxes (as in the US after 1933). If the level of taxation is low, and especially if the government inspires little confidence, the public will continue to use the gold-backed money, and buy the inconvertible money at tax time. But this strategy will pose the risk that there may be a shortage of tax-paying money at tax time, driving up its price. If the level of taxation is high, this could impose a serious, unexpected loss. If this loss, adjusted for its probability, is larger than the carrying costs of the inconvertible money, the public will accept and use that money.

Once it decides to accept and use the inconvertible money, however, Gresham's Law comes into play. The weaker currency will be accepted, but it will also be passed along as fast as possible, building up holdings only for tax-paying. The gold-based money will also be accepted, but being judged sounder, it will tend to be held as an asset, so it will gradually drop out of circulation.

A system based on bank money has no 'anchor'. Since banks are in business for profits, they will create loans to meet any creditworthy demands, so bank money cannot easily be constrained in quantity. To maintain the value of such money, however, prices and wages must remain steady in terms of the unit of account. To keep money wages and prices steady, therefore, it has seemed that demand must be kept weak, creating an overhang of unemployed labor and excess productive capacity. It is clear that this is wasteful; to argue that it is unnecessary, however, we must show how the value of bank money could be anchored some other way. Such a proposal will be suggested in the last section of this chapter.

The absence of an anchor also leaves the interest rate floating free. There is no supply function tying the quantity of money to reserves and reserves to the interest rate. Reserves are the balances banks hold with the central bank; these will fluctuate with the state of trade and with the government's tax and spending activities. Excess or deficiencies in the reserve balances will lead to sharp fluctuations in overnight rates. The central bank therefore has to smooth this out. Whatever rate the central bank sets in the market for its loans will automatically become the minimum rate. In short, in order to *smooth* the basic interest rate, the central bank has no choice but to *peg* that rate.

In a closed economy[15] with a pure system of fiat and balance-sheet money, the two 'prices' determined above by supply and demand – the value of money and the interest rate – will now be determined outside of, or apart from the market; they will be what economists call 'exogenous'. The command of the nominal unit of account – the dollar or the pound or the peso – over goods and services is a convention that ties the accounting system of the economy in question to its world of production and exchange; in practice, of course, this will always be given by history. The unit of account at any time will be worth so much in goods and services, because this is what has been established in practice, historically deriving from the metallic system. But once the tie to precious metal has been broken, there is no market, no organized system of pressures, to keep the level of this unit stable at the given initial value. It is what it is because of the arbitrary facts of history, but no market forces will keep it that way. This opens the door to inflation. But there will be no automatic response. The interest rate is no longer set by supply and demand.

M SYSTEMS AND C SYSTEMS CONTRASTED

Goodhart's contention is that the euro is based on M theory. We have suggested that M systems – in practice, associated with earlier forms of capitalism – are characterized by built-in, self-stabilizing mechanisms, which, however, have to be regulated and supplemented by the Mint or the central bank. Fiscal policy is not so effective in such systems, so stabilization is left to monetary management, where the chief purpose will be to prevent inflation.

But the money in the modern world is not based on gold or silver, nor do modern monetary systems behave like M systems. This has implications for the idea of an OCA. C theory would not base the case for an OCA on 'efficiency'. The argument would tend to be that a certain group of countries are so closely integrated that they move through the phases of the business cycle together, so that monetary and fiscal policy would tend to affect them in the same ways. Moreover, policies would be stronger and more effective for being co-ordinated.

This is a very different way of thinking. To see its implications, let's draw the contrasts between M- and C-thinking about monetary systems. The relevant differences can be summarized in regard to real and money wages, deposits and reserves, finance, interest and capital values, and the role of the central bank.

Real Wages and Money Wages

In the old system prices were determined in two steps. The money unit of account was fixed in metal by the minting process, and then the wage was set in terms of the unit of account, which meant that it was set in coined money. This had an important implication: when money is tied to intrinsic value, setting the wage in terms of money fixes the real wage. So if the wage in terms of metallic money is determined in the labor market by supply and demand, this settles the real wage and the distribution of income. That is, once the wage is set in terms of a money article that is itself produced by mining and minting, the rate of profit and prices are fixed also.

The easiest way to see this is to consider a highly simplified system, in which wages are paid in gold. In every industry outputs will be produced and wages will be paid in gold. But the industry that produces gold (we assume in suitable form for use as a medium of exchange), likewise pays wages (and any other costs) in terms of gold. But its output is also gold. Profits are output minus wages (and other costs), so profits will also be realized in gold. Profits over the sums advanced gives the rate of profit; so when the wage is fixed in gold, the rate of profit is set in the gold industry. Competition requires that in all other industries prices must be such as to yield this same rate of profit. So: fixing the wage in terms of gold fixes the rate of profit and all prices (Nell, 1998a, pp. 229–32, 2000).[16]

But when money is not tied to commodity production the connection between wages and prices no longer holds. Fixing the money wage does not fix the real wage. The real wage is the money wage divided by the price level, and the two parts are no longer inseparably connected. Supply and demand in the labor market may affect the money wage, but they do not settle the real wage. The mark-up, the percentage by which business sets prices above wage costs, still has to be determined. Prices and money wages are determined separately.

By contrast, as we shall see shortly, many conventional economists assume the validity of marginal productivity theory. The real wage is expressed as a ratio of money wages to an index of prices. If this is to remain equal to a constant – the equilibrium marginal product – both numerator and denominator must grow at the same rate. Price and money wage movements must be equal. But conventional marginal productivity theory is highly suspect.[17] Yet arguably it is simply a mistaken account of an actual phenomenon. For a version of marginal productivity appears to hold in the economy of early capitalism – but only there

(Michie, 1987; Nell, 1998b). In such conditions the pressure of effective demand pushes the economy to a position where the real wage equals the marginal utilization product of labor, but this comes about precisely through different speeds of adjustment of money wages and prices, that is, different rates of inflation (Hicks, 1989; Nell, 2001). In modern, fully industrialized capitalism, however, there is no requirement that the real wage should equal the marginal utilization product, indeed since the marginal product is generally constant over the range of normal utilization, this could not be achieved. So there is no market pressure at all to pull rates of wage and price inflation together. We can therefore expect them typically to differ. This means that inflation will normally be non-uniform and so will have consequences for distribution.

Since bargaining processes are likely to be different in different countries, inflationary pressures may well end up being different, even if the phases of the cycle are the same. A uniform euro-wide anti-inflationary policy may be inappropriate – unless it is a preventative one, of the kind we shall suggest in concluding.

Bank Deposits and Reserves

The monetary system of a modern, industrial economy is based on the fiat of the state, and on the balance sheets of banks. The chief form of money is bank liabilities, which the state guarantees in various ways and will accept in payment of taxes. These liabilities are created in the course of normal business. Banks, of course, receive deposits and re-lend them.[18] To focus on this, however, is to miss the essential aspect of modern money – its creation and cancellation in the process of circulation. Banks *create* deposits in response to the demand for advances for working capital, chiefly to pay wages. The deposit is a liability, but the loan is a corresponding asset. The books balance. The bank, of course, must have adequate capital to cover its risks, and it must be part of a system that will enable it to manage its liquidity problems. But the money supply is inseparable from the demand for money. Within a wide range the monetary system imposes no constraints. It simply adapts.

Banks as well as government create money on demand. Banks create deposits by making loans to qualified borrowers. Banks create deposits up to the point permitted by their capitalization, meaning the amount of independent capital they have – for this is what will cover liabilities in the event of a failure. So the amount of capital a bank must have is the amount that will cover its risk. Given an adequate capitalization, then, a bank will create deposits by making loans. The deposits are liabilities, the loans are assets. So assets and liabilities balance; provided the bank is sufficiently well capitalized – able to cover its risks – there is no problem of solvency. What a bank must be able to do, then, is clear the checks written against its deposits, and such clearing requires adequate liquidity. Liquidity, rather than solvency, is the characteristic problem of a modern bank.

A modern banking system, then, must be able to guarantee liquidity – deposits must be fully liquid, that is to say, always and everywhere acceptable. Which means that checks must always clear. But why should anyone accept a check drawn on a bank they never heard of, or even if they have, is half a continent away? Even assuming that the signer of the check is known and believed to be good for the money, how do the recipients know that the bank is sound? The answer *has* to be that the check will be good because someone guarantees it even if the bank is in trouble. That must be someone sufficiently powerful and sufficiently well-known, which means the government or an agency of the government, such as the Federal Reserve. Such backing will ensure that the check will clear, provided, of course, that the credit of the signer is good. Liquidity is what the central bank guarantees.[19]

Essentially bank deposits are accepted as currency because they are backed by the state. They are needed because they can be used to pay taxes; the fact that taxes must be paid, of course, rests on the power of the state to tax. (In Russia today taxes can be evaded, and the ruble has been supplanted in many places by the dollar or the mark, which are desired because they can be used to buy imports.) Bank deposits, and the monies which the state spends, are created at the point at which they enter circulation, and they are canceled at the time they are removed from circulation. When a loan is repaid, a bank liability – money – is canceled; when a loan is rolled over, it is canceled and recreated. When taxes are paid and the tax check has cleared, the government's account at the Fed is reduced – money is canceled. Creation and cancellation of money is not quite the same thing as supply and demand – for one thing, market forces tend to bring demand and supply into alignment, but they do not act in anything like the same way on creation and cancellation. The supply-and-demand terminology, appropriate to the craft economy, does not accurately describe what takes place in the modern monetary system. It is better to say that money is created and canceled in the process of circulation.

Neither the bank deposits nor the paper are convertible into gold or other metals; they cannot be taken to the banks and turned in for anything of intrinsic value. They do not constrain behavior in the way convertible reserves did. Modern reserves are simply balances at the central bank; their only actual function is as 'clearing balances' – otherwise they simply serve as a tool by means of which the Central Bank can influence banks' behavior.

As a result, of course, there are no automatic market mechanisms that will tend to maintain the value of money. The market offers no system for stabilizing the price level. Inflation will have to be prevented or controlled by discretionary policy – or some other automatic stabilizer will have to be found.

Financial Systems

The financial system of the early capitalist economy was fairly simple. Bonds were sold to raise money for large-scale long-term capital projects such as building railroads. Government bonds were even more important. There was also a fairly small stock market. In early capitalism the financial system mobilizes savings to finance investment. In such an economy investments were judged by their potential profitability, compared to the interest charges. Growth did not so directly affect financial markets; rather than the growth rate, it was the profit rate that had to be compared to the interest rate. Businesses borrowed from banks, or issued bonds, to raise capital. To be able to service the loans or bonds they had to earn profit on that capital at a rate that would enable them to do so. Given a favorable climate for profits, business depreciation allowances could be channeled into sinking funds, to finance production of long-lived capital goods; other business savings – profits – then tended to flow into investment, and household savings were mobilized to underwrite housing construction and the production of durable goods, as well as being made available for business investment.

The financing of modern corporate industry reflects the ways it differs from the small-scale business of the earlier system. Long-term funds have to be raised on a huge scale; short-term funds have to be mobilized at a moment's notice. As demand changes, funds have to be canceled or shifted rapidly between activities. The day-to-day operations of the system, as well as its long-term health, rest on a complex set of markets for financial instruments providing various kinds of claims to streams of income with various maturities; these streams may be used for many purposes. Speculation on their value takes place. Some of them also carry voting rights in regard to corporate governance, so the financial system also provides the market for corporate control. Growth is reflected in share price appreciation; the growth rate and the interest rate are related to one another both in the money markets and in financial markets.

Banks are constrained by bank capital, where such capital is held to cover normal risks. Having adequate capital is required by the state, as a condition of state support for the banking system. This is a sensible precaution, limiting the indirect liability of the state, and it provides protection against moral hazard problems. But it is a rather loose constraint. Individual banks can easily raise additional capital when they need to cover the risks of potentially profitable additional lending. On the other hand it is more difficult for the system *as a whole* to raise further bank capital in an expansion. This will require a general rise in interest rates, yet such a rise may simply drive up prices, especially in a boom. And this may leave *real* rates unchanged, providing no additional real profit out of which to accumulate additional capital.

But the fact that money creation through lending is constrained by bank capital rather than real reserves creates a problem in regard to asset-price inflation. For the value of bank capital increases when stock and bond prices rise. So more money can be created; but this money may be used for speculation, further driving up asset prices. The result can be a self-sustaining asset inflationary spiral. The rise in asset prices will tend to pull up interest rates, but only in the wake of the price increases; that is, after the fact. This will not be enough to act as a corrective.

The Position of the Central Bank

To repeat, once the link to intrinsic value (cost of production plus seigniorage) is broken, there is no identifiable process by which the unit of account is connected to real goods and services. The connection, in fact, is simply given by history and tradition. Nor is there any market process that will maintain that value. Breaking the link implies that reserves are no longer held for the purpose of redemption; reserves have become simply clearing balances. The Fed can demand that banks hold a certain fraction of reserves – but it cannot limit the absolute quantity of reserves without endangering the clearing of checks. In short, without real reserves the central bank cannot control the quantity of money, so has no tools for controlling inflation, other than the nominal rate of interest. But this has only a limited effect; investment and demand for consumer durables properly respond to the real rate – always allowing for money illusion.[20] An important implication: central banks have less power over the economy than many suppose. The popular press suggests – and Wall Street appears to believe – that the Chairman of the Fed can determine the direction of the economy. Perhaps on occasion, but not as a normal course of events. The only tool available, the nominal rate of interest, arguably is simply not up to the job.

A little reflection will explain this. First there is no reason to doubt the traditional Keynesian judgment – that neither investment spending nor consumer durable purchases respond reliably to variations in nominal interest rates. Indeed, both *should* only be sensitive to changes in real interest rates.[21] Second, stabilization is multi-faceted. Central banks have to prevent recessions, as well as defend against inflation. If the economy is characterized by a Phillips curve, then recession will be the price of controlling inflation. However, if there is no reliable relationship between inflation and unemployment – as in recent decades – then there are *two* independent target variables to be controlled with *one* policy tool.

Indeed it is worse than that. In the later part of the postwar period, after the ending of most capital controls, the nominal rate of interest became an important factor in managing and defending the value of the currency in international markets. A recession might call for a reduction of the interest rate, to stimulate domestic investment. But such a reduction could then trigger a sell-off of the domestic currency; this would cause a withdrawal of foreign capital, leading to a Stock Market decline. The lower exchange rate would then lead to an increase in import costs, and so to widespread price increases, triggering inflation. In short the policy called for by domestic needs could easily conflict with the appropriate international stance.[22]

If there is a Phillips curve, then inflation can only be controlled *at the expense* of unemployment, unemployment curbed only by allowing inflation. If consumption moves with the Stock Market, reflecting wealth effects, then cutting back consumption requires curbing the Stock Market. Controlling inflation this way could well turn out to be appallingly expensive, but to make matters worse – it might not work the way policy-makers expect, or indeed, at all. For neither the Phillips curve nor the wealth effect relationships are reliable. Not only may they shift; they may sometimes not even be evident at all. So depending on them to constrain spending may not be effective.

On top of everything, it is the traditional responsibility of the central bank to maintain order in financial markets, which is now understood to include the Stock Market. Actual and anticipated interest rate changes now have powerful effects on stock prices. These effects have to be taken into consideration, adding yet another target variable to those the central bank must consider when making changes in interest rates. How many target variables can be managed with one policy tool?

What the central bank *can* reliably do, is create a recession by raising the nominal rate higher and higher until spending is cut back significantly. However, it can't reverse the course of the economy; raising rates will shut it down, but cutting them may not start it up. The one policy tool the central bank has does not work symmetrically.

Economic policy cannot be left to rest on the powers of the central bank. And, indeed, the supporters of the euro have recognized this is setting the harsh fiscal conditions that member states must meet. These conditions effectively establish a permanent stance of fiscal austerity, which will tend to prevent the development of demand-based inflationary pressures, but by the same token will also lead to low capacity utilization and slow growth.

POLICY AND THE CHARTALIST POSITION

The euro is not an M system; it is a C system, but an unusual one, in that it is not backed by the sovereign power of a state, and does not have the backing of a tax system or a fiscal policy. The design of the system, especially in regard to fiscal constraints, appears to be intended to make the euro behave like an M currency. In particular, it will not be prone to inflation.

This is perhaps not as surprising as it might seem. There is a famous claim that one could be a Chartalist in theory, and still support a Metallist position in practice. To quote Schumpeter:

> An economist may, for instance, be fully convinced that theoretical metallism is untenable, and yet be a strong practical metallist. Lack of confidence in the authorities or politicians, whose freedom of action is greatly increased by currency systems that do not provide for prompt and unquestioning redemption in gold of all means of payment that do not consist of gold, is quite sufficient to motivate practical metallism in a theoretical c[h]artalist... (1954, 289)

One could reject the Metallist theory, supporting Chartalism, yet in practice support currency systems that require prompt redemption *in order to put a check on Governments' tendencies to overissue*. The Metallist commitment to redeem would be a policy commitment. It would establish an *automatic* regulatory system; but, although automatic, it would still be a matter of policy. A Chartalist would not subscribe to the view that metallic money spontaneously generated itself through the market. Currencies are established and maintained by the state, but the policies that ensure this can either be discretionary or could be set up to run automatically.

In today's world, of course, the problem is not a tendency to overissue – although monetarists still want to try to control the money supply. But in modern monetary systems, in which banks create deposits by making loans, that is not a feasible objective – as Goodhart and others have long argued. But it is still necessary to seek a curb on the tendency of markets to fall into self-sustaining inflation, including asset inflation.

Inflation may also have political roots, and Metallism has a political side. It has often been allied to a strong form of *laissez faire*, holding that defense of markets, property and wealth – which requires a sound currency and safe banks – must keep democratic forces at bay, lest they undermine efficiency in pursuit of equity. Markets, on this view, are not only stabilizing; they stabilize at an optimal level, and government intervention will only lead to suboptimal positions. Democratic forces could push for interventions in the name of stability, yet in truth be trying to reap rewards, for example for labor, that cannot be justified by economic efficiency. This could then set off inflation. To prevent such democratic forces from gaining a foothold, monetarists and their allies have argued that, as far as possible, adjustment should be placed in the care of automatic or self-regulating market mechanisms. And this is what the real money system offered. But it is not what the euro provides.

In Schumpeter's time currencies still had backing. No longer. There is simply no basis for a Metallist position, whatever might have been true in the past. Yet the belief in the automatic self-regulating properties of markets dies hard; no matter how badly out of line it is with current reality. There is little evidence of a price mechanism in the advanced economies today, and none at all of any kind of self-regulating adjustment in financial markets. Far from regulating themselves, contemporary financial markets appear to be prone to asset price bubbles. Nor can these markets be stabilized by simple interest rate adjustments. This is partly because the nominal interest rate is too weak or is inappropriate as a policy tool. But it is also because there are far too many conflicting demands on the central bank. It has one policy tool, and a wide and sometimes changing list of objectives and priorities.

But the euro does not rely exclusively on the weak policy tool of the central bank. In fact it relies on fiscal policy, but not on *discretionary* fiscal policy. Instead it has *a policy of built-in austerity*. The ability of governments to run deficits and pile up debt is severely restricted. This is a policy stance, rather than a policy. It is not responsive to changing conditions. It will tend to prevent demand-pressure inflation; and it will curb other kinds, to the extent that they can be reined in by running the economy with a lot of slack. So it is unlikely to prevent cost-inflation. And it is outrageously expensive.

CONCLUSION

Metallism simply has no basis in today's world. Nor is there justification for any doctrines, like monetarism and its relatives, that are grounded on Metallism, or on belief in the self-adjusting properties of monetary systems. Yet M theorists do have a point when they argue that discretionary policies are at the mercy of politics, and can lead to instability and inflation. But they have not come up with an automatic adjustment. Instead they offer the combination of a rigid fiscal stance with the discretionary policy of an independent and supposedly expert central bank, relying on the weak and asymmetrical policy tool of the nominal interest rate. This is not the answer – instead they should have come up with an alternative plan of automatic self-regulation, something more like what the old M system provided. As we shall see, this is what the ELR can offer today.

By contrast, Chartalists take the position that the state must manage the monetary system. Once the metal-based system has been abandoned, there is no longer any protection against inflation. So the managers have to take action. Relying on the effects of the nominal interest rate will not be sufficient. The European system has made it virtually impossible to draw on discretionary fiscal policy. The fiscal stance taken is expensive and rigid.

Goodhart's conclusion – namely that the euro cannot be supported by monetary policy alone, even with an austerity fiscal stance – is consonant with recent events and may very likely turn out to be correct. But the errors in setting up the euro are most probably not due to an excessive belief in the efficiency of money, or the ability of markets to generate it spontaneously, but rather arose because issues of stabilization were ignored. This seems to have happened because of an insufficiently examined belief in the self-adjustment of markets, probably well-grounded (to some extent) in earlier eras, and justifiable in terms of M theory, which was arguably applicable in those eras. But M theory does not apply today, for the good reason that metal-based monetary systems proved insufficiently flexible and have been replaced by pure C systems. These do not have any self-regulating properties. Nor is the policy tool, the nominal interest rate, adequate to the task of managing the economy. The old Keynesian contention, that fiscal policy must be at the center of economic management, needs to be re-examined, or, perhaps, re-invented.

However, fiscal policy need not necessarily be discretionary. There is no need to abandon the idea of automatic self-regulation. M theorists are surely right to emphasize the desirability of self-regulating systems. But a rigid fiscal stance, combined with an independent but nevertheless discretionary monetary policy, is no substitute for a flexible self-regulating system.

And such systems can be found. The budget of the central government, for example, will tend automatically to move countercyclically – welfare spending falls in the boom, while tax receipts increase. This has been recognized for decades. But governments have come to fear that an expansion may trigger inflation – hence the rigid fiscal stance prescribed for the euro.

Yet this need not be the case. An automatic fiscal response can be combined with wage stabilization. The key to this is to treat a portion of government employment as a 'buffer stock', hired at a fixed wage (which effectively becomes a market-enforced minimum wage) when the economy is weak, and released to better-paying jobs when the economy is strong. This then will stabilize the lower end of the wage scale, and since wage and salary relativities tend to hold steady over time, it will likely stabilize the whole wage structure. To set this up it is necessary to commit the government to hire anyone willing to work at a fixed wage, creating a special Public Service Employment Program for the purpose. When the economy weakens, labor will flow into this program, working at jobs that are socially useful, but not normally profitable – environmental clean-up, teachers' assistants in primary schools, meals on wheels, various kinds of support for private industry, and so on – including training and retraining programs. When the economy recovers, labor will flow out to the private sector. Several policy packages of this kind have recently been proposed (Harvey, 1989; Wray, 1998; Nell and Majewski, forthcoming).

These proposals, outlining what is often called an employer of last resort, offer both an automatic countercyclical fiscal response and a kind of 'buffer stock' stabilization of the money wage. This is not just another promising direction in which policy might move; it provides a plausible replacement for the automatic stabilizer that M systems had.

NOTES

* This chapter draws on Chapter 5 of *Leviathan's Wallet*, written jointly by myself and Ray Majewski. Thanks to Warren Mosler and to members of the Transformational Growth and Full Employment Program at the New School for comments and support.

1. It is widely assumed that when competitive markets are stable, they tend towards 'optimal' positions, that is, to positions which reflect what the market participants 'want'. Neoclassical theory tries to demonstrate this rigorously. Unfortunately, it turns out not to be true under normal assumptions. General equilibrium models characteristically have multiple solutions, even an infinite number, some or all of which may be unstable. Moreover, it is very difficult to define a role for money in such models.

2. All the same, real money was normally coined by monarchs in denominations defined by the royal mints.

3. In Nell (1988, 1998a, 1998b) systematic differences between a 'craft economy' (including craft-based factories) and a 'mass production' economy are examined. The two systems are considered in 'pure' form and shown to adjust differently, the first depending on a price mechanism, the second on a multiplier-accelerator. This analysis does not have to be accepted, however, to agree that there are many significant differences between early, small-scale capitalism and the modern industrial corporate system.

4. As Berkeley pointed out (Johnston, 1970) a country rich in gold and silver but poor in industry is not truly wealthy. It cannot consume the gold and silver any more than Midas could; it will soon spend its metal reserves on imports from industrious nations, and then it will have nothing.

5. The importance of clearly distinguishing between the unit of account and its embodiment in coins can be illustrated by reference to the disastrous British Recoinage of 1695. Following Locke's advocacy, the worn and underweight – and so undervalued – old coinage was more or less completely replaced by new coins of full weight. Money was more valuable, so prices fell. But *debts* were reckoned in the unit of account; hence the burden of debt was increased throughout the kingdom, with unfortunate effects on commerce and trade – the exact opposite of what had been intended. Locke may fairly be accused of not having understood the difference between the coinage and the unit of account (Johnston, 1970, VIII).

6. As Walras, Marshall, Pigou and Fisher all held, cf. the long discussion in Patinkin, 1965, Ch VIII, and Supplementary Notes C, D, F, and G. If, as is likely, the value – or supply price – from mining and minting reflects constant costs over the relevant range, then another characteristically Classical result holds: value is governed from the supply side and quantity from the demand. (Cf. Garegnani, 1989)

7. Supporters of the Loanable Funds approach may object, but there is little evidence that saving has ever been very responsive to interest. More importantly, there is a theoretical objection. When interest increases, wealth-holding households find their income higher, but by the same token, business firms find that their profit income net of interest is down. When everyone has adjusted to the change, wealth-holding households may save more, but businesses will be saving less. On the assumption that all capital income is saved, these changes will cancel. If wealth-holding households consume a portion of capital income, but businesses, in the light of competitive pressures, save it all, then a rise in interest would *reduce* saving.

8. This provides an explanation for what Keynes called 'Gibson's Paradox', namely the strong and centuries-long correlation between the level of prices and the interest rate (Keynes, 1930, Vol II). It also shows the market interest rate fluctuating around a long-term norm, so that booms and slumps will tend to average out.

9. Note that fiscal policy cannot be very effective here. A deficit does provide a stimulus, but at the same time it will shift the demand for reserves up, raising interest rates; a surplus provides a drag, but will lower interest rates.

10. Wicksell (1898) developed this idea. If the 'money rate of interest' lay below the 'natural rate of return', then the economy would have a tendency to inflate, if the money rate were above the natural rate the economy would deflate. If there are no real reserves to constrain the system, the inflation and deflation will tend to continue indefinitely.

11. In fact, the Mint had a small liability; it had to issue new, full-weight coins to replace any worn or underweight coins presented to it.

12. Historically fiat money has usually been introduced as a temporary expedient in wartime, sometimes with reasonable success, as with 'greenbacks' in the US Civil War, sometimes disastrously, as in the case of the 'assignats' of the French Revolution.

13. Government can be large or small; banking can be privately managed or state-managed. But when banks are no longer constrained by real reserves, their credibility depends on state backing. The state therefore insists on banks having sufficient capital to cover their normal risks, and regulates them accordingly. In this sense bank-created currency is an indirect liability of the state.

14. The account of circulation makes it possible to identify a specific sum of money or credit-money, and show that this amount, appropriately advanced, will 'monetize' all transactions in the economy, including the realization of profits. Given assumptions about technology and institutions, this sum of money and the sequence in which it moves can be shown to be unique. It provides a precise definition of 'velocity'.

15. A closed economy need not be taken to mean an economy without foreign trade or factor – capital or labor – flows. Rather it is one in which trade and factor flows are prevented from exercising any influence over economic magnitudes – prices, quantities and income flows.

16. It's easy – and important – to see that this will not be the case in a C system. The analogy to mining and minting would be banking. But the output of banking is not money or even loans. It is financial services, which are intangible. Wages and salaries and other costs are paid in money; but the value of financial services – their earning power – depends on the *rate of interest*.

17. When presented in full dress as high-powered pure theory, it turns out to suffer from a logical flaw, as demonstrated in the 'Capital Critique' debates (Garegnani, 1970; Harcourt, 1972; Laibman and Nell, 1977). Statistical and econometric studies are either inconclusive, or show that real wages are mildly pro-cyclical today. Institutional analyses show that businesses do not think in marginal productivity terms when making hiring decisions.

18. That banks receive deposits which they re-lend is easily understood. But such a process cannot be the basis of a pure system of accounting money. For a re-lending process to begin, there must be some initial money coming from outside the banking system which is then deposited with it. Suppose there is no such money; the banking system is the sole supplier of deposits. Then the deposits must be created by banks. Suppose the government deposits money with the banks; the same questions arise – did the money come from outside the government, or did the government create it? If the latter, then how? We shall see that the central bank creates deposits for the treasury, balanced by treasury securities, the interest on which the central bank returns to the treasury. Government and the banking system work together to create and cancel money.

19. An important part of the guarantee is provided by deposit insurance, but this, too, is normally provided by the state, and, if it were private, in a major crisis it would have to be underwritten by the state.

20. In the very short run, a change in the nominal rate will normally – but not always – imply a similar change in the real rate. Once a longer stretch of time is considered, however, this cannot be assumed.

21. Consumers will not be likely to curtail their purchases of durable goods because of a rise in nominal interest if their incomes have gone up proportionately. Similarly businesses will not feel compelled to cut back spending if their money profits have risen in the same proportion as interest charges.

22. Indeed, the policy problem may be even more difficult. Consider two countries, A and B, that trade with each other, with a flexible exchange rate. An imbalance develops, so that A runs a trade deficit with B. Its exchange rate falls, imports are more costly and prices begin to rise. In B a surplus emerges and imports are cheaper. To control inflation and keep the exchange rate from falling too far, A raises nominal interest rates. But because of inflation this has only a small effect on *real* interest rates. So a large increase will be necessary – and if large enough this may induce a recession. But a recession will very likely bring the Stock Market down. With inflation up, a weak exchange rate and a recession impending, even with

nominal interest rates very high at least some financial capital will flee from A to B, where a trade surplus and a strong exchange rate offer a safer climate, even though nominal rates are lower. Such movement is likely to trigger a downswing in stock prices and further capital movements. To stem this, interest rates will have to be raised further, which will only make things worse domestically. As short-term funds move the reserve position of A weakens relative to B adding further impetus to the flight to quality. In short, there may be circumstances in which flexible exchange rates prove to be de-stabilizing.

REFERENCES

Deleplace, Ghislain and E.J. Nell (1996), *Money In Motion*, London: Macmillan.

Garegnani, Piero (1970), 'Heterogeneous capital, the production function and the theory of distribution', *Review of Economic Studies*, 37: 407–36.

Goodhart, Charles, Chapters 1 and 9, this volume.

Harcourt, G.C. (1972), *Cambridge Controversies in Capital Theory*, New York: Cambridge University Press.

Harvey, Philip (1989), *Securing the Right to Employment*, Princeton: Princeton University Press.

Hicks, Sir John (1967), *Critical Essays in Monetary Theory*, Oxford: Clarendon Press.

Hicks, Sir John (1989), *A Market Theory of Money*, London: Macmillan.

Johnston, Joseph (1970), *Bishop Berkeley's QUERIST in Historical Perspective*, Dundalk: Dundalgen Press.

Keynes, John Maynard (1930), *Treatise on Money*, 2 vols, London: Macmillan.

Laibman, David and E.J. Nell (1977), 'Reswitching, Wicksell effects and the neoclassical production function', *American Economic Review*, 63: 100–113.

Michie, Jonathan (1987), *Wages in the Business Cycle*, London: Frances Pinter.

Nell, Edward (1988), *Prosperity and Public Spending*, London and New York: Unwin Hyman.

Nell Edward (1996), *Making Sense of a Changing Economy*, New York and London: Routledge.

Nell Edward (1998a), *The General Theory of Transformational Growth*, Cambridge: Cambridge University Press.

Nell Edward (ed.) (1998b), *Transformational Growth and the Business Cycle*, New York and London: Routledge.

Nell Edward (2000), 'Monetizing the classical equations', New School working paper, forthcoming 2003, *Cambridge Journal of Economics*.

Nell Edward (2001), 'Notes on Hicks and Horizontalism', in Louis-Philippe Rochon and Matias Vernengo (eds), *Horizontalism*, Cheltenham, Edward Elgar.

Nell, Edward and Raymon Majewski (forthcoming), *Leviathan's Wallet*.

Patinkin, Don (1965), *Money, Interest and Prices*, 2nd edn, New York: Harper and Row.

Schumpeter, J.A. (1954), *A History of Economic Analysis*, New York: Oxford University Press.

Wicksell, Knut (1898), *Interest and Prices*, translated 1936 by R.F. Kahn, reprinted (1962), New York: Augustus Kelley.

Wicksell, Knut (1911), *Lectures on Economic Theory, Vol. 2*, translated 1934–5 by E. Classen, reprinted in London: Routledge and Kegan Paul.

Wicksell, Knut (1989), *Interest and Prices*, translated by R.F. Kahn, London: Macmillan.

Wray, Randall (1998), *Understanding Modern Money*, Cheltenham, UK and Northampton, MA, USA: Edward Elgar.

7. Money as a social institution: A heterodox view of the euro

Robert Guttmann

When Robert Mundell won the 1999 Nobel Prize in Economics, the media – always in need of coining a phrase, which helps concretize the otherwise elusively abstract work of economists – called him the 'father of the euro'. Notwithstanding his significant contributions to supply-side economics and the modeling of macroeconomic adjustment processes, the Columbia University professor won distinction above all with his work on Optimal Currency Areas (Mundell, 1961) of which the creation of a single-currency zone within the European Union could be considered the most ambitious application to date.

With Mundell's *opus maior* thus celebrated and the euro project well under way, it is an opportune moment to take a closer look at an important contribution appearing recently in the *European Journal of Political Economy* by Charles Goodhart of the London School of Economics (Goodhart, 1998). In this article Professor Goodhart attacks Mundell's notion of Optimum Currency Areas (OCA) as well as its applicability for Europe's single-currency project currently under way. He builds his argument in very original fashion by putting the OCA concept into the context of traditional monetary theory and presenting an alternative view of money, which leads to a radically different interpretation of the euro's introduction and repercussions.

Goodhart's article raises a number of crucial questions concerning money which deserve a lot of reflection and debate. In April 1999 a panel of economists, historians, and political scientists had the opportunity to discuss them with Professor Goodhart in a one-day conference at the New School University in New York, and my comment here is an outgrowth of this memorable event.

THE AMBIGUOUS ORIGINS OF MONEY

Most economists view the evolution of money exclusively in terms of economic cost minimization efforts by the private sector (Menger, 1892). Different forms of money have emerged over time, because they offered potential users lower transaction and adjustment costs than hitherto existing media of exchange. This Mengerian conceptualization of money, termed by Goodhart the 'M view', lends itself very conveniently to the construction of neoclassical equilibrium models about the market's inherent capacity for stable and efficient self-regulation. It highlights the neutrality of money *vis-à-vis* the rest of the economy as a merely technical means with which to facilitate transactions. It is an approach that preserves very well the neoclassical tradition of mathematical modeling. And it downplays, often even ignores, the role of government in the management of money as if the latter were beyond any political considerations and should not be hampered by those. There is, in other words, also an ideological aspect to the M view, one that corresponds to the orthodox economist's love for free markets unimpeded by government meddling and constraints.

In his 1998 paper Goodhart attacks the M view from a variety of angles. For one, he disputes that money emerged in the way presented by the M team, deriving its origins instead from early religious and other communitarian practices, which predated trade. He also points to clear contradictions in the M team theory concerning history's most important money forms, stressing here the considerable transaction costs of metal money as well as the inseparable linkage between the state and fiat money in the form of paper notes. Based on these criticisms, Goodhart concludes that a different approach to money, known as the Cartalist (or Chartist) view, provides a much more accurate and meaningful framework with which to explain the origins and subsequent development of money. This so-called 'C view' highlights the role of the state, and with it political considerations, in the management of money. An inherently interdisciplinary approach shared by historians, anthropologists, political scientists, but only a minority of (mostly heteredox) economists, the C view links money to the state apparatus. That linkage concerns above all political sovereignty, of which control over the national currency is perhaps the most vital expression, as well as the state's fiscal authority which is greatly abetted by its management of money creation. Goodhart develops both of these connections with the aid of many literature references and historic illustrations to argue the superiority of the C view over the M view.

The starting point of contention between the two competing views is the question concerning how money originated in the first place. The C view, accepting the fact that money probably emerged long before any organized state apparatus had taken root, looks at religious and other intra-communitarian practices for an answer. One such early use of money concerns the settlement of disputes in which the injured party obtains the payment of a fine by the party committing the criminal act for compensation of injury or property damage. Such wergeld had the advantage of resolving conflicts and preventing tit-for-tat escalation of violence among feuding clans, which threatened to tear apart relatively small and interdependent settlements. The practice soon spread to other interpersonal relationships, such as payments of a dowry in arranged marriages or payments for slaves. In addition, money also emerged in religious practices, often replacing sacrificial practices or payments in kind, which turned temples into commercial centers of the ancient world. Once priests began to lend out the wealth they had amassed from gifts offered during religious ceremonies, they needed a commodity serving as monetary standard which third parties would accept as means of payment.[1]

An important byproduct of placing the origins of money in these inter-societal activities of religion and restitution is the attention it focuses on the means-of-payment function of money. This function, emphasized by Karl Marx (see Marx, 1967, Chs. 22 and 25) and largely ignored by most other economists working on money, concerns the settlement of obligations rooted in custom (for example gifts in religious practices, marriage dowries) or arising from debt contracts. It seems to me that this function of money is absolutely vital, not least in the context of the international monetary system. Cross-border transactions, whether involving trade or investments, represent – from the point of view of monetary transfers – payment obligations from one country to another. Any deficits from one country to another must be settled by corres-ponding money transfers from the deficit country's central bank to the surplus country's central bank. Here money functions as means of payment. The problem is that any system using national currencies as international money violates this function. In such a system the country issuing the national currency serving as international medium of exchange (for example the US-dollar after World War II) has the advantage of being able to pay for its external deficits with other countries in its own currency. Such deficits, which the key-currency issuer must run to provide the rest of the world with adequate liquidity, are automatically financed by foreigners holding the key currency as reserve. In other words, the country issuing the world money has to run balance-of-payments deficits and can automatically finance them by what is in effect an interest-free line of revolving credit supplied by the rest of the world holding reserves of its currency. Its deficits with other countries are thus never really settled, in the sense of having to give up a portion of one's income to pay for one's debt obligations. This is a major structural flaw of our current interna-tional monetary system and explains some of its destabilizing propensities (see Guttmann, 1997).

Let us now return to the debate over the origins of money. Unfortunately, Goodhart focuses his historical account on metal money and makes only a couple of passing references to agrarian money. The latter, a money form which surely preceded metals by several millennia, is the form of money highlighted by the M view. It emerged gradually in the wake of trade when the drawbacks of barter in terms of price formation and double coincidence of wants began to limit exchange activity below its potential.[2] With barter transactions growing more complex and sophisticated, people had an incentive to simplify the process. They surely realized that basic goods which were in strong demand, and in limited supply, maintained a steady value or even rose in value in relation to other products. Wheat was such a product; barley, too. Gradually, people began to save small quantities of, say, wheat to facilitate barter. Now they did not have to offer exactly the good desired by the other party to obtain the product they wanted. They could instead simply offer some of the hoarded wheat to the other party of the trade who, knowing the durable value of the wheat, would be willing to exchange his product for the grain. It also seems logical that parties to trade would increasingly assess the 'price' of goods in terms of that standard article that everyone knew, used, and had an appreciation of, such as wheat or barley. From the limited evidence available, we know that this process of turning certain widely used commodities into a generally accepted medium of exchange took place first in the Middle East (the so-called 'fertile crescent' connecting the Jordan Valley, Eastern Turkey, and Iraq like an arch), about 7000 to 8000 years ago.[3] We also know that there was a tremendous variety of commodities used as money early on. They comprised products used for ornamentation (for example beads, precious stones, other types of jewelry), animal products widely used by humans for protection or clothing (for example hides, wool, furs), useful tools (for example circular stones, nails), and above all agricultural products, such as cereals, grains, liquids (for example oil, wine, beer), honey (for sweetening), salt (for preservation of food), as well as cattle for large trans-actions such as acquiring a wife, purchasing a slave, or paying tribute.

The proliferation of such agrarian money forms in prehistoric societies lends itself to support the M view, because the process emphasizes the search for cost minimization by market agents no longer willing to accept the burdens of barter. Indeed, every major textbook in economics tells the same story, the invention of money aimed at overcoming the high transaction costs involved in barter. But if agrarian money was so efficient by comparison, why was it then replaced by metal money, a money form whose need for verification of fineness and weight made it arguably more costly than, say, wheat or other fairly homogeneous commodities serving as medium of exchange? Goodhart (1998, p. 11) raises this question, but fails to answer it. Let me try to come up with an answer on his behalf.

Agrarian money forms fell out of favor, because they suffered from major shortcomings prone to destabilize prehistoric societies. For one, those in a position to produce the product representing money must have had a huge advantage over those not able to do so. While everyone else always had to sell something socially useful first in order to acquire any money, the producers of the commodity serving as generally accepted medium of exchange had immediate access to money, by the very act of production. The introduction of such an institutionalized advantage for some eroded the primitive communism

of collective production efforts and common property found in early settlements. We can surmise that the appearance of money nourished instead the
notions of private property and production for profit. The period of money's first
appearance, around 5000 BC, coincided with the emergence of privately owned
farmland in the same geographic area, the Eastern Mediterranean. Owners of
money must at that point have been able to purchase land and so turn themselves
into producers of money, surely a lucrative proposition. Apart from producing
the medium of exchange and thus gaining direct command in the marketplace,
the producers of money also profited each time that the value of their product
increased and caused other (that is, non-money) goods to become cheaper.
Since land was in many instances the raw material for the creation of money,
as was surely the case with all agricultural or animal-based money-forms, the
struggle over its control had to be intense at times. Attacks on weaker communities by stronger settlements to take land and other resources useful for
money creation must have been more common than in the era of barter.

An even more important flaw of early forms of commodity money, in
particular agricultural money forms such as wheat or barley, was the propensity
of their producers for excess supplies thereof. Individual producers had an
incentive to produce a lot of the commodity serving as medium of exchange in
order to enhance their own purchasing power. But what appeared to make sense
on the micro level of single producers had disastrous consequences when considering the macro level of the aggregate. Together, the efforts of individual
producers to create more money often ended up devaluing that money.
Whenever the supply of money outpaced the output of tradable goods, prices
would rise across the board so that each unit of money would end up buying
less. Since it now took more money to buy the same quantity of goods, the
collective attempt to produce more commodity money usually proved self-
defeating while destabilizing prehistoric economies with an inflationary shock.

In sum, we do not know for sure how money first emerged – whether as the
result of religious and other cultural practices in accordance with the C view or
in the wake of trade to overcome the limitations of barter as emphasized by the
M view. Its emergence predates recorded history, thus leaving us bereft of
conclusive evidence. We can, however, surmise that agrarian forms of money,
stressed by the M view as proof of its cost-minimization theorem, contained
the disadvantages of inequality, social stratification, aggravation of conflict,
and excess supply (in addition to recurrent supply disruptions due to the vicis-
situdes of nature). All these are shortcomings usually associated with the
private-commodity dimension of money. In other words, whenever money takes
the form of a commodity produced by private agents seeking to profit from its
issue, it will exhibit these destabilizing tendencies of unequal access and pro-
cyclical supply. That argument seems to me an effective channel for

counter-attacking the standard M view, because it highlights the other, less sanguine side of leaving the evolution of money in the hands of private agents.

THE CONTRADICTORY DUAL NATURE OF MONEY

What neither the C view nor the M view recognize adequately is that money is a social institution which humans themselves introduced to facilitate their economic activities and regulate their social relations. When viewing money as such rather than simply as a good or asset, we take it for granted that one is dealing here with a man-made construct subject to change. We also view money as an integral part of the economy, a fundamentally endogenous variable that cannot be separated from the rest of the economy as the dominant (M view) paradigm wishes us to believe.

Perhaps the most important implication of the social-institution view of money I am suggesting here is recognition of its contradictory dual nature. Money combines two different aspects that are opposed to each other and whose conflicts, if left unchecked, can wreak havoc with the stability of our economy. On the one hand, money serves as a public good, because its proper functioning – in terms of the modalities of its creation, its smooth circulation, and its stable valuation – yields such large social benefits that you would not want anyone to be deprived of those. On the other hand, money has always contained elements of a private commodity inasmuch as it gets created by private agents seeking to profit from that privilege. Today the private agents empowered to create money are the commercial banks and other bank-like depository institutions (for example thrifts, credit unions). Those institutions create new money whenever they use their excess reserves accumulated in the course of taking deposits to make a loan on which they earn interest. The very act of money creation (via credit extension) is thus a major source of income creation for those institutions.

The dual nature of money is contradictory to the extent that the private-commodity aspects of money, if allowed to manifest themselves unimpeded, may very well engender consequences that undermine the public-good qualities of money. For example, if some market agents were empowered to create money and thereby were in a position to finance their spending with new money, they would gain a decisive advantage over all those market agents unable to do the same. Today we have resolved this equal-access problem by locating the creation of money outside the marketplace, in the banking system. Banks issue mere tokens (for example an empty book of checks) and then transfer those via credit to borrowers in whose hands the tokens become money as soon as the loan gets spent on goods, services or assets.[4] We still have a financial-exclusion problem violating the equal-access requirement of money as a public good.

Banks continue to deny credit to many businesses considered less creditworthy, particularly the smaller and/or newer ones, while also depriving the poor of access to checking accounts.

Another destabilizing consequence of money's private-commodity dimension is the tendency for banks to overextend credit during boom periods in pursuit of greater profit and then cut back lending sharply amidst the first troubling signs of over-extension, such as in response to sudden defaults. This boom–bust pattern of bank lending gives rise to a markedly pro-cyclical money supply that reinforces the business-cycle dynamic of ups and downs in our economy. To the extent that the banks' propensity for credit over-extension during boom periods feeds bubble-like speculation or overproduction, the private-commodity aspect of money ends up destabilizing our economy on a recurrent basis.

Finally, the private-commodity aspect of money manifests itself also in the fact that in the hands of private issuers, competing with each other for market share and motivated by profit, money itself becomes an object of innovation and product development. At times, such innovative activity gives rise to new money forms, which have profound (and often unintended) repercussions for the operation of our economic system. The Eurocurrencies market, which established itself in the early 1960s as a globally organized and unregulated banking network, is one example of such monetary innovation with far-reaching consequences. Cybercash may be another example, emerging over the coming decade in the wake of the 'Internet Revolution' to facilitate burgeoning e-commerce. Whatever form such monetary innovation may take, it will certainly be driven by considerations of attractiveness. People are notoriously wedded to the prevailing money forms, having vested a lot of public trust in them and have become deeply attached to them through habituation from constant use. A new money form must therefore have some kind of irresistible advantage, be it convenience and lower transaction costs or the prospect of greater stability, for the public to accept it in lieu of established money forms. Of course, the excesses associated with the private-commodity dimension of any particular money form may render the latter so problematic that the public is ready for a better substitute, a point correctly highlighted by Goodhart's discussion of dollarization in high-inflation countries (Goodhart, 1998, pp. 419–21).

The M view's emphasis on cost minimization is therefore perhaps not as irrelevant as its C view opponents often claim, since new money forms – even those introduced by the state – must gain public acceptance and trust, and thus contain some degree of attractiveness. A more effective critique of the M view would be to stress that money creation left in the hands of private agents tends to encourage excesses which are detrimental to the performance of our economic system.[5] This line of argumentation goes through a different route to arrive at the C view's central point linking money to public authority. The C view stresses control of money creation as a pillar of state power, both as a symbol of national sovereignty vested in the government and as a mechanism for its fiscal authority to impose tax payments on agents in its jurisdiction. The social-institution view of money, by contrast, arrives at the link between money and state through the need of having to balance the contradictory dual nature of this institution. To the extent that the private-commodity dimensions of money all threaten its public-good quality by accentuating inequality of access and cyclical instability, they have to be kept in check. Otherwise money does not operate efficiently and undermines the stability of the economy. Such containment of money's more destabilizing features has come to be vested in the hands of the government as the only non-market agent capable of counteracting market forces. Today the monetary authority of the state, the central bank, aims to safeguard the public-good quality of money with a combination of monetary-policy tools manipulating the money-creation ability of banks, financial regulations designed to affect structure and behavior of banks, lender-of-last-resort mechanisms to counteract financial crises, and international monetary arrangements which guide the participation of the national economy in the world economy.

The state management of money began early on with the introduction of metal money. Goodhart (1998, p. 412) explains why mints have almost always been under government control because of security concerns and verification requirements. I would add here that the very introduction of metal probably provided itself impetus for an enormous centralization of power, especially when compared with the inherently decentralized agrarian money forms which metal money came to replace. Metal had to be mined, and ownership of the mines was surely confined to a tiny elite of wealthy landowners who by means of that control alone could exercise considerable power. The mining of metal provided those operating the mines with monopoly access to a whole new generation of superior weaponry made of metal. By imposing metal pieces as medium of exchange, the mine-owners could extend their power into the sphere of commerce and so become true rulers. In that sense it is fair to argue that the very imposition of metal money acted as a source of state power. The more or less simultaneous appearance of metal money in three regions (Egypt, Sumer and China) more than five millennia ago coincided with the establishment of dynastic empires in each of these areas, the first nation states in human history. As can be seen in the bimetallic standard introduced by the Code of Menes (c. 3100 BC) as the foundation for centuries of Pharaonic rule along the Nile, the imposition of metal money served to legitimate state power in the hands of a single ruler whose authority was inexorably linked to his guarantee of its value. While Goodhart is correct in pointing out the difficulties involved in verifying weight and fineness of the money's metal content, we can also presume that even the earliest wardens of metal money worked hard to standardize the various metal shapes circulating as medium of exchange – a process which became much easier with the invention of minted coins in Lydia around 700 BC. And they surely interfered with the relative supplies of different metals serving as money to maintain their guaranteed relative prices. To the extent that they succeeded in standardizing metal-money shapes and maintaining their relative valuation standards, the rulers enjoyed the public trust in the money forms under their control as an endorsement of their authority, a legitimization of their rule.

Given these connections, it is not surprising that all the great subsequent empires of antiquity – the Babylon of Hammurabi, Solon's Athens, Rome in the aftermath of its wars with Carthage – established their imperial power by guaranteeing the value of their metal-money pieces, maintaining that guarantee of monetary stability for long periods of time, and extending the circulation of this state-managed money territorially as a vehicle of expanding the empire's reach.[6] As we know, centuries of responsible rule eventually ended in mismanagement in which increasingly desperate rules, having overextended themselves and facing consequently urgent funding problems, began to abandon the value guarantee by debasing their currency. The last vestiges of the Greek empire collapsed in hyperinflation when Alexander the Great decided, shortly before his untimely death in 323 BC, to release the gold hoard he had captured eight years earlier in Persepolis. And Nero's debasement of Rome's coins in 64 AD set the stage for four centuries of money mismanagement and eventual hyperinflation, which ended with the fall of the Eternal City in 476 AD. Even though Goodhart (ibid., p. 412) is correct in stressing the importance of dynastic rule for extending the time horizon of single rulers and thus assuring greater time consistency, the very nature of dynastic rule concentrating absolute power in the hands of a single monarch eventually corrupted the successors of the dynasty's founding fathers. Corrupt leaders abandoned their responsibility for public-good quality of money by regarding the public till as their private domain, a special case of money's private-commodity dimensions taking over to the detriment of society's well-being. It has been a long process of constant struggle, lasting at least until England's Bank Charter Act of 1844, to develop sufficiently accountable and democratic government structures for the public's interest in sound money to be safeguarded by a responsible monetary authority of the state.

This gets us to the transition from metal money to fiat money. Involving paper notes that are no longer convertible into gold or silver but serve as money by mere government decree (for example legal tender laws), such fiat money is the domain of the state. It is understandable that the C view regards fiat money as direct proof of its theory's superior relevance, a money form which seemingly contradicts the M view of monetary innovation as a result of private cost minimization efforts (Goodhart, 1998, pp. 416–18). Then again, for much of its historic existence, until the final breakdown of the gold standard in 1931, fiat money was a money form of dubious quality and ill equipped to gain public trust in durable fashion. It was usually introduced in an emergency situation when war had forced suspension of the gold standard and governments were under considerable pressure to finance the war-induced explosion of budget deficits. Unable to increase taxes in commensurate fashion for fear of eroding public support of the war, governments opted instead for a more indirect way via higher inflation devaluing the government's debt and increasing tax collections. This inflation tax, a byproduct of war-induced hyperinflation, works for a while until people lose confidence in money's stability and start to adjust their behavior in a destabilizing fashion, a cumulative process of self-realizing inflationary expectations which ends in the chaotic wildfires of hyperinflation.

Is it therefore surprising that the government often had to reinforce its fiat, the legal decrees imposing such inconvertible paper notes as money, by other means of imposition such as allowing payment of taxes and other obligations to be made only in fiat money or forcing its soldiers to accept payment in the new paper currency? The lack of public trust in fiat money during the 18th and 19th centuries is well illustrated in the fact that each of these experiments in direct state management of money – from the American Continentals of the Independence War and the assignats in post-revolutionary France to the (somewhat more cautiously managed) US greenbacks of the Civil War – was terminated shortly after the end of war with a return of the country in question to the gold standard.

It should be understood that fiat money, for so long not even a very durable variant of inconvertible paper notes functioning as money, is only part of a much broader story concerning a fundamental change in money form from commodity-money to credit-money (see Guttmann, 1994). That story began in earnest in the city-states of Renaissance Italy – Siena, Genoa, above all Florence – where banks resumed during the 13th century the ancient Roman practice of circulating depository receipts for gold storage as medium of exchange in lieu of the gold coins themselves. Now no longer bound to a specific person but usable as money in the hands of any 'bearer', those notes enjoyed wide circulation within the local sphere of medieval Italy's city-states. They were seen 'as good as gold' provided the banks could make good on their convertibility commitment. Those institutions discovered, however, that under normal circumstances only a fairly small portion of their deposits would be withdrawn on any given day. Only a fraction of the stored gold thus had to be covered by notes. This realization prompted bankers, after all profit-driven actors, to issue a lot more notes than were backed by specie reserves in acts of lending in order to enhance their interest income. Fractional-reserve banking is a relatively early invention, dating back centuries. Medieval history is full of evidence of panic runs on banks rumored to be overextended (see Morgan, 1965; Kindleberger, 1978; Boyer-Xambieu et al., 1994) as well as authorities responding to public unrest by establishing giro banks whose supposedly conservative practices would keep the public's savings safe.[7] The public-good quality of such early forms of private bank money was anchored in their automatic convertibility with precious metals, a linkage inclined to reestablish itself recurrently in banking crises during which the overblown supply of paper money was violently shrunk back to its metallic base.

This precarious coexistence of gold and private bank notes began to change in the early 18th century when the Bank of Amsterdam, then one of Europe's leading banks, experienced several defaults on its loans and found itself unable to assure depositors payment in coin on demand. By this time, however, the public had already become so used to the convenience of making payments through the bank that its deposits continued to circulate and be accepted at face value for many years thereafter even though they were no longer fully backed by gold reserves. What this example made clear was that private bank money in paper form had finally become anchored as a medium of exchange in its own right, because it was too convenient to give up. Hence it is perhaps important to remember that the introduction of inconvertible paper notes did not coincide with that of fiat money.

During the 18th century we see further consolidation when the Bank of England, set up as a government-sponsored giro bank in 1694 and an institution with which Professor Goodhart has himself been associated as a member of its governing board, managed to concentrate issue of bank notes in its hands and create a sophisticated interbank system of reserve transfers for the circulation of its notes across the British territories. Turning itself so into a bank for other banks, the Bank of England became the first central bank and a pioneer of the modern payments system with which to clear checks, assure the automatic convertibility between different money forms, and transfer reserves. There was now an infrastructure in place for the management of fiat money and private bank money when the gold standard finally bit the dust in 1931.

To be sure, that transition from a regime of commodity-money relying on specie-flow adjustments to a regime of state-managed credit-money required further refinements and adjustments, as evidenced by Roosevelt's reforms of money and banking during his New Deal (for example Emergency Banking Act of 1933, Glass-Steagall Banking Act of 1933, Bank Act of 1935). But once these institutional changes were in place, the central banks of the industrialized nations were in a position to manage the coexistence of government-issued fiat money and private bank money. After the end of World War II they did so in growth-promoting fashion by focusing on low interest rates, fixed exchange rates, and ample provisions of liquidity injections with which to monetize a portion of the nation's debts in support of continuous excess spending. The gold standard had been successfully replaced by a more flexible alternative in which inconvertible paper notes issued by central banks or commercial banks in acts of lending could function effectively as endogenously elastic credit-money.[8]

What is most remarkable about this story is not fiat money, but the state's management of the public–private mix of credit-money. The central bank, besides maintaining the automatic convertibility of all legitimate money forms in circulation through its operation of the payments system, also manipulated the money-creating ability of profit-seeking banks by determining their (excess) reserves to be used for money creation. It imposed regulatory restrictions on the structure and operation of banks and acted as lender-of-last-resort for troubled banks to manage financial crises. Finally, central banks also created with Bretton Woods a cross-border payments system among themselves through which funds could be transferred across borders to meet international payments obligations. Each of these five areas of central bank intervention aimed at maintaining the public-good quality of a money form which in large measure was created by profit-seeking agents and therefore subject to unequal access and cyclical behavior. The fiat-money portion of this monetary aggregate has always been fairly small, usually not more than 20 percent.

Once again we are compelled to highlight state management of money in terms of balancing its otherwise contradictory public-good and private-commodity dimensions. The connection between state and money goes beyond the C view's emphasis on political sovereignty and fiscal authority. It must also include that balancing act by the central banks *vis-à-vis* commercial banks issuing their own money in pursuit of additional interest income. The C view should extend its analytical and conceptual framework toward the state's management of money's contradictory dual nature. Such an extension would make it easier to argue that the M view's emphasis on private-sector cost min-imization is relevant, yet must at the same time remain always subordinate to the imperatives of public authority over money. Market regulation and the motive of private gain are inclined to undermine the effectiveness of money just as much as irresponsible government rule may do. Therefore they have to be kept in check, and this is the job of a central bank as the institution repre-senting the monetary authority of the state.

Theoretical inclusion of money's contradictory dual nature would also provide more space for consideration of monetary innovation, much of it driven by the private sector. We would then be better able to analyse the 'regulatory dialectic' driving this process where private-sector institutions develop new money forms (for example NOW accounts, money-market deposit accounts, money-market fund shares) and the central bank scrambles to extend its regulatory reach over those (see Kane, 1981). Some innovations may escape the regulatory reach of the monetary authorities as a result of which the private-commodity aspects of those new money forms become too prevalent to the detriment of stability and equity in our economic system. We have seen this happening with the Eurocurrency market, a globally integrated and unregulated banking network operating without regulatory constraints (at least until the 1988 Basle Accord), which has been a key factor in every major global financial crisis since its take-off in the 1960s. Another example may be cybercash, electronic money created and circulating on the Internet, which will soon take center stage to challenge the regulatory capabilities of the monetary authorities. Both of these innovations have made the lack of state authority over money an urgent issue for which the C view, as composed now, may not yet have adequate answers.

THE PARADOX OF THE EURO

Some of these limitations of the C view come out clearly in Goodhart's discussion of the European Union as an Optimum Currency Area on the basis of which its single-currency project now under way has been justified. He is correct in pointing out that Europe's monetary union violates the principles of political sovereignty and fiscal authority vested in money as a matter of state interest (ibid., pp. 420–23). This begs the question why Europe's leaders, most notably French President Mitterrand and German Chancellor Kohl, would have embarked on such an adventure of folly of replacing their cherished national currencies with an uncertain, potentially inadequate instrument which in addition would rob them of control over three of the four most effective macroeconomic adjustment mechanisms on a national level – the country's exchange rate, monetary policy and budget deficits. Goodhart does not really address this question in the detail it deserves.

The single-currency plan first emerged in the late 1960s, the subject of heated discussions, which ended with the Werner Report (1970). Implementation of that report's principal recommendation for adoption of a single currency was derailed by the collapse of Bretton Woods and subsequent turmoil in foreign exchange markets. When flexible exchange rates took hold after March 1973, the movement of capital out of dollars and into marks threatened to tear the European customs union apart because of the rapid appreciation of the mark against other European currencies. The Germans had already taken measure to protect themselves by linking the currencies of their smaller neighbors to the mark, the so-called 'snake', but England, France and Italy ended up not participating in this experiment. Those countries pursued instead a 'competitive devaluation' strategy, which left them in the end with higher inflation and interest rates. When they finally hooked up their currencies (except the British pound) to the mark, with creation of the European Monetary System in 1979, the EC had introduced a fixed-rate regime which even included a new supranational money form of limited official use as store of value and unit of account, the European Currency Unit (or Ecu). This system worked quite well, and its success provided an infrastructure of institutions and conventions on which to build a single-currency project.

Such a project became a necessity when the EC ratified the Single European Act of 1987. One key aspect of this common-market initiative was liberalization of capital flows within the EC by 1991. Belatedly, perhaps, Europe's politicians realized that you cannot have fixed exchange rates, autonomous monetary policy, and free cross-border mobility of capital all at the same time (see Padoa-Schioppa *et al.*, 1987). Something in this 'impossible triangle' had to give, propelling them towards a single currency which would resolve the exchange-rate and monetary-policy questions at the same time. The revival of the Werner Report gave them a blueprint for implementation of a single currency, especially since that report had resolved one of the most contentious questions with a Solomonic compromise. At the time, the Germans had argued that monetary union could only come about after having achieved an adequate degree of convergence among its members. The French disagreed, stressing the speedy implementation of a single currency itself as a vehicle for accelerated integration and convergence. This is the great 'chicken-or-egg' question underlying Mundell's OCA concept. A century earlier the Americans had answered this question decisively by imposing a national currency during the Civil War which later on became the pillar of a nationally integrated economy. The Germans themselves seemed to have switched to the French view in 1990 when they pushed through a hastily organized monetary union with East Germany as the first step towards reunification. The compromise proposed in the Werner Report provided for a multi-phased introduction of the single currency, with each phase contingent on measurable progress in the convergence of several performance indicators. That same idea was two decades later adopted in the Maastricht Treaty of 1991, which set in motion a ten-year, three-phase process for the introduction of the euro. We are now in the final stage, with the actual phase-in of the euro under way and to be completed by July 2002.

While made possible by the success of the European Monetary System and made necessary by the imminent liberalization of capital flows, the introduction of the euro was also the result of political considerations. The entire project of European integration had from its very beginning, the days of Adenauer, Schumann and Monnet in the immediate aftermath of World War II, been predominantly political in nature. It was designed to meet such directly political objectives as making for a lasting peace between traditionally hostile neighbors, anchoring Germany in the Western alliance, and undercutting the threat of communism. Weakened by a long period of military conflict and finding themselves squeezed by two feuding superpowers, the West Europeans wanted to strengthen their vulnerable position by forming a tightly integrated bloc of countries speaking with one voice. Yet, and here the project found itself from the onset in a structural contradiction, the project could not be perceived in such overtly political terms. For that the attachment to the nation state was still too powerful, fueled not least by deep-rooted fears of being dominated by bigger neighbors in any supranational structure of federalism. Given that the idea of a united Europe has always been propagated by authoritarian leaders intent on subjugating the rest of the continent under their rule – from Caesar and Charlemagne to Napoleon and Hitler, such fears are not irrational. People are attached to local cultures and relate to their nation state with patriotic pride, but they are suspicious of transnational structures which diminish the political sovereignty of their member states. In light of such resistance the political construction of the European Union has always lagged behind the initiatives of economic integration, building up a 'democratic deficit' concerning the EC's policy-making institutions – an arrogant commission of unelected bureaucrats, a quarrelsome council of ministers clashing over divergent national interests, and finally an elected parliament of limited power and influence. This deficit did not help make the federalist idea of a United States of Europe more attractive.

The construction of the euro has exhibited the same contradiction. On the one hand, the project was clearly of a political nature, motivated by the desire of France and its southern neighbors to relax the grip of Germany's anti-inflationary Bundesbank on their economies, by Germany's need to deepen its economic dominance through more integrated markets, and a collective aspiration to challenge the dominance of the dollar. The euro was also seen as the logical next step in European integration, following the transformation from a customs union into a common market. A single market needs a single currency. The more far-sighted European leaders of the time, certainly France's Mitterrand, Germany's Kohl and EC Commission President Delors, understood also that the creation of a single currency would put in place a new reality that would foster greater steps towards political union.[9] In that regard the Maastricht Treaty already provided for a common foreign and security policy, a strengthening of the European Parliament, and greater reliance on weighted-majority voting to overcome the dominance of national interests and the resulting inertia amidst constant veto threats in a system of unanimity voting rules. These were first steps in the direction of political union and will certainly not be the last. But the idea of a political union cannot be put on the table openly, because anti-federalist sentiments are still too strong – much like they were in the United States during the early 19th century.

Against this background, the C view's criticism of the euro project gains new meaning and context. One cannot be too upset about the absence of political sovereignty expressed by the euro. This monetary innovation from above is by design a supranational construct whereas political sovereignty remains vested in the nation states making up the single-currency zone. A joint undertaking by a group of neighboring states, monetary union is seen by the majority of

European leaders as a first step in the direction of political union, a tool with which to force member states into greater cooperation and coordination. A similar argument applies to the fiscal-authority question so dear to the C view. Fiscal federalism does not yet exist in Europe, with national budgets dwarfing the EU budget. But the single market itself requires increasing harmonization of tax regulations and rates, as for instance in the case of the value-added tax for price equalization purposes. We can also imagine that the EU budget will play a much greater role in the future than it does today as the EU takes on responsibility for a massive transfer of structural funds to lesser developed regions, large-scale EU-wide infrastructure investments, and the standardization of income-maintenance programs among member states. Yet while the member states retain for the time being control over their budgets, the modalities of the euro deprive those countries of monetizing the public debt through open-market operations of their local central bank. Instead they are forced into the euro-denominated bond market which, even though already surprisingly deep with liquidity after only one year, may make adequate deficit-financing hard to come by during EU-wide downturns when budget deficits rise automatically while the bond market may freeze amidst a spreading credit crunch. How will the European Central Bank react when it faces fiscal crises in some member states which require targeted liquidity injections as used to be provided by their national central banks' open-market purchases of government securities? In the meantime, EU members are committed to a high degree of fiscal discipline, crystallized in the promise to keep budget deficits below 3 percent of their gross domestic product. In that sense, it strikes me, they have already lost a good deal of fiscal authority without any adequate replacement on the federal level of the EU put in place yet.

One of the great ironies with regard to the euro project is that, in the absence of any political justifications that might trigger a tidal wave of anti-federalist sentiments, the euro had to be sold to a skeptical public with a different twist. Here it was useful that the European Central Bank (ECB), the first major EU-based policy-making institution, could be represented as a politically independent institution which would not be swayed by pressure from politicians to pursue a course with which it did not agree. While the ECB has the structure of the Fed, it will have the cold heart and single-minded head of the German Bundesbank, the price the rest of Europe paid to get the Germans on board. Confining the policy objectives of the ECB by statute to price stability is in my opinion a mistake.[10] Better would have been a broader range of goals, much like the Fed has to pursue, balancing price stability with the requirements of economic growth and maximum employment.

Such a more nuanced monetary policy would go a long way toward legitimating the central bank as deserving of its independence. Otherwise, I fear, a rigid ECB will inevitably suffer at one point from its own democratic deficit and see its policies come under heavy attack. Formal independence is not the same as political autonomy built informally on the basis of public respect.

The other way monetary union has been sold to the public is by putting strong emphasis on the advantages of a single currency for European producers and consumers, thus in terms of precisely those private-sector cost reductions stressed by the M view.[11] The public has bought the argument even though a large majority of Europeans wonder how much the single currency will benefit the largest corporations disproportionately more than anyone else in the union. The credibility of the argument that the euro will make it easier for the Europeans to challenge the key-currency status of the dollar depends on the relative strength of the new currency, with a highly valued euro perhaps squeezing European producers too hard. The ECB will have its hand full trying to manage this tension.

In general, I believe that the euro may well eventually bring about the cost reductions and efficiency gains promised by the M view. This, however, does not justify framing the legitimation of this endeavour exclusively in terms of the rationales generally pushed by the M view. Even though the single currency may make it easier to get there, the European Union does not comprise an Optimum Currency Area yet. For that there are still too many institutional and cultural barriers to resource mobility (for example language barriers preventing people from moving from one country to another, a fragmented Internet) and, I suspect, not yet enough symmetry in adjustments to external shocks as evidenced by the difference the collapse of the Soviet Union made to Finland compared to, say, Portugal. The cost reductions promised by the M view must be weighed against possible cost increases from the implementation of the euro, such as higher prices in increasingly oligopolistic industries, eroding regulatory powers of national governments over issues of local interest, as well as greater adjustment costs when the process of adjustment is channeled predominantly through the labor markets rather than through fiscal policy or through monetary policy aiming to lower the prices of money (that is exchange rates and interest rates).

The problematic dominance of the M view in the construction of Europe's single currency goes beyond propaganda to the heart of the matter, the institutional framework of the euro and its European Central Bank. That structure has been put into place by hard-core monetarists whose narrow view of money has led to some troubling aspects worth pondering. I wish to go here beyond my earlier complaint about the ECB's single-minded focus on price stability, a classic fingerprint of monetarism. What concerns me even more, bringing once again my social-institution view of money to bear, is how the ECB has been constructed as a monetary authority. I doubt whether it has yet the capability of a truly effective central bank. Let us remember that for the purposes of managing the public-good quality of money against threats from its private-commodity forces, a central bank has to do more than just conduct monetary policy. It also acts as a bank regulator, intervenes in financial crises as lender-of-last-resort, and represents the country (or in this case a group of 11 countries) in the international monetary system. The ECB may not yet be constituted properly with regard to two of these monetary regime dimensions.

Most obviously, the ECB still has to prove its ability to be an effective lender-of-last-resort. True, the European Union has put into place a system of uniform bank deposit insurance, much like the US Federal Deposit Insurance Corporation, but that system has yet to be tested in terms of its ability to remove failed banks, intervene proactively when troubled banks have not yet failed, and discourage excessive moral-hazard risks. The ECB itself will surely be able to play an active lender-of-last-resort role in system-wide crises requiring across-the-board liquidity injections as well as *vis-à-vis* individual banks through its standing facilities of short-term credit. But less clear is its ability to intervene in country-wide financial crises, because it lacks the capability of direct targeting of its credit to specific countries. If it is not empowered to bail out individual governments through open-market operations, how much autonomy will the regional branches of the European System of Central Banks (ESCB) have to inject funds into their local member-nation economies? Most likely, as we have seen with the evolution of the Fed, the Bundesbank and other central banks, good intentions of a decentralized central bank structure get swept aside by the exigencies of centralizing the multi-dimensional state management of money in the hands of the governing board at the head of the central bank structure.[12] Yet country-wide financial crises may still be a likely occurrence in the absence of an economically and politically integrated zone in which symmetric adjustments and synchronized business cycles prevail.

Effective crisis management also requires strong supervisory capabilities vested in the central bank for proactive action and collection of 'early-warning' information, and here the picture of the ECB as bank supervisor is quite murky. Since those supervisory and examination responsibilities were to be carried by a separate EU agency responsible for banking regulations as well as the new deposit insurance system, the ECB's supervisory role has been confined to a marginal role of advice and special tasks. That super-regulator has yet to see the light of day, and the deposit insurance system, new as it is, still has a significant learning curve to go through.

Talking about bank regulation, it strikes me as noteworthy that the ECB has been deprived of regulatory powers. The Fed fought very hard recently to safeguard its supervisory and regulatory powers over at least the leading banks, willing to hold up comprehensive bank reform legislation in US Congress for more than a decade to win that point. It justified this stubborn defense of its traditional turf on the grounds that bank regulation and supervision were of vital importance to the conduct of monetary policy as well as the central bank's role of crisis manager. European leaders would have done well to listen to the Fed's arguments more carefully when they designed the ECB. Instead, they disconnected bank regulation institutionally from monetary policy as if these two central bank functions could really be separated without problem. There is, of course, a story behind that decision which is worth reflecting on. When the EU set out to implement its single-market initiative between 1987 and 1992, its officials faced the challenge of harmonizing many national rules and regulations across the community. They soon found out that this was an extremely arduous, slow and consuming exercise, involving endless negotiations between regulators still wedded to the national interest, steeped in different cultures, and resentful of the loss of sovereignty. Indeed the task proved so difficult and the deadlines set so tight that the officials opted for an alternative where the member countries would simply accept each other's domestic regulatory regime reciprocally. But that so-called 'home country' principle left the national differences in rules and regulations intact, to be harmonized at a later date when and wherever possible.

In the area of banking and financial-services regulation such harmonization has not yet taken place, and an EU-wide regulatory agency remains an unfinished agenda. Of course, liberalization of cross-border capital movements in the single-market initiative provided impetus for creation of an integrated EU-wide banking system which implementation of the euro will complete. In the face of this evolution the EC Commission passed the Second Banking Directive in December 1989 which offered a framework for pan-European universal banks, but left (mutually recognized) member country regulations intact. Each Euroland member state will therefore operate with its own bank regulations for some time to come, leaving untouched a rather divergent set of institutions, regulations and practices across the European Union. That lack of homogeneity will also impair the ECB's conduct of monetary policy. Since the transmission of such a policy operates through adjustments in the balance sheets of banks, the impact of a supposedly uniform monetary policy will differ between member states whose banks have traditionally used asset management strategies (for example Britain, Italy, Austria) and those member states where liability management techniques prevail among banks (for example Germany, France). Moreover, now that the restructuring of Europe's financial-services industry has gone from national consolidation to cross-border mergers in preparation for a single-currency zone, this lack of harmonization of the regulatory apparatus will create administrative, organizational and equity problems in cumulative fashion. It will surely slow down EU-wide restructuring of banks and capital markets as well as financial innovation, areas where the Europeans lag behind the Americans. Once the combination of common market and single currency has driven the movement far enough towards an oligopoly of large universal banks, integrated stock markets, and greater reliance on corporate bonds, the fragmented structure of bank regulations will have to be reorganized towards pan-European uniformity and more widely diversified banking operations.

The most optimistic assessment we can make with regard to Europe's new monetary regime is that we are dealing here with an experiment still in the making, a longer-term project of which the implementation of Maastricht's economic and monetary union was just the first phase. Fiscal federalism will become a more important issue, together with implementation of a social charter to alleviate adjustment pressures in the labor market. Additional reforms of EU's new monetary authority will be necessary to give it appropriate supervisory, regulatory and lender-of-last-resort capabilities as well as a broader range of policy objectives to balance. These changes will come about not by design, but as ad hoc responses to structural imbalances and crises demanding action. Being essentially political, such a process of institutional reform escapes the M view's exclusive criterion of private-sector cost reduction even though that framework of thinking always helps rationalize steps in the direction of reform. More appropriate is the C view, with its inclusion of political aspects and fiscal authority in the evaluation of new money forms. Even better is to extend the C team theory with the notion of money as a social institution, which emphasizes the institutional prerequisites for a successful integration of money by balancing its public-good and private-commodity dimensions. Such an extension focuses attention on the multidimensional intervention modalities of the central bank, thus allowing us to address some of the yet unresolved issues surrounding the construction of Euroland.

NOTES

1. Aglietta and Orléan (1982) compare prehistoric practices of sacrifice and modern market mechanisms to show how the introduction of money links both modes of societal organization. In a later work these two economists of the French regulation school provide a collection of readings which offer fascinating accounts of money's origins in intercommunitarian practices preceding trade (Aglietta and Orléan, 1998). See in this context especially the articles by Charles Malamoud, Mark Anspach, Jean-Marie Thiveaud and Jean Andreau.
2. Barter is cumbersome for two reasons. First of all, in barter each good carries numerous prices, as it gets priced in terms of any other good with which it is potentially exchangeable. And the whole formation of prices is a highly subjective affair, likely to involve a lot of haggling between buyers and sellers. More importantly, barter will only come about when each party to the exchange has what the other party wants and at the same time wants what the other party has. This double coincidence of wants involves major search costs and restricts trading activity greatly.
3. Using archeological evidence, Leon Festinger (1983) provides a fascinating account of the beginnings of trade in prehistoric settlements of the Eastern Mediterranean.
4. The tokens issued by banks (that is empty checks) only become money in the hands of others, their borrowing customers. The issuing banks cannot use these tokens for their own spending purposes. In other words, they cannot write checks drawn on themselves. Banks must pay for their purchases of goods and services out of their own revenue. Similarly, the government

cannot create money directly to fund public expenditures. The central bank as issuer of currency is for that reason institutionally separated from the rest of the government.

5. Karl Polanyi (1944), in his brilliant discussion of the transformational qualities of capitalism, warns of the dangers arising from that system's tendency to turn nature, humans and money into commodities and so subject them to the follies of market regulation. When nature is transformed by private property rights and market valuation of land, when humans become wage-laborers exposed to the incertitudes of the labor market, when money creation is dominated by the profit motives of its private issuers for the purposes of capital accumulation, capitalism cannot escape its crisis-prone propensities for cycles and inequality. Polanyi has characterized the excessive commodification of land, labor and money as capitalism's 'satanic mills', a phrase designed to highlight its dangers.

6. The Code of Hammurabi, a series of laws and decrees issued by Babylon's most important ruler in 1745 BC, dealt with the confluence of war-induced hyperinflation and huge reconstruction expenditures through a monetary reform which restored barley as sole medium of exchange in rural areas and so concentrated the circulation of silver in urban areas. In 594 BC Athens' great reformer Solon introduced a coin and promised to chop off the hands of anyone found debasing the new coin, including himself. This value guarantee helped the city-state develop a remarkably sophisticated economy and become the dominant power in the Eastern Mediterranean. Rome's leaders, facing hyperinflation in the wake of the Pyrrhic and Punic Wars, introduced the silver denarius in 268 BC with an iron-clad guarantee as to its value (in terms of weight and fineness) which brought about a long period of stable money and rapid economic growth.

7. Giro banks were explicitly forbidden to make loans in excess of their deposit base. In reality, the giro banks of Renaissance Italy and later Northern Europe proved frequently just as unreliable as privately owned commercial banks. Subject to political pressures by the same city governments that had set them up in the first place, the giro banks often ended up making loans to the authorities which were no longer covered by their available specie reserves.

8. We might want to characterize inconvertible paper notes, issued either by governments or commercial banks, as credit-money inasmuch as they are created in acts of credit extension and thus for the duration of their existence tied to debt.

9. In that context it is worthwhile to remember that these same leaders decided at the time to rename the European Community (EC) as the European Union (EU) – a name surely expressing not only economic and monetary union, but also political union (at least as a tendential process of institutional change).

10. Regarding its single policy focus on price stability the European Central Bank resembles the Bundesbank much more than the Federal Reserve whose statutes require the balancing of price stability with growth and employment conditions as simultaneous objectives to pursue.

11. This strategy emerged very clearly from the very onset when the EC Commission introduced the idea of a single currency to the public. Publication of the crucial Delors Report (1989) and the Commission's own study (1990) both framed the rationale for such an ambitious step, compared to maintaining the status quo, purely in terms of econonic costs and benefits.

12. The structure of the EU's new central bank is in a formal sense quite decentralized, combining the national central banks and the European Central Bank into a seemingly well-balanced European System of Central Banks. But in practice this ESCB is likely to be directed from its administrative center, the Governing Council of the ECB at its Frankfurt headquarters.

REFERENCES

Aglietta, M. and A. Orléan (1982), *La violence de la monnaie*, Paris: Presses Universitaires de France.

Aglietta, M. and Orléan, A. (1998), *La monnaie souveraine*, Paris: Odile Jacob.

Boyer-Xambeu, M.T., G. Deleplace and L. Gillard (1994), *Private Money & Public Currencies: The 16th Century Challenge*, Armonk (NY): M.E. Sharpe.

Commission of the EC (1990), 'One market, one money', *European Economy*, 44, October.

Committee for the Study of Economic and Monetary Unions (Delors Report) (1989), Report on Economic and Monetary Union in the European Community, Luxembourg: Office for Official Publications of the European Communities.

Festinger, L. (1983), *The Human Legacy*, New York: Columbia University Press.

Goodhart, C.A.E. (1998), 'The two concepts of money: implications for the analysis of optimal currency areas', *European Journal of Political Economy*, 14, 407–32.

Guttmann, R. (1994), *How Credit-Money Shapes the Economy*, Armonk (NY): M.E. Sharpe.

Guttmann, R. (1997), 'The International Monetary System', in R. Guttmann (ed.), *Reforming Money and Finance: Towards a New Monetary Regime*, Armonk (NY): M.E. Sharpe, pp. 14–23.

Kane, E. (1981), 'Impact of regulation on economic behavior: Accelerating inflation, technological innovation, and the decreasing effectiveness of banking regulation', *Journal of Finance*, 36, 355–67.

Kindleberger, C. (1978), *Panics, Manias, and Crashes*, New York: Basic Books.

Marx, K. (1967), *Capital*, Volume III. New York: International Publishers. First published in German in 1895.

Menger, K. (1892), 'On the origin of money', *Economic Journal*, 2, 238–55.

Morgan, V. (1965), *A History of Money*, Harmondsworth (UK): Penguin Books.

Mundell, R. (1961), 'The theory of optimum currency areas', *American Economic Review*, 51, 657–64.

Padoa-Schioppa, T. et al. (1987), *Efficiency, Stability and Equity*, Oxford: Oxford University Press.

Polanyi, K. (1944), *The Great Transformation*, Boston: Beacon Press.

Werner Report (1970), Report to the Council and the Commission on the realization by stages of Economic and Monetary Union in the Community. Supplement to Bulletin of the EC, 3.

8. Neglected costs of monetary union: The loss of sovereignty in the sphere of public policy

Stephanie Bell

INTRODUCTION

In his 1998 article 'The two concepts of money: Implications for the analysis of Optimal Currency Areas', Charles Goodhart analysed the theoretical justification for European monetary union, the Optimum Currency Area (OCA) theory. In his paper, he focused on two opposing theories of money – the Metallist and the Chartalist theories – and concluded that, although the OCA paradigm was grounded in the Metallist tradition, the Chartalist theory was both more compelling (empirically) and more accurate (historically). By resurrecting the Chartalist theory of money, Goodhart has reminded us that there is a fundamental connection between a nation's power over its currency and its power over public policy. Although he did not personally delve into this connection, he suggested that 'we need to consider carefully what problems this may portend for the future Euro single currency area' (1998, p. 425).

In this chapter, I attempt to provide the careful consideration that Goodhart recommended. Specifically, this chapter is concerned with the extent to which Lerner's 'functional' approach to public policy is tenable under the institutional arrangements that now govern the eurozone. Generally speaking, economists writing on the euro tend to take one of two positions: (1) they maintain that the loss of independent monetary policy is the most severe cost imposed on member states but that the benefits of monetary union outweigh these costs, or (2) they contend that the fiscal constraints imposed under the Stability and Growth Pact impose the most severe costs on member states. In this chapter, it is concluded that the most severe restriction of policy choice derives not from the inability to adjust interest and exchange rates or from the 3 percent deficit-to-GDP limitation imposed under the Stability and Growth Pact but from the decision to abandon chartal monies in favor of a currency which member states and their central banks are unable to create at will. This conclusion directly supports

Goodhart's recognition that sovereignty over policy choice is a function of sovereignty over money.

LERNER'S VISION

In 1941, Abba Lerner wrote an essay entitled 'The economic steering wheel: The story of the people's new clothes'. In the opening paragraph, he invited the reader to enter a fantasy world, where mad motorists on Mars perpetually flirted with death by submitting themselves to the mercy of an unconventional interplanetary highway system. In the scenario he described, automobiles were guided by a high-tech system of specialized braking devices and cleverly crafted roads rather than by living beings (Martians) that could skillfully direct their vehicles by employing the use of a steering wheel. Instead, these motorists relied on high curbs that were designed to maneuver wayward vehicles back onto the road. Most autos would bounce erratically from curb to curb, their passengers averting disaster despite having forsaken the power to control their own destiny.[1] Likening this state of affairs to a bad dream, Lerner suggested that Earthlings should be grateful that their fate is governed by more sensible (if less sophisticated) methods.

While the transportation system on Earth was deemed preferable, Lerner maintained that 'when it comes to maintaining their economic system', humans are as reckless as the mad Martians because they allow 'their economic automobile to bounce from the curb of depression to the curb of inflation in wide and uncontrolled arcs' (1941, p. 271). Specifically, he indicted the human race for failing to devise a mechanism capable of systematically regulating the level of employment.

Lerner's approach was generally consistent with Keynes's. Most importantly, he maintained that the level of output and employment (that is effective demand) was determined by the amount of total spending, and, like Keynes, he believed that capitalist economies were inherently demand-constrained. Thus, Lerner viewed unemployment as the result of insufficient aggregate demand, which, he believed, could be eliminated by adopting a 'functional' approach to public policy. Lerner explained this approach in his 1943 article 'Functional Finance and the Federal debt'. He said:

> The central idea is that government fiscal policy, its spending and taxing, its borrowing and repayment of loans, its issue of new money and its withdrawal of money, shall all be undertaken with an eye only to the *results* of these actions and not to any established traditional doctrine about what is sound or unsound. This principle of judging only by *effects* has been applied in many other fields of human activity, where it is known as the method of science as opposed to scholasticism. The principle of judging

fiscal measures by the way they work or function in the economy we may call Functional Finance (1943, p. 39; emphasis in original).

Thus, if full employment was to be achieved, the government would have to abandon any pre-existing bias toward 'sound' finance and grip hold of the steering wheel of Functional Finance. Like a motorist with the ability to control the speed and direction of its automobile, Lerner suggested that policymakers could guide the pace of economic activity, steering the economy away from danger (recession) and toward prosperity by implementing policy according to two fundamental principles (or 'laws').

The first law of Functional Finance placed upon the government the responsibility for maintaining the total rate of spending on goods and services at the level necessary to purchase all of the output that a fully employed labor force could produce. In elucidating this law, Lerner explained that when spending was at the requisite level, it would prevent both inflation and unemployment (that is there would be full employment and price stability). In order to increase total spending, he suggested that the government increase its own expenditures or reduce taxes so that private spending would increase. Similarly, the government could cut its spending or raise taxes in order to reduce the total rate of spending.

The second law of Functional Finance decreed the specific *manner* in which the shortfall in total spending was to be eliminated. Specifically, Lerner proposed that the government borrow only in the event that private spending would otherwise generate excessive aggregate demand. Since he believed that there would ordinarily be insufficient aggregate demand, he felt that under ordinary circumstances it would be unnecessary for the government to offer bonds in exchange for *existing* funds. Instead, he believed that bonds should be sold to the central bank or to private banks 'on conditions which permit the banks to issue new credit money based on their additional holdings of government securities, [which] must be considered for our purposes as printing money' (Lerner, 1943, p. 41).

In Lerner's view, policymakers were not taking full advantage of the economic steering wheel. Too much of the time, the economic auto was allowed to stray from a full employment path. But, said Lerner, the government could prevent this by keeping its hands on the wheel so that it could react appropriately to unforeseen obstructions in the road. Thus, by adjusting its taxing/spending, purchase/sale of bonds, and creation/destruction of money, the government could keep the economy on a path toward full employment.

Although Lerner's approach appeared to be tenable regardless of the monetary system in place, it will be argued in this chapter that a nation can undertake Functional Finance only under certain specific monetary arrangements. Since I have already demonstrated (Bell, 2000) that the US monetary system is amenable to Functional Finance, my objective here is to consider the prospects for Functional Finance under an alternative monetary system. If Functional Finance represents the ultimate in policy freedom, then it is instructive to inquire whether nations who adopt alternative monetary arrangements retain this degree of freedom. Although we could apply our analysis to a variety of monetary arrangements (that is currency boards, a gold standard, or other systems of fixed exchange rates), our focus here will be on the monetary system that now governs the eurozone.[2]

WHY A CURRENCY UNION BUT NOT A POLITICAL UNION?

Monetary union was considered a logical and necessary counterpart to economic union.[3] Indeed, EMU stands for 'economic and monetary union', not 'European monetary union', as it is often mistakenly defined. Moreover, because Europe had been moving toward economic union for some time, plans to introduce a single currency began well before the Treaty on European Union (or Maastricht Treaty) was drafted. In fact, as Coffey notes, 'a full economic and monetary union (EMU) [was] agreed upon by the Heads of Government of the original six founder Member States of the European Economic Community (EEC) in Den Haag at the end of 1969' (1993, p. 1). Table 8.1 shows that a broad process of integration actually began even before 1969.

Table 8.1   Predecessors to the 1992 Treaty on Monetary Union (Maastricht)

1951:	Union of Coal and Steel Producing Industries
1957:	Treaties of Rome – established a European Common Market
1965:	Treaty on Economic European Union
1973:	Alignment of European Currencies – adopted after the end of the Bretton Woods system
1979:	European Monetary System (EMS)
1990:	Delors Proposals – suggested a program for future monetary integration

It is not coincidental that this process began just after World War II. While economic and political cohesion became important after the war, the idea of a United States of Europe, which was revived by Churchill in 1946, had to be abandoned due to resistance from the Communist bloc.[4] Thus, Europe's integration plans were limited to Western Europe, where a number of post-World War II treaties and agreements helped to pave the way for economic and monetary union. But it was the Maastricht Treaty, agreed upon by the European

Community (EC) heads of government in December 1991 and signed on 7 February, 1992, which actually laid out the process by which the euro was to be gradually implemented.

Today, 11 of the 15 countries in the European Union (EU) have relinquished control of their domestic monetary policies and abandoned their individual currencies. Old currencies such as francs, marks and lira will continue to exist until mid-2002, but only as irrevocably fixed units of the new euro currency, which will replace them altogether by June 2002. Table 8.2 shows the three-phase process by which this change is taking place.

Table 8.2   Stage three of the Treaty on Monetary Union

Phase One – 1 January 1999
- Conversion rates between national currencies and the euro become irrevocably fixed.[5]
- Legislation on the euro into force.
- Foreign-exchange and money markets switch over.

Phase Two – 1 January 1999 – December 2001
- The ECB begins to operate.
- All new issues of public debt are denominated in euros.
- Financial markets switch over.

Phase Three – 1 January – July 2002
- Euro notes and coins will be brought into circulation.
- National currency notes and coins will be gradually withdrawn.
- All bank accounts will be euro-denominated.
- The euro will be used for salaries, welfare services and retail trade.

With the completion of stage three, sovereign currencies, which will be gradually withdrawn from circulation, will cease to carry the status of legal tender, and the introduction of the euro as the common currency of the eleven participating countries will be complete.

As the heading indicates, the purpose of this section is to explain both the reasons for adopting a single currency and the rationale for stopping short of full political union. A general answer to the first part of this question has already been given: a single currency was believed to be a logical and necessary counterpart to economic union, something Europe has been moving toward since the mid-twentieth century. More specific support for the single currency often focuses on two (related) benefits – the reduction of transaction costs and the elimination of exchange rate risks. The former is considered by Eudey to be 'the most important' benefit of moving to a single currency (1998, p. 14). The benefit, of course, is that a single currency makes it possible to move within a single monetary area 'without having to exchange money every hundred kilometers' (Vaclav, 1997, p. 1). In other words, a French citizen bound for Italy need not exchange francs for lira in order to purchase goods and services while in Italy, since the euro will circulate in both regions. The other oft-cited benefit – the elimination of exchange rate risks – means that this same traveler will not become a victim of an unexpected devaluation or revaluation.[6] Additionally, it is often believed that monetary union will strengthen the single market, promote convergence of national economies, and encourage investment in the eurozone.

Against these benefits, a host of costs have also been identified. The loss of independent monetary policy (that is the ability to control interest and exchange rates) and the resulting constraints imposed upon fiscal flexibility typically rank high when making an inventory of the costs of monetary union. The EUR-11, having chosen to adopt the euro, must have believed that the benefits of monetary union outweighed the (non-trivial) costs of moving to a single currency. This belief was based on the Optimum Currency Area (OCA) theory, which suggests that the benefits of monetary union should be balanced against the costs of forfeiting interest and exchange rates as adjustment mechanisms.

The most notable contributions to the study of Optimum Currency Areas have been made by Mundell (1961), McKinnon (1963), Kenen (1969), Fleming (1971), Onida (1972), Corden (1972), Magnifico (1973), and Presley and Dennis (1976). For Mundell, an Optimum Currency Area 'is precisely a region in which there exists factor mobility' (Coffey, 1977, p. 43). According to Mundell, exchange rates would fluctuate to equilibrate conditions *between different currency areas*, but factor (labor) movement would equilibrate conditions *within a particular currency area*.[7]

McKinnon (1963), while not rejecting the role of factor mobility, tended to emphasize the degree of 'openness' of the economy as a criterion which should be used to define an OCA. The idea seems logical, as Coffey notes, 'since these countries – whose economies are open or very open ones – were conducting half of their trade with each other' (1993, p. 1). Kenen (1969), in contrast, focused on the degree of 'complementarity' as a crucial characteristic. Magnifico (1973), like Kenen, also emphasized complementarity, arguing that it was important for nations to exhibit a 'similar propensity to inflate'.

In sum, Mundell originally maintained that as long as labor was highly mobile, it would not be risky to relinquish monetary sovereignty in favor of a common currency. Since then, others have extended this criterion to include openness to trade, capital mobility, and wage/price flexibility. Together, these criteria form what many economists' today use to determine the feasibility of an OCA. Thus, in its modern form, a currency union is considered advantageous if goods and services, capital, labor and prices move in the appropriate directions following asymmetric shocks.[8] Assuming these adjustments take place as required, the regions would become *self-stabilizing*, and the loss of monetary sovereignty would become irrelevant. As the OCA theory is frequently used to justify European monetary union, an expectation that the EUR-11 satisfied the OCA criteria could be listed as a final reason for the adoption of the euro.

Now that we have some understanding of the various forces that influenced the decision to adopt the euro, we must inquire as to why the EUR-11 decided to stop short of full (political) union. As Eric Helleiner notes, 'most nation-states in the contemporary world have attempted to maintain a distinct currency which is both homogenous and exclusive within their territorial boundaries' (1997, p. 2). However, in the case of European monetary union, the currency union spans 'a set of sovereign states with relatively little federal centralisation of either political powers or of fiscal competences' (Goodhart, 1996c, p. 1083). Our objective is to understand why, in an environment where 'all separate nation states larger than Panama, Liberia or Liechtenstein have a *single* currency' (Goodhart, 1996c, p. 1084), the consensus became 'One Market, One Money', rather than 'One Nation, One Money'.

Along with the argument that 'one market needs one money' (European Commission, 1990), the EUR-11 conceded to the idea that a single federal authority should have the exclusive right to manage this money (Treaty, Article 105a). However, they did not demand an analogous transference of power with respect to fiscal authority. In fact, says Wilhelm Nolling, 'the political intention of the Treaty is to *subordinate* the Community's economic and fiscal policies' (1993, p. 143). Thus, fiscal authority remains the responsibility of individual member state*s*, while monetary policy, which is primary, is now the responsibility of the European Central Bank (ECB). This separation has created an unprecedented divorce between the monetary and fiscal authorities, a divorce motivated by a desire to establish a monetary authority with 'absolute independence from government' (Goodhart, 1998, p. 409).

Philip Arestis and Malcolm Sawyer (1998) argue that the monetarist theory underlies the desire for strict central bank independence. Godley also sees the monetarist influence, suggesting that 'it took a group largely composed of bankers (the Delors Committee)' to decide that 'governments are unable, and therefore should not try, to achieve any of the traditional goals of economic policy, such as growth and full employment, (1992, p. 39). All that can legitimately be done, according to this view, is to control the money supply and balance the budget' (ibid.). Both of these beliefs – that the central bank can control the rate of inflation and that the levels of output and employment are set on the supply-side of the economy – are central tenets of monetarism. Under the monetarist view, the economy is naturally driven toward equilibrium by a set of highly efficient and fast-acting forces so that activist policies are both unnecessary and unwise. Thus, at least part of the reason for the 'divorce' has to do with the fact that monetarists do not believe there is a role for fiscal policy.[9] A compatible motivation is given by Jerry Jordan, who argues that 'Europe's move to a single market for capital, goods, and labor is part of a worldwide trend toward greater reliance on unfettered markets for the allocation of productive resources' (1997, p. 1).[10]

THE TERMS OF THE DIVORCE

In a very real sense, the Maastricht Treaty is like a divorce contract; it allocates various rights and responsibilities among the 'divorcing' fiscal and monetary institutions. By submitting to the conditions laid out in the Treaty, member states have agreed to hand over certain powers and to abstain from certain behaviors. As Ramon Torrent notes, 'one does not need to be a specialist to understand the extraordinary importance and implications [of this] not only in terms of the institutional equilibrium and balance of powers within the European Union but also in terms of economic policy' (1999, p. 1229). The purpose of this section is to describe the institutional framework within which fiscal and monetary policies are to be conducted and to explain the terms (that is the rules and conditions) under which they must be carried out.

The establishment of the European System of Central Banks (ESCB) marks the most important institutional modification to have occurred on the monetary side. Comprised of the European Central Bank (ECB) and the National Central Banks (NCBs) of all 15 countries within the European Union (EU), the ESCB is controlled by the Governing Council and the Executive Board, the decision-making bodies of the ECB.[11] The Executive Board consists of the President, the Vice-President and four other members, while the Governing Council includes the members of the Executive Board and the Governors of the National Central Banks (NCBs).

Under Title II, the Treaty states that 'the primary objective of the ESCB shall be to maintain price stability' (Article 105).[12] This objective is to be pursued indirectly, through control of the money supply. In addition, the Treaty specifies a number of secondary responsibilities, which include:[13]

- defining and implementing monetary policy within the Community
- conducting foreign exchange operations consistent with the provisions of Article 109
- holding and managing the official foreign reserves of the member states
- promoting the smooth operation of the payments systems.

Under the new framework, NCBs – like the Bundesbank and the Banque de France – have been relieved of their authority to conduct independent monetary policy. Under current arrangements, the Governing Council formulates monetary policy for the entire eurozone, while the Executive Board is charged with the implementation of the Community's monetary policy (Article 109a). The NCBs, having lost the power to conduct independent monetary policy, are primarily operating arms of the ECB.[14] Figure 8.1 describes these relations.

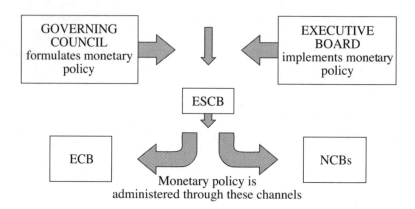

Figure 8.1   Decision-making bodies of the ESCB

In order to achieve its objectives, the ESCB has a variety of policy instruments at its disposal. First, it has the power to conduct open market operations. In addition to initiating these operations, the ESCB also decides on the instrument to be used and the terms and conditions under which the operation will be executed.[15] The *General Documentation on ESCB Monetary Policy Instruments and Procedures* (1997), specifies four kinds of open market operations:

1. *Main Refinancing Operations* – Regular liquidity-providing reverse transactions with a weekly frequency and a maturity of two weeks
2. *Longer-Term Refinancing Operations* – Liquidity-providing reverse transactions with a monthly frequency and a maturity of three months
3. *Fine-Tuning Operations* – Executed on an ad hoc basis in order to smooth the effects on interest rates caused by unexpected liquidity fluctuations in the market
4. *Structural Operations* – Executed whenever the ECB wishes to adjust the structural position of the ESCB *vis-à-vis* the financial sector

A second instrument of monetary policy, the short-term interest rate, follows from the ESCB's willingness to provide or absorb overnight liquidity at marginal lending/deposit facilities, known as standing facilities. Two standing facilities are available to eligible counterparties on their own initiative:[16]

- *Borrowing Facility* – Counterparties can use the marginal lending facility to obtain overnight liquidity from the National Central Banks against eligible assets. The interest rate on the marginal lending facility normally provides a *ceiling* for the overnight market interest rate.
- *Lending Facility* – Counterparties can use the deposit facility to make overnight deposits with the National Central Banks. The interest rate on the deposit facility normally provides a *floor* for the overnight market interest rate.

The third instrument is control over minimum reserve requirements on accounts with the ESCB.[17] The ESCB's minimum reserve system applies to credit institutions in the euro area and is based on a system of lagged reserve accounting (LRA) similar to the US system.[18] These three things – open market operations, overnight lending/borrowing rates, and minimum reserve requirements – make up the set of instruments through which the Treaty grants the ECB power to conduct monetary policy.

While the Treaty clearly describes the manner in which monetary policy is to be implemented, it does not include such a precise blueprint for the implementation of fiscal policy. This is not only because fiscal policy remains the responsibility of member states but also, as argued above, because the Delors Committee was comprised primarily of monetarists, who tend to view the economic system as inherently stable and who consider fiscal policy a fairly impotent and unreliable tool. Thus, rather than sketching out a program for the implementation of countercyclical fiscal policy, the Treaty imposes a set of rules and guidelines that are designed to *constrain* the use of discretionary fiscal policy. Specifically, by agreeing to the terms set out in the Maastricht Treaty, member states have subjected themselves to three distinct fiscal constraints.

First, member states have agreed to exercise a certain degree of *self-restraint* when it comes to matters of fiscal policy. The Treaty encourages 'close coordination of Member States' economic policies' (Article 3a), asking member states to 'regard their economic policies as a matter of common concern and ... [to] coordinate them within the Council, in accordance with the provisions of Article 102a' (Article 103).

To be convinced that member states have responded to this plea for self-restraint, one need only consider the position of the French government.[19] At the close of 1998, French officials published a document titled *Multiannual Public Finance Programme to the Year 2002: A Strategy for Growth and Employment*. In it, officials laid out the principles that they believe should govern public policy over the next three years. With respect to fiscal policy, they openly commit themselves to the principles of 'sound' finance, stating that 'larger deficits occurring in years of low growth are [to be] offset by smaller deficits in years of high growth' (French Republic, 1998, p. 9).[20] For the period 2000 to 2002, the officials set targets for real expenditure for the general government. The targets were set in line with what the officials believed represented a desirable trend in the government debt ratio over a full economic cycle. Assuming their targets are met, general government expenditures in France will grow at just 1 percent per year (in real terms) over the three years of the program.[21]

The government's budget policy follows from the conventional wisdom that government deficits, by raising prices and interest rates, will 'crowd-out' private sector activity. Two controversial elements are central to this view. The first is the (positive) correlation that is supposed to exist between budget deficits and prices. The problem with this argument is that deficit spending, like additional spending by households or firms, should put upward pressure on prices only if the additional demand is borne by an already fully employed industry or economy, hardly a concern of the present-day EUR-11. Second, the conventional view requires a (negative) correlation between investment and the rate of interest. But this, too, is problematic as demonstrated by the capital critiques and by Fazzari (1993). Nevertheless, the French position is consistent with the ideological bias embedded in the Treaty and, hence, with the monetarist/sound finance perspective that favors fiscal discipline rather than Functional Finance.

The second constraint on fiscal policy derives from the Stability and Growth Pact. Proposed by former German Finance Minister Waigel, the pact makes more explicit the budgetary limits and financial penalties for non-compliance with Maastricht rules regarding fiscal discipline. The pact, which was ratified at the June 1997 Amsterdam Summit, strengthens the surveillance of member states by forbidding countries from running deficits in excess of 3 percent of GDP and requires that debt-to-GDP ratios be maintained below 60 percent. One reason for these limits is the European Council's belief that they mark 'an essential condition for sustainable and non-inflationary growth and a high level of employment' (quoted in Spiegel, 1997, p. 1).[22] Both Issing (1997) and Semmler (1999) recognize that member states are not encouraged to take advantage of the 'freedom' to *persistently* run small deficits but, instead, are to offset deficits by running surpluses in subsequent periods in order to generate balanced budgets over the business cycle. Issing, who is the Chief Economist of the ECB, notes:

> If, for instance, the 3 percent criterion for the budget deficit were prescribed as a statutory upper limit for national governments having joined the monetary union, the authorities in each country would be responsible for ensuring the necessary leeway. In buoyant economic conditions, the budget deficit would thus have to be much lower

in order to provide fiscal policy makers with the appropriate scope for running up higher deficits in periods of recession (Issing, 1997, p. 11).[23]

As Parguez (1999) contends, encouraging balanced budgets is related to the fear of negative spillover effects (that is externality effects), which are thought to occur as one country's budget deficit, working through its impact on interest rates, affects economic conditions in other EU nations.

In the event that a country does not fulfill the two fiscal criteria – for the budget deficit and public indebtedness – the excessive deficit procedure pursuant to Article 104(c) will apply. Under the *Excessive Deficit Procedure*, deficits exceeding 3 percent of GDP are subject to a fine as declared by the European Council upon a report by the European Commission and a judgment by the Monetary Committee. Specifically, the Stability and Growth Pact commits EMU members to government budget positions that are close to balance, and the *Excessive Deficit Procedure* allows the Council to:

- demand that recalcitrant governments 'publish additional information, to be specified by the Council, before issuing bonds and securities; to invite the European Investment Bank to reconsider its lending policy towards the Member State concerned;
- require the Member State concerned to make a non-interest-bearing deposit of an appropriate size with the Community until the excessive deficit has, in view of the Council, been corrected;
- impose fines of an appropriate size' (Article 104c).

There is strong disagreement regarding the severity of the deficit-to-GDP and debt-to-GDP constraints. For example, Pasinetti argues that 'the "pact" may entail severe costs on two counts: because it prevents expansionary policies in periods of recession and mass unemployment ... and because, on top of that, it even imposes heavy fines' (1997, p. 9). Arestis and Sawyer concur, suggesting that the objective deficit-to-GDP 'constraint on the budget deficit clearly limits the use of national fiscal policy for demand management purposes' (1998, p. 2). DeGrawe (1996) and Eichengreen and von Hagen (1995) also oppose the objective constraint, arguing that member states should be free to pursue independent fiscal policy without arbitrary limits or penalties.[24] In contrast, Mosler (1999) suggests that the objective constraints are relatively unimportant, since member states are unlikely to be able to secure financing for deficits in excess of 3 percent of GDP except, perhaps, over very relatively short periods of time.[25]

The final constraint on fiscal freedom, mandated under *Article 104* of the Maastricht Treaty, is the requirement that central governments abandon the use of 'overdraft facilities or any other type of credit facility with the ECB or with the central banks of the Member States' (Article 104). Article 104 forbids both the ECB and the NCBs from lending *directly* to member states or buying securities *directly* from them. Moreover, it states that the ECB should be mindful of this rule when carrying out monetary policy so that it does not engage in operations that would amount to the *indirect* monetization of debt.[26] Additionally, Article 104 includes a provision that neither the Community nor any other member state shall be 'liable for or assume the commitments of central governments, regional, local or other public authorities, other bodies governed by public law, or public undertakings of any Member State, without prejudice to mutual financial guarantees for the joint execution of a specific project' (Article 104b). This provision is often referred to as the no-bailout clause, because it implies that even if a member state finds itself unable to service its debt commitments, the ECB is not permitted to assist it by purchasing a portion of its outstanding bonds.

Since NCBs are now forbidden to issue Treasury bonds on behalf of the government, and the ECB is forbidden to monetize (directly or indirectly) government debt, governments wishing to deficit-spend must now float bonds on the capital market, where they must compete with the financing needs of private borrowers. It is for this reason that Mosler (1999) wonders whether the Stability and Growth Pact and the Excessive Deficit Procedure are even needed in order to constrain government spending. It may well be that financial markets – if they can price risk correctly – will be able to impose discipline by constraining public spending without the need for penalties for fiscal violations (Eichengreen and von Hagen, 1995).

Focusing on the role of the Excessive Deficits Procedure, Eichengreen and von Hagen (1995) contend that it exists because the Treaty's no-bailout provision is not considered credible. If it were, it would be sufficient, they maintain, to warn member states that the ECB will not step in to stave off a crisis that might result from a scenario such as the one described below:

> The scenario the framers of the treaty had in mind presumably runs as follows ... Imagine that a government of a member state – call it Italy for illustrative purposes – experiences a revenue shortfall. It finds it difficult to service its debt. Bondholders concerned about the interruption of debt service begin to sell their bonds, depressing their price and forcing the Italian government to raise the interest rate it offers when it attempts to roll over maturing issues. The rise in interest rates further widens the gap between government revenues and expenditures, exacerbating the fiscal problem. Problems in the bond market threaten to spill over to other financial markets, because, for example, higher interest rates depress equity prices. In the worst-case scenario, the collapse of asset prices and the impact of higher interest rates on corporate profitability and the performance of outstanding loans can threaten the stability of the banking system (Eichengreen and von Hagen, 1995, p. 224).

Peter Kenen argues that the purpose of the financing constraint is either intended to 'reinforce the ban on "excessive" budget deficits' or to 'reinforce the independence of the ECB by giving it better control over the money supply' (1995, p. 70).

In sum, the Maastricht Treaty specifies the responsibilities and limitations of the newly created ESCB and the individual member states. The decision-making bodies of the ESCB are responsible for the formulation and implementation of a single monetary policy within the eurozone. Thus, NCBs can no longer alter interest or exchange rates in response to changing domestic conditions. Rather, they must accept the policy that is formulated by the governing council and implemented throughout the eurozone. In addition to assenting to the loss of monetary autonomy, member states have consented to a variety of constraints that limit their fiscal autonomy. They have agreed to pursue fiscal policy in accordance with the guidelines established by the European Council and to implement it without recourse to overdraft accounts or financial assistance from any central bank.

IMPLICATIONS FOR SOVEREIGNTY OVER POLICY

The purpose of this section is to demonstrate that despite the attention that critics have paid to the second constraint – the 3 percent deficit-to-GDP limitation – the third constraint – the one imposed by financial markets – actually results in a far more serious limitation of policy choice. Specifically, by forsaking their monetary independence and agreeing to the terms set out in Article 104 of the Maastricht Treaty, the national fiscal authorities of the EUR-11 voluntarily relinquished the power to conduct fiscal policy according to the principles of Functional Finance.

Godley recognizes the significance of this, arguing that the abdication of monetary authority has brought 'an end to the sovereignty of its component nations and their power to take independent action on major issues' (1992, p. 39). Sawyer (1999) also appreciates the relationship between sovereignty over policy choice and sovereignty over money. He recognizes that by severing this relationship, 'national governments will no longer have the ability to "print money" to pay interest on bonds, and their ability to pay depends on their ability to levy the necessary taxation' (Sawyer, 1999, p. 11). This means that member states must (ultimately) rely on tax revenues in order to finance spending and/or validate past spending (that is service debt).

Thus, unlike the US government, which really faces no external budget constraint, the EUR-11 governments truly do face financing constraints. Two important implications follow from this. First, member states *must* secure the funds required to spend in excess of current receipts before they can engage in deficit spending. Although the US government *could* spend first and drain reserves later (by selling bonds), EUR-11 governments *must* sell bonds first.

Thus, their ability to deficit-spend depends upon the willingness of private banks to extend credit in advance. Second, unlike the bonds issued by the US government, the obligations that are issued by EUR-11 governments are no longer default-risk-free. As Parguez recognizes, this means that markets will make lending decisions on the basis of their perception of member states' creditworthiness, which is based on a state's ability to 'pledge to balance its budget, to get a zero *ex post* deficit, so as to protect the banks against the risk of accumulating public debt' (1999, p. 72). Since markets will perceive some members of the EUR-11 as more creditworthy than others, financial markets will not view bonds issued by different nations as perfect substitutes. Therefore, high-debt countries may be unable to secure funding on the same terms as their low-debt competitors. This was recognized by Lemmen and Goodhart, who suggest that 'governments with above-average deficits and debt will find that they have less financial flexibility within EMU than [was previously] the case' (1999, p. 77).

Suppose, for example, that Italy or Belgium – with debt-to-GDP ratios of 115.1 and 116.1, respectively, at the close of 1999 – decided to pursue expansionary fiscal policy in order to stimulate GDP and combat high domestic unemployment. If capital markets demand high rates of interest in order to hold Italian or Belgian government debt, then it is easy to see how these governments could be forced to abandon expansionary policy. As Kregel (1999) notes, an attempt by Italy to expand domestic demand would lead to a deterioration of the Italian fiscal deficit and, hence, 'credit risks rising on Italian securities' (p. 40). Jordan states the implications succinctly:

> The risk for the fiscal authorities of any member country is that the 'dismal arithmetic' of the budget constraint leaves few palatable alternatives. If the yield on government securities demanded by markets exceeds a country's nominal income growth, then interest expense on the outstanding debt must become a relatively larger burden (Jordan, 1997, p. 3).

Again, the 'burden' can persist because EUR-11 governments cannot create spendable deposits internally (that is 'print' money) in order to meet rising interest costs. Thus, unlike the US government, which can *always* meet any dollar-denominated commitment as it comes due, the EUR-11 governments must finance their excess spending by selling bonds. Looking at the budget constraint $G - T = \Delta B + \Delta M$, then, we see that deficits must be covered by borrowing (that is $\Delta M = 0$ for purposes of government finance). But if interest payments are becoming a significant portion of a member state's total outlays, it may be difficult to convince financial markets to accept new issues in order to service the growing debt.[27]

While some (for example Eichengreen and von Hagen, 1995) have argued that member states can still service higher debt levels because they retain the power to alter tax rates, others recognize that EUR-11 governments are seriously constrained in this regard. Jordan, for example, argues that 'the prospect of higher taxes would cause the factors of production to migrate ... [so that] ... higher tax rates could, eventually, shrink the tax base' (1997, p. 3).[28] Taylor also disagrees with Eichengreen and von Hagen, suggesting that, despite 'their substantial revenue-raising powers,' member states will 'be increasingly constrained by the pressure of "fiscal competition" operating [under EMU]' (1999, p. 16).

Again, this 'fiscal competition' is the direct result of Article 104. Because member states can no longer create spendable deposits internally (that is 'print' money), they must compete for euros by selling bonds to private investors (including private banks) who will not view the various obligations as perfect substitutes. Thus, governments must float bonds on the capital market, where they must compete with debt instruments offered by other (government and non-government) entities. The result, as Taylor recognizes, is that 'debt issuance by Euroland's governments [will] take place in a new environment of market discipline' (1999, p. 16).

The ability of financial markets to impose discipline on member states depends upon two important factors. First, the no-bailout rule must be seen as reasonably credible. If it is, then markets will 'treat lending to EMU governments in much the same way that they approach lending to the regional governments of existing federal monetary unions' (Taylor, 1999, p. 16). Second, markets must be well informed and efficient in their pricing of credit risk. If they are, they will be able to 'exert effective new safeguards against persistently high borrowing' (ibid.).

To the extent that these conditions are met, lenders may assign different quality or risk premiums to the obligations of member governments 'whose ability to service debt seems less assured than other nations' (Stevens, 1999, p. 5). Thus, even though the ECB, through its willingness to provide (absorb) liquidity at marginal lending (deposit) facilities, will set the short-term interest rate, 'bonds issued by different national governments, denominated in euros, may attract different credit ratings and hence different interest rates' (Sawyer, 1999, p. 11). As Lemmen and Goodhart (1999) explain, this means that 'credit risks will replace market risks ... as the principal source of relative risk in government debt markets in EMU' (p. 77). As a consequence, obligations issued by EUR-11 governments begin to resemble those issued by state and local governments in the United States, where risk premiums 'rise sharply with the ratio of state debt to state product. States with high debt-to-output ratios can become effectively rationed out of the market' (Jordan, 1997, p. 3).

Thus, the traditional (institutional) link between the treasury and the central bank has been severed under the new monetary arrangements, which means that unlike currencies that are 'creatures' of their issuing states, 'the Euro will be a pure-private money, created at the sole request of private agents by banks obliged to comply with the targets set by the Central Bank, [and] sustained by the expectations of the financial markets!' (Parguez, 1999, p. 66). Whereas the franc, the mark, the lira and so on used to derive their legitimacy from the state (that is from their acceptance in payment of taxes), financial markets are now 'the ultimate source of legitimacy for the [euro]' (ibid., p. 72).

Having broken the (Chartalist) link between sovereignty over currency and sovereignty over public policy, member states must rely on the willingness of commercial banks or other financial institutions when floating new issues; they cannot create spendable balances the way the US Treasury can. Therefore, government debt issued by the EUR-11 countries is forced to compete with other forms of debt (for example commercial paper, bonds issued by private firms, the debt of other member states). In the event that a member state finds itself unable to locate sufficient funding, it will be forced to run a balanced budget. Imposing fiscal constraints on member governments in order to encourage discipline is, of course, wholly inconsistent with the idea of Functional Finance.

CONCLUSION

Before entering the currency union, NCBs had command over their own currencies and could alter interest and/or exchange rates in an attempt to stabilize their economies. Now, however, they must accept the monetary and exchange rate policies that are handed down by the ESCB. Moreover, member states have agreed to allow the ESCB to make the pursuit of *price stability* its overriding objective in implementing monetary and exchange rate policies. They did not, however, insist that a federal agency be made responsible for stabilizing *output* and *employment* in times of crises.

Currently, 'the federal budget for the European Union is not used as a tool to address recessions or overheating, either in particular countries or in Europe as a whole' (Eudey, 1998, p. 17). It is as if policymakers decided to set the economic speedometer at 55 mph, even though it might be wise to speed up (or slow down), depending on current (economic) driving conditions. Although some groups (for example monetarists) probably find this limited role for fiscal policy comforting, others have been critical of the lack of attention it has received. Wynne Godley, for example, states:

> The incredible lacuna in the Maastricht program is that, while it contains a blueprint for the establishment and modus operandi of an independent central bank, there is no blueprint whatever of the analogue, in Community terms, of a central government (Godley, 1992, 40).

This is significant because, as Jordan explains, 'the sustainability of any monetary regime depends on the fiscal regime in which it operates' (1997, p. 4). The reader will recall that the fiscal regime in which the EUR-11 must operate is characterized by three distinct constraints that have been imposed as part of the currency union. However, as Hughes-Hallet and Scott note:

> Empirical research has shown that monetary union is particularly dependent on its supporting fiscal policies in that, in the absence of sufficiently larger or frequent interventions, economic performance will rapidly deteriorate in the union's constituent economies (1993, p. 72).

Because of the deficit-to-GDP constraint, many critics of the European currency union have concluded that it will be impossible for the constituent governments to provide the kind of large-scale intervention that would be needed to stimulate depressed economies. These critics do not seem to be objecting to the existence of fiscal discipline in general, but to the particular upper limit – 3 percent deficit-to-GDP – that has been imposed under the Stability and Growth Pact.

This view begs the question: is the upper limit the *primary* obstruction to flexible policy? If it were, then raising it (or lifting it all together) should renew significant fiscal flexibility. But it is not clear that the 3 percent limit is really constraining deficit spending in the EUR-11. Indeed, one might conclude, given that the unemployment rate in the euro area averaged 10 percent in 1999, that many member states would have at least exercised their right to run deficits equal to 3 percent of GDP. As Figure 8.2 reveals, however, none of the EUR-11 governments even came close to running up against the 3 percent deficit-to-GDP limit.

We cannot know for sure whether each member state's budgetary position reflects its preferred stance or whether larger deficits would have been run in the absence of financial market discipline. It seems clear, however, that even if member states were able to jettison the objective deficit-to-GDP limit and to abandon any self-imposed fiscal restraints that stem from a bias for 'sound' finance, no member of the EUR-11 would be capable of conducting policy according to the principles of Functional Finance.

The reader will recall that Lerner proposed that the government undertake two functions. First, the government was to ensure that the level of total spending was sufficient to purchase all of the goods and services that a fully employed system could produce. Now, if spending by households, firms and foreigners typically generated a spending gap of no more than 3 percent of GDP *and* governments were able to borrow enough to close this gap, then it would be possible for the EUR-11 governments to implement Lerner's first law. However, Article 104 prevents member states from closing the gap in accordance with his second

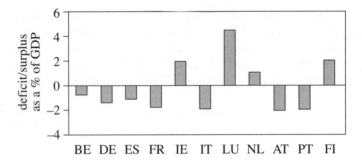

Source: *Monthly Bulletin* (September), http:www.ecb.int

Figure 8.2   EUR-11 deficit-to-GDP (1999)

law, which precludes borrowing unless the private sector would otherwise spend enough to bring about full employment.

Implementing policy according to the principles of Functional Finance means using taxes and bonds 'simply as instruments, and not as magic charms that will cause mysterious hurt if they are manipulated by the wrong people or without due reverence for tradition' (Lerner, 1943, p. 51). It means deciding whether to tax/spend, buy/sell bonds, create/destroy money, and so on by considering which operation is likely to yield the most desirable effects on the macroeconomy. In other words, policymakers should decide on a policy objective – for Lerner this was full employment and price stability – and then use whatever means are deemed most constructive, given the goal. As the EUR-11 'possess none of the instruments of macro-economic policy, their political choice is confined to relatively minor matters of emphasis – a bit more education here, a bit less infrastructure there' (Godley, 1992, p. 39).

Going back to Lerner's vision of policymakers as stewards of the economic automobile, it is clear that member states, by abandoning their sovereign currencies, have indeed forsaken control of their economic steering wheels. There are, perhaps, only two ways to regain this control.[29] First, the institutional arrangements could be reformed. For example, the ECB (or a newly-established lending institution) could be required to aid member states in their pursuit of a broad set of policy objectives by assisting in the co-ordination of monetary and fiscal policy. This has been proposed by Arestis *et al.* (2000), Sawyer (1999), and Kregel (1999). The crucial point is that member states need to be able to avert the financial constraint, imposed under Article 104. This would enable member states to regain control over their *individual* steering wheels.

Second, the EUR-11 could unite politically. As Godley suggests 'the counterpart of giving up sovereignty should be that the component nations are constituted into a federation to whom their sovereignty is entrusted' (1992, p. 40). Under political union, the power to tax would be transferred to the EU, and its budget could be used to co-ordinate policy according to the principles of Functional Finance. This, essentially, means allowing a federated European government to control the economic steering wheel on behalf of the entire EUR-11. Either way, it seems that the link between control over money and control over policy must be reestablished if nations are to recapture control of their economic steering wheels.

NOTES

1. I say 'most' because the system tended to fail about 10 percent of the time. Burned vehicles and dead motorists were efficiently deposited in nearby fields.
2. The 'Eurozone' (or EUR-11) refers to the geographic territory throughout which the Euro has been adopted. This geographic area includes Austria, Belgium, Finland, France, Germany, Ireland, Italy, Luxembourg, the Netherlands, Portugal and Spain. The countries within the European Union that opted out of EMU – Sweden, Denmark, Norway and the UK – retain the power to conduct independent monetary policy.
3. For an alternative perspective, see Goodhart (1996a), in which it is argued that a single currency is not a *necessary* consequence of a single market.
4. Although 11 countries have adopted the euro, Alan Meltzer argues that it is not really Europe (as a whole) but France and Germany (in particular) that were important. Specifically, he calls EMU 'a way to bind France to Germany and Germany to France' (1997, p. 17).
5. During the transition period, all national currencies will be denominations of the euro, which is denominated in 100 cents. The euro can only be used for non-cash purposes during the transition period and will replace all national notes and coins by July 2002.
6. This was true even before the euro began to circulate (physically), since the values of all eurozone currencies were *fixed* in relation to the euro.
7. Mundell received the Nobel Prize in Economics, in part, for his 1961 article on 'Optimum Currency Areas'.
8. Although our purpose is to provide insight into the decision to adopt a common currency (that is a monetary union), the above also sheds light on the decision to adopt common economic policy. The idea of a one-size-fits-all policy follows from the idea of factor mobility. Thus, as long as factors are viewed as sufficiently mobile, there is a symbiotic relationship between an OCA and an EMU. Peter Coffey, who is critical of this conclusion, points out that an optimum currency area is different from an economic and monetary union. The former implies the linking of individual currencies through fixed exchange rates while the latter implies 'common economic, fiscal and monetary policies as well as a common currency' (1977, p. 41). In Coffey's view, it does not necessarily follow that an optimum currency is conducive to a full economic and monetary union.
9. As Meltzer notes, another reason for maintaining fiscal power at the national level may have to do with the fact that 'Europe, or even Germany and France, are unwilling to mention political union or federation as a feasible near-term prospect' (1997, p. 17).
10. Both views are incompatible with Functional Finance, which views the reliance on unfettered markets and the opposition to discretionary fiscal policy as conceptually similar to the removal of one's hands from an automobile's steering wheel.
11. The ESCB 'denotes all the central banks in the European Union that have access to Target, and includes not only the European Central Bank and the 11 euro-area central banks, but also the central banks of England, Sweden, Denmark and Greece' (Weller, 1999, p. 43).
12. In October 1998, price stability was defined as 'a year-on-year increase in the Harmonised Index of Consumer Prices for the euro of below 2%' (ECB).

13. Among the more conspicuous duties often conferred upon governments, but for which the ESCB bears no responsibility, are the pursuit of high rates of growth and employment and a responsibility to act as 'lender-of-last-resort' in times of crises. For this reason, many economists (Arestis and Sawyer, 1998; Zaretsky, 1998; Kregel, 1999; Parguez, 1999; Lemmen and Goodhart, 1999) have been critical of the duties with which the ESCB has been charged.
14. The NCBs will continue to perform many of their original functions, but they 'now engage in monetary policy operations only when and as instructed by the ECB' (Stevens, 1999, p. 1).
15. Unlike the Federal Reserve, Stevens argues that the ECB lacks 'a deep market for securities in which to conduct policy operations', requiring it to operate in a variety of public and private debts (1999, p. 2).
16. Use of the standing facilities is subject to the fulfillment of certain access criteria.
17. The reserve requirement went into effect at the beginning of Stage Three. The requirement has been set at 2 percent of individual credit institutions' liabilities. The liabilities against which credit institutions must hold reserves include: overnight deposits, deposits with an agreed maturity or period of notice of up to two years, debt securities issued with an agreed maturity of up to two years and money market paper (Mfi-assets.hotline@ecb.int). A lump-sum allowance of 100 000 euros can be deducted from this amount in order to determine the final reserve requirement.
18. Under the ESCB's requirements, 'compliance with reserve requirements is determined on the basis of the average of the end-of-calendar-day balances on the counterparties' reserve accounts over a one-month maintenance period' (http://www.ect.int/pub/pdf/gedo98eu.pdf).
19. France was chosen because official documents (in English) were easily obtainable, not because the French government is unique in its commitment to fiscal restraint.
20. The French, then, are pursuing a balanced budget over the course of the business cycle. Interested readers are encouraged to consult a paper on the Australian experience by George Argyrous (1998), in which it is argued that 'trying to eliminate a deficit and force a surplus through outlay reductions biases the business cycle downward so that on average a deficit persists' (p. 9).
21. Currently, public spending is over 50 percent of GDP.
22. Despite the Council's stated objectives, Kregel (1999) maintains that the Stability Pact ensures that priority is given to wage and price stability over high growth and employment.
23. Parguez actually argues that the Growth and Stability Pact 'leads to the conclusion that fiscal surpluses should be the rule to enhance the value of the currency' (1999, p. 66).
24. The limits are referred to as arbitrary because there was no technical (or even theoretical) reason for choosing 3 percent and 60 percent as the upper limits for the deficit-to-GDP and debt-to-GDP ratios. Indeed, as Bean (1992) notes, the limits were chosen primarily because 3 percent and 60 percent happened to be close to the average that prevailed when the Treaty was signed.
25. As we will see, Mosler's position derives from the relative importance he places on the third form of fiscal constraint – the one imposed by financial markets.
26. Parguez calls the suppression of any interference in the process of money creation the '*sine qua non* condition for the ability of the ECB to impose the Euro' (1999, p. 65).
27. Governments can attempt to match these rising expenditures by raising tax rates or by permanently reducing their non-interest outlays (or some combination of these).
28. Jordan's scenario is, perhaps, highly implausible since, as we shall see, labor has been extremely immobile within the eurozone.
29. Abandoning the euro is not considered an option, since Europe's rules bar any country from doing so.

REFERENCES

Arestis, Philip and Malcolm Sawyer (1998), 'Prospects for the single European currency and some proposals for a new Maastricht', draft manuscript.

Arestis, Philip, Kevin McCauley and Malcolm Sawyer (2000), 'An alternative stability pact for the European Union', Jerome Levy Economics Institute, Working Paper No. 296.

Argyrous, George (1998), 'Can expenditure cuts eliminate a budget deficit? The Australian experience', *Levy Institute*, Working Paper No. 248, pp. 1–11.

Bean, Charles (1992), 'Economic and Monetary Union in Europe', *Journal of Economic Perspectives*, **6**, Autumn, pp. 31–52.

Bell, Stephanie (2000), 'Do taxes and bonds finance government spending?', *Journal of Economic Issues*, **19**(3), 603–20.

Coffey, Peter (1993), 'The European Monetary System and Economic and Monetary Union' in *Main Economic Policy Areas of the EC – After 1992*, 4th Revised Edition, Peter Coffey (ed.), Dordrecht: Kluwer Academic Publishers.

Corden, W.M. (1972), 'Monetary integration', *Essays in International Finance*, Princeton.

DeGrawe, Paul (1995), *The Economics of Monetary Integration*, Oxford: Oxford Unversity Press.

ECB (1998), 'The Quantitative Reference Value for Monetary Growth.' press release, 13 October.

ECB (1999), monthly bulletin, July.

Eichengreen, Barry and Jurgen von Hagen (1995), 'Fiscal policy and monetary union: Federalism, fiscal restrictions, and the no-bailout rule' in *Monetary Policy in an Integrated World Economy*, edited by Horst Siebert, Schriftleitung: Harmen Lehment.

Eudey, Gwen (1998), 'Why is Europe forming a monetary union?', *Business Review*, November/December.

Fazzari, Steven (1993), 'Investment and US fiscal policy in the 1990s', *Jerome Levy Economics Institute*, Working Paper, No. 98.

Fleming, J.M. (1971), 'On exchange rate unification', *Economic Journal*, September.

Fleming, J.M. (1999), 'Functional finance and full employment: Lessons from Lerner for today', *Journal of Economic Issues*, **33**(2), 475–82.

French Republic (1998), 'Multi-annual public finance programme to the year 2002: A strategy for growth and employment', ftp://ftp.oat.finances.gouv.fr/pub/2002us.pdf

Godley, Wynne (1992), 'Maastricht and all that: letter from Europe', *London Review of Books*, **14**(19), October.

Godley, Wynne (1997), 'Curried EMU – the meal that fails to nourish', *The Observer*, 31 August.

Goodhart, Charles (1996a), 'The two concepts of money and the future of Europe', unpublished paper.

Goodhart, Charles (1996b), 'The approach to EMU' in *Making EMU Happen. Problems and Proposals: A Symposium*, edited by Peter Kenen, August.

Goodhart, Charles (1996c), 'European monetary integration', *European Economic Review*, **40**, 1083–90.

Goodhart, Charles (1998), 'The two concepts of money: implications for the analysis of optimal currency areas', *European Journal of Political Economy*, **14**, 407–32.

Helleiner, Eric (1997), 'One nation, one money: Territorial currencies and the nation state', http://www.sv.uio.no/arena/publications/wp97–17.htm

Hughes-Hallet, Andres and Andrew Scott (1993), 'The fiscal policy dilemmas of monetary union' in *Main Economic Policy Areas of the EC – After 1992*, 4th Revised Edition, Peter Coffey (ed.), Dordrecht: Kluwer Academic Publishers, pp. 65–101.

Issing, Otmar (1997), 'A German perspective on monetary union' in *A Single European Currency?*, Washington, DC: The AEI Press, pp. 7–12.

Jordan, Jerry L. (1997), 'Money, fiscal discipline, and growth', speech for Federal Reserve Bank of Cleveland, 1 September.

Kenen, Peter B. (1969), 'The theory of Optimum Currency Areas', in R.A. Mundell and A.K. Swoboda (eds), *Monetary Problems of the International Economy*, Chicago: Chicago University Press.

Kregel, Jan (1999), 'Currency stabilization through full employment: Can EMU combine price stability with employment and income growth?', *Eastern Economic Journal*, **25**, 35–47.

Lemmen, Jan J.G. and Charles A.E. Goodhart (1999), 'Credit risks and European government bond markets: A panel data econometric analysis', *Eastern Economic Journal*, **25**(1), Winter, pp. 77–107.

Lerner, Abba P. (1941), 'The economic steering wheel: The story of the people's new clothes', *The University Review*, June, pp. 2–8.

Lerner, Abba P. (1943), 'Functional finance and the federal debt', *Social Research*, **10**, 38–51.

Magnifico, G. (1973), *European Monetary Unification*, London: Macmillan.

McKinnon, R.I. (1963), 'Optimum currency areas', *American Economic Review*, **53**.

Meltzer, Alan H. (1997), 'An American perspective on monetary union' in *A Single European Currency?*, Washington, DC: The AEI Press, pp. 13–21.

Meltzer, Alan H. (1999), *The Launching of the Euro: A Conference on the European and Monetary Union*, Annandale-on-Hudson, The Bard Center.

Mosler, Warren (1999), *The Launching of the Euro: A Conference on the European and Monetary Union*, Annandale-on-Hudson, The Bard Center.

Mundell, R.A. (1961), 'A theory of Optimum Currency Areas', *American Economic Review*, **51**.

Nolling, Wilhelm (1993), *Monetary Policy in Europe after Maastricht*, New York: St. Martin's Press.

Onida, F. (1972), *The Theory and Policy of Optimum Currency Areas and their Implications for the European Monetary Union*, SUERF.

Parguez, Alain (1999), 'The expected failure of the European Economic and Monetary Union: A false money against the real economy', *Eastern Economic Journal*, **25**, 63–76.

Pasinetti, Luigi L. (1997), 'The myth (or folly) of the 3% deficit/GNP Maastricht "parameter"', unpublished paper 1997, presented in the Luigi Einaudi Lecture, 18 April 1997, at the Academia Nazionale dei Lincei, Rome.

Presley, J.R. and C.E.J. Dennis (1976), *Currency Areas: Theory and Practice*, London: Macmillan.

Sawyer, Malcolm (1999), 'Minsky's analysis, the European single currency, and the global financial system', *The Jerome Levy Economics Institute*, Working Paper No. 266, pp. 1–18.

Semmler, Willi (1999), 'The European Monetary Union: success or failure in practice?', January.

Spiegel, Mark M. (1997), 'Fiscal constraints in the EMU', *Federal Reserve Bank of San Francisco, Economic Letter*, No. 97–23, 15 August, http://www.frbsf.org/econrsrch/wklyltr/e197-23.html

Stevens, Ed (1999), 'The euro', *Federal Reserve Bank of Cleveland Economic Trends*, Jan. 1, www.clev.frb.ordresearch/com99/0101.pdf.

Taylor, Christopher (1999), 'Payments imbalances, secession risk and potential financial traumas in Europe's monetary union', draft manuscript.

Torrent, Ramon (1999), 'Whom is the European Central Bank the central bank of?: Reaction to Zilioli and Selmayr', *Common Market Law Review*, **36**, 1229–41.

Vaclav Klaus (1997), 'European Monetary Union and its systemic and fiscal consequences', *A Single European Currency?*, Washington, DC: The AEI Press, pp. 1–6.

Weller, Benedict (1999), 'Special feature: The euro in the world economy', *Central Banking*, **9**(3), February, 39–45.

Zaretsky, Adam M. (1998), 'Yes, this EMU will fly, but will it stay aloft?', *Federal Reserve Bank of St. Louis*, http://www.stls.frb.org/publications/re/1998/c/re11998c3.html

9. A reply to the contributors

Charles A.E. Goodhart

INTRODUCTION

I feel honoured and privileged that so many fine economists have felt moved to comment upon, to criticize, and to extend my original paper on 'The two concepts of money'. I appreciate and have learnt from each of their papers; though, not surprisingly, I do not agree with everything in every paper (though I do with the greater part of all of them). It has been encouraging for me that extension and commentary has been more common than criticism, though this has been partly due to the fact that those who have felt sufficiently interested to participate have mostly been fellow-members of the minority heterodox group of Cartalist (or Chartalist) thinkers on monetary issues. But a minority, such as our own, who can claim to include among its membership such thinkers as Plato, Adam Smith, Schumpeter and Keynes, is not in immediate danger of extinction. Perhaps my best and simplest response would have been to say a heartfelt 'thank you' to all the contributors, and to leave it at that.

But I doubt if that is quite what Ed Nell and Stephanie Bell are expecting and hoping from me. Since I am extremely grateful to them, first to Ed for organizing a seminar on this subject at the New School for Social Research in New York in the Summer of 1999, and second to Ed and Stephanie both for organizing, editing and writing a Preface for this book. I had better gird up my loins and attempt a proper response.

Given that each of the contributors was independently reacting to my original paper, there was inevitably considerable overlap in their comments. Therefore rather than comment on each author/chapter in turn, I shall try to group the material into major themes, and react to the arguments in each theme separately. Following the line of analysis of my own paper, the main themes of the chapters and the book as a whole are the following:

I. The historical genesis of money.
II.a. The nature of the analytical divisions and differences between M theory and C theory.
II.b. The policy implications (within a closed economy), of adopting C theory rather than M theory.

III. An assessment of the remarkable[1] institutional characteristics of the new EMU (Economic and Monetary Union) system in Europe, against the background of C theory (rather than the Optimal Currency Area (OCA) extension of M theory).

Amongst the authors, Hudson (Chapter 3) mostly concentrates on (I) and then (II.b) above, Helleiner (Chapter 4) on (II.a), Wray (Chapter 5) on (I) and (III), Nell (Chapter 6) on (II.a) and (II.b), Guttman (Chapter 7) on (I) and (II.b), and Bell (Chapter 8) on (III). That listing, of course, leaves out Mehrling (Chapter 2), who, rather than commenting on the topics raised by my paper, writes most perceptively on how this issue fits into the wider development and corpus of my own work as a monetary theorist and historian. I could not wish for any other or better analyst of my own work than Perry. As his studies on Schumpeter and Fisher Black have shown, he has an outstanding capacity to see the world through the lens of his protagonist in each case. As one of his few (still-living) subjects, I can happily testify to that.

(I)   THE HISTORICAL GENESIS OF MONEY

As Mehrling states, I am a historian by training and preferred approach, but I have not myself done any detailed, or original, research on the conditions for the emergence of money in ancient history. Nevertheless anyone with any serious concern for historical, anthropological, numismatic and social analysis cannot but be struck by the contrast between the wealth of empirical support for C theory, and the absence of such for M theory (which latter could be described as hand waving in spades!).

In this context I greatly appreciated, and learnt much more, from the historical studies of both Hudson and Wray, both of whom have done far more original and extensive work in this field than I have. I particularly liked the emphasis that both placed on the pre-market role of money as a means of settling debts, to someone a person has injured, for marriage obligations, or (increasingly) to the state. As was mentioned several times, 'The verb "to pay" originally meant to pacify, to make peace...' (see Hudson, p. 47 and Wray, p. 97).

From amongst the many fascinating historical details in these two chapters, I was myself especially struck by two. First, Hudson argues that the monetary crisis that helped to break the Roman empire was not excessive government spending, but a collapse of the tax base. Thus he writes, p. 53,

> The Roman treasury was bankrupted by wealthy landowners using their control of the Senate to shift the fiscal burden onto the classes below them. Lacking the means to pay, these classes were driven below the break-even point. As debt deflation drained

the economy of money, barter arrangements ensued. Trade collapsed and the economy shrunk into local self-sufficient manor units.

The second insight that I particularly liked was that by Wray (p. 103). He noted that the state can only impose obligations, and hence define money (through which such obligations can be redeemed), on its own subjects. Hence there remains a problem of resolving international debts, whether arising from trade, capital flows, the need to pay foreign mercenaries to prosecute war, and so on. So, Wray states that,

> Thus, the King of England needed something of high and easily recognized value to conduct foreign wars, and precious metals fit the bill. As discussed above, use of full bodied coin in this instance would be more akin to bartering gold for military provisions than to use the money to purchase them. It is not surprising, we believe, that Mercantilism, the international gold standard, and large-scale foreign wars all developed at about the same time.

Amongst the three authors dealing at any length with the historical genesis of money, the one that I feel least comfortable with is Guttman. There are several reasons for this. First, he buys the M-theoretical historical viewpoint that indirect commodity barter in agrarian products such as wheat, cattle, and so on, in order to facilitate exchange, pre-dated the emergence of money. Thus he writes (pp. 140–41):

> With barter transactions growing more complex and sophisticated, people had an incentive to simplify the process. They surely realized that basic goods which were in strong demand, and in limited supply, maintained a steady value or even rose in value in relation to other products. Wheat was such a product; barley, too. Gradually, people began to save small quantities of, say, wheat to facilitate barter. Now they did not have to offer exactly the good desired by the other party to obtain the product they wanted. They could instead simply offer some of the hoarded wheat to the other party of the trade who, knowing the durable value of the wheat, would be willing to exchange his product for the grain.

In contrast, Hudson, Wray (and I) all argue that money first arose as an acceptable way of resolving inter-communal debt obligations, and only subsequently (when money's functions had thus become accepted and ratified as a unit of account and means of payment), became widely adopted in market transactions.

Guttman's historical argument, however, then faces him with a problem. If agrarian commodity money was such an efficient cost-reducing mechanism, why did it then become replaced by (precious) metallic money? Guttman accepts that metal, even stamped coin, was 'a money form whose need for verification of fineness and weight made it arguably more costly than, say, wheat or other fairly homogeneous commodities serving as a medium of exchange' (p. 141).

He then argues that agrarian money fell out of favour for two reasons, 'short-comings prone to destabilize prehistoric societies'. The first was that ownership of the means of producing such monetary commodities, for example land-owners, led to increased class (communal) divisions and strife. Probably so, but as Guttman later recognizes, that same effect was greatly enhanced by the shift to metallic money. Thus he writes (p. 145),

> the very introduction of metal probably provided itself impetus for an enormous cen-tralization of power, especially when compared with the inherently decentralized agrarian money forms which metal came to replace. Metal had to be mined, and ownership of the mines was surely confined to a tiny elite of wealthy landowners who by means of that control alone could exercise considerable power. The mining of metal provided those operating the mines with monopoly access to a whole new generation of superior weaponry made of metal. By imposing metal pieces as medium of exchange, the mine-owners could extend their power into the sphere of commerce and so become true rulers. In that sense it is fair to argue that the very imposition of metal money acted as a source of state power.

Second, he argues that a flaw in the use of commodity money was that it encouraged 'excess supplies thereof' (p. 142). But this is surely wrong. While it is easy (though still contentious) to argue that mining to produce monetary gold or silver is, ultimately, a waste of scarce resources, any institutional incentive to produce a surplus of food that can be used to transfer (human) resources into manufactures, arts, education and other services, would surely be a huge benefit for society as a whole.

In so far as money inherently arises, as most Cartalists argue, out of a debt/credit nexus, it must have real effects, if only because the assumption of debt/credit relationships will change real variables. In that respect Cartalists dispute the view of monetarists that money is only a neutral veil, a cost-reducing lubricant of exchanges, which, were it not for certain imperfections and frictions in the real world, could allow analysis of real (non-monetary) and monetary analysis to be separated completely in a (classical) dichotomy. This thought leads on naturally to the next stage, an assessment of the current analytical dif-ferences between M and C theories.

(II.a) THE ANALYTICAL DIFFERENCES BETWEEN C THEORY AND M THEORY

As Stephanie Bell (2001) notes, any agent, whether sovereign, subsidiary government, firm, collective body (for example charity), or individual, can issue debt. What then distinguishes those debts that are generally acceptable in third party exchanges, as a means of payment, as money, from those that are not? The answer that Cartalists give, and that is repeated in many of these chapters, is the *power* of the state not only to impose obligations (taxes, duties, fines) on their subjects, but also to define the instrument in which such obligations may be redeemed/paid. Since failure to meet such obligations involves a penalty (a further fine, imprisonment, and so on), this leads to a demand for such instruments, whether this be hazel twigs (see Wray) or any other (non-counterfeitable) nominal instrument, which demand the government then meets by paying for goods and services by issuing such instruments. If the government issues more such money in expenditures than it requires in payment of taxes, that is it runs a deficit, then the value of its money in terms of such goods and services will tend to decline, that is there will be inflation, and vice versa (unless the current deficit is financed by interest-bearing bond sales, which shifts the problem of deficit finance inter-temporally).

There are a number of associated issues. First, a matter which will be of importance again when we come to heading III, subsidiary governments can impose debt (tax) obligations on their subjects, but have to accept that payment for such obligations is fully met by receipt of the money of a higher level, *sovereign* government. The adoption of EMU transforms the member states in the eurozone into such subsidiary governments, at least in such an economic context. Second, there is the question (again see Bell, 2001) of what makes bank (demand) deposits generally acceptable as money, to which the answer is, surely, the (unquestioned) convertibility of such deposits into the government's base (high powered) money at par. What the factors are, and their relative weights, that maintain faith in such convertibility (such as cash reserves, capital, deposit insurance, official regulation, and so on) is a subject that need not detain us further here, though it is raised in Bell (2001) and some of the chapters here.

The greater the power of the state over its inhabitants, the more the government can require its subjects to use and to value a nominal instrument of its choice as money, independently of any separate commodity value in an alternative use. When a government loses power, perhaps because it is losing a civil war (as with the Confederate States), or because it is dealing with other sovereign states, the more the transactions have to be with full-bodied commodity money (for example gold) or by barter.[2]

M theorists emphasize the importance of the acceptability of an instrument in exchange, as much as, or even more than, C theorists. But they run into severe problems when they seek to address the question of what makes a monetary instrument acceptable in the first place. Trial and error in the historical process of conducting exchanges with agrarian commodity money (see Guttman) would be a superficially plausible story, were it not for the fact that it appears to be historically invalid, at least in most cases. But that story fails to account for the shift to precious metals, still less for the jump to fiat money.

So, there are two key divisions between C theory and M theory. The latter emphasizes the role of private sector markets, and of efficiency considerations in minimizing transactions costs. The former emphasizes the role of the state and para-statal institutions, and the importance of power relationships. If one wants to distinguish theoretical positions, as I did in my original paper, the natural tendency is not only to emphasize, but even perhaps to exaggerate, such distinctions.

Several of the contributors of chapters to this book have criticized me for such exaggerated emphasis on the above key distinctions, and after reading their case against my rather simple and stark theoretical distinctions, I can only plead 'guilty as charged'. In particular I very much liked and accept the more nuanced approach put forward by Eric Helleiner (Chapter 4). His arguments that the creation of a single territorial currently greatly reduced 'fiscal trans-action costs'[3] (see pp. 80–81), and could provide a symbolic, pictorial means of unifying the population served by that single currency, see pp. 83–4, is not only clearly historically correct, but also, as Helleiner records in his final section on 'Relevance for understanding EMU', accounts for much of the drive to the euro single currency in Europe today. Another point, which he makes and I accept, is that much of the demand for domestic currency reform, unification and simplification into a national currency system (primarily in the 19th century) came from bottom-up (rather than top-down), from the poor who had generally been ill-served by 'the often terrible quality and inadequate quantity of "small change money" of the pre-industrial monetary order' (p. 82), and by industri-alists whose 'larger economic spaces on a national-scale... were no longer well served by traditional monetary systems' (p. 82). Again, he also notes that the growth of transnational enterprise has put industrialists in the forefront as advocates of wider regional currency areas, such as the euro.

All the above points are well-taken. A more contentious argument is whether C theory was adopted (in the 1930s) by those who consciously wanted to manage money, for example to avoid depression or to hasten industrialization, and whether the adoption of the euro derives in part

> from the fact that it will make life more difficult for national policymakers who are committed to 'outdated' Keynesian macroeconomic policies. In some cases, enthusiasm for this objective has come from state officials who themselves became disillusioned with Keynesianism in the context of both the stagflationary experience of the 1970s and the rational expectations revolutions in the discipline of economics in recent years. Also encouraging the abandonment of this kind of monetary policy, however, have been the difficulties of pursuing it in the new environment of globalized financial markets. (Helleiner, p. 86)

This latter is in the vein of the several Cartalist writers, notably in this book, Hudson, who see M theorists as involved in a kind of political conspiracy theory (for example to reduce the role of the state). We shall return to this latter issue later.

Ed Nell (Chapter 6) also criticizes me, and Cartalists more generally, for concentrating unduly on questions relating to the acceptability and efficiency of monetary instruments (for example for fiscal policies and for exchange). The main thrust of his chapter is to enquire which monetary system is more likely to provide (price) stability. Nell notes that, not only is the (unbacked) debt and fiat money of the state subject to inflation and repudiation, but also that a full metallic (gold or silver) monetary system has certain inherent self-stabilizing features.[4] If the value of commodities and services falls in terms of the metallic money (that is, prices rise, so an ounce of gold will buy fewer goods) for whatever reason (say a new technological discovery for refining gold), then the incentive to supply new gold (either from non-monetary 'hoards' or from new mining) will decline. Less gold will be supplied, and the price level will revert towards the 'equilibrium'. Such supply-side effects, especially on new gold production from mining, could take a very long time to occur, (and be overwhelmed by 'shocks', such as of new discoveries and mining technologies). But, if there were sufficient belief in the ultimate efficacy of such equilibrating effects, the dynamic speed of such equilibration could be expedited by expectations operating on flows in and out of hoards, and on interest rates; just as M theorists down the centuries have, and continue to, argue.

One argument that has been used by Cartalists (and is raised by Nell, p. 117, and others in this book) is that expectations need *not* be stabilizing. It is clear that asset price/inflation bubbles and debt/deflation spirals can continue very damagingly for much too long (for recent examples one has only to look at Nasdaq and Japan). In my view there are good grounds for belief that, even given the propensity for such spirals, a (metallic) monetary system is ultimately self-stabilizing, via real balance effects, effects on incentives to supply new metallic money, limits to the extent of bubbles (or of deflationary fears), but in a sense such theoretical arguments are academic. What is clear is that a (metallic) monetary system, left to itself, does not necessarily operate optimally; but whether interventionist 'management' will improve, or worsen, the working of the system is a separate question.

History matters; and it matters far more to Cartalists than to Monetarists, who like Kiyotaki and Wright (1998) often inhabit an abstract, algebraic world. As Ed Nell's introductory quotation indicates, perhaps Sir John Hicks was also, at heart, a Cartalist. Anyhow, the two great monetary experiences of the 20th century were the collapse of the Gold Standard in the 1930s and the endemic fiat-money inflation after World War II, reaching its apogee in the 1970s. Even though the reasons for the former, the collapse of the Gold Standard, was somewhat special rather than necessarily generic (on all this see Eichengreen (1992)), it did herald the temporary triumph of 'managed money'.

The inflation of the 1960s and 1970s revealed that money could be mismanaged,[5] rather than well managed. This led to a battle between the M theorists, who wanted money to be subject to some new automatic control mechanism (K% rule, monetary base growth rule, restored Gold Standard, and so on) and the C theorists who sought to keep monetary policy managed in a discretionary fashion, but just managed much 'better' than in the past. The technique that has now generally triumphed for such better management is for governments to define an objective of price stability, and then to delegate its achievement to an operationally independent central bank. From my point of view that represents an eminently desirable finishing point, a just-about optimal combination of M and C theories, with C theory (naturally) having the upper hand.

But to many of the contributors to this book, the concentrated focus of current monetary policy on medium and longer term price stability is too narrow. This brings us naturally to the next section.

(II.B) THE POLICY IMPLICATIONS OF ADOPTING C THEORY RATHER THAN M THEORY

One of the strong points of C theory is that, within this context, monetary and fiscal policies are intimately connected; one implication is that it would be extremely difficult and dislocating for a central bank to try to stabilize monetary growth (and price inflation) in the face of large government deficits. The attempt to do so, via very high real interest rates, would not only reduce investment and growth, but also lead to such increasing interest payments on government debt as to threaten its longer-term sustainability. This is accepted by all C theorists, and by the contributors to this book. By contrast, M theorists are generally ambivalent on this point, sometimes arguing, as Friedman has done, that the determinants of monetary growth (that is base money and the multiplier) can be analysed strictly separately from fiscal considerations; while at other times M theorists have argued that a necessary condition for automatic, rule-based, monetary management to work is a constraint on government deficits, as in the Amsterdam 'growth and stability' Treaty requirement, as originally introduced by Theo Waigel, the German Minister of Finance. C theorists in contrast see the need, not for a fixed *constraint*, but for an 'appropriate' *adjustment* of fiscal policy to allow both short-run equilibrium of output and for medium-term price stability.

The importance of fiscal balance to the achievement of price stability is reiterated (correctly) by many contributors to this book, for example Hudson, Chapter 3, pp. 64–5, Wray, Chapter 5, pp. 105–6, and Nell, Chapter 6, pp 133–4. This leads some Cartalists (again see Wray) to question whether price stability may be *more* the responsibility of fiscal, than of monetary, policy. In my own view, responsibility for price stability has to be shared between the two arms of policy; in some specific cases, however, responsibility for a breakdown in price stability can be attributed *ex post* primarily to failures in one, or other, of the two arms of policymaking. But, *ex ante*, what is important is to get an appropriate balance between the two, so that price stability can be achieved at the same time as a sufficient proportion of GDP can be allocated to productive investment (whether in the private or public sectors).

C theorists see money creation as arising from a debt/credit nexus. Whereas the main cause of debt/credit creation (and of money) has usually arisen from the (excessive) financial requirements of the state, one should never forget that much, nowadays the majority, of credit expansion arises from the private sector assumption of debt. Such private sector credit expansion is generally based on (collateralized by) financial and real assets, and predominantly used to buy financial, and real assets.

This means that monetary expansion (and contagion) is intimately connected with asset price fluctuations (both real assets, such as houses, property and investment goods, as well as financial assets). Causation is, of course, interactive and two-way. Just as monetary expansion drives (asset price) inflation, so also asset price inflation raises bank profitability and capital, see Nell, Chapter 6, pp. 129–30, thereby encouraging further expansion. Thus for a C theorist it comes naturally to view price stability within the context of an index (or indices) that should include asset prices, whereas (mainstream) M theorists, for a variety of reasons, tend to define, and measure, price stability in terms of indices that exclude (most) asset prices, and encompass, as far as possible, only prices of current goods and services. This contrast is well captured in a number of chapters here, notably in Hudson, Chapter 3, pp. 67–72, and Nell, Chapter 6, pp. 129–31. Perhaps the main area of disagreement amongst C theorists is over the question of what the medium-term objectives of (monetary) policy should be. This is not a problem for (mainstream) M theorists, who overwhelmingly subscribe to the view that (over the medium, and longer) term real variables are primarily determined by real, supply-side factors (absent major monetary disasters, such as hyperinflation, serious deflation) so that all that nominal, monetary policies *can* deliver over such a longer-term horizon is price stability.

I tend to agree with this view (always noting the qualification about avoiding monetary disasters) and I see no contradiction between holding to C monetary theory, and in believing that the primary function of monetary policy in the medium and longer runs should be the achievement of price stability. But several of the contributors to this book would want monetary policy to have a much wider remit, incorporating specific concern and responsibility for employment, growth, and so on.

Nell, Chapter 6, p. 124, argues that a fiat money system has no anchor, so 'To keep money wages and prices steady, therefore, it has seemed that demand must be kept weak, creating an overhang of unemployed labor and excess productive capacity. It is clear that this is wasteful; ...'. Similarly Wray, p. 106, states that 'Modern governments typically use unemployment to fight inflation'.

Although some of the contributors, notably Bell, Chapter 8, and Guttmann, Chapter 7, would agree that the objectives of monetary policy should be widened, both Nell and Wray would allocate responsibility for the achievement of full employment more to fiscal policy, via the state acting as the (buffer-stock) employer-of-last-resort. I have considerable doubts and reservations about this set of proposals, mainly on efficiency and allocative grounds, but it is not central either to my own initial paper nor to these other contributions, so the issue can, perhaps, be left over here. Where I do strongly agree with Nell is that the power of monetary policy, and of interest rates, to 'determine the direction of the economy' has been greatly exaggerated, notably in the US press; when this becomes evident, as it may in 2001/2002, there may well be a severe popular reaction.

In the most extreme of the contributions on the policy implications of monetary theory, Hudson, Chapter 3, suggests that M theory, at least in its monetarist guise, is politically and ideologically driven; 'Dressed up as positivist economics, monetarism is an anti-government ideology, ... The past half-century has seen an ideological war fought over whether planning should be done by governments or by financial engineers in the banking, insurance and stock-broking industries, and their representatives in the central banks and finance ministries' (p. 62), and there is much along similar lines. There is *some* truth in this tirade. The exclusion of the central role of government, of legal and social institutions, and so on, from M, and from much of the rest of mainstream theory, is not only an egregious mistake but also leads to policy errors, for example as recently occurred in Russia. But Hudson puts it all in such an aggressive fashion, and so ignores the valid counter-arguments, about the failures of governmental intervention, the corruption of power, and so on, that it puts my teeth on edge. In addition, I greatly deplore the, almost personal, attacks on Robert Mundell and his Nobel Prize award. I happen myself to believe that Optimal Currency Area (OCA) theory is not a satisfactory tool for understanding the actual basis for the adoption of currency areas, or to assess the likely workings of EMU, but Mundell's achievements in international monetary economics are manifold, and fully worthy of recognition.

This brings us onto the final main area of discussion, which is EMU.

(III) AN ASSESSMENT OF THE NEW ECONOMIC AND MONETARY UNION (EMU) IN EUROPE

Those contributors to this book who mention EMU, and most do, appear to share my reservations and doubts about the new system, particularly the divorce between placing the monetary powers at the central, federal level, whilst leaving the main fiscal competencies at the national level. Wray (p. 107), descibes EMU as

> a unique and scary experiment, and one that comes at a particularly bad time – just as Europe, the USA and the rest of the world prepare to spiral down into deep recession, if not depression. By divorcing money from fiscal authority, the individual European nations will probably have to retrench, precisely when they should adopt expansionary policy.

The two final contributions to this book, Chapter 7 by Guttmann and Chapter 8 by Bell, are primarily about these issues, that is assessing the implications and characteristics of the eurozone from the stand-point of C theory. Mostly I agree with their analyses, but I do have some minor differences of viewpoint. For example, Guttmann argues (p. 153), that widening the objectives of the ECB, to include growth and employment, would lessen attacks on its independence arising from its 'democratic deficit'. I take exactly the opposite view, which is that concern about the 'democratic deficit' is much greater when a central bank has goal independence, in addition to operational independence. That said, Guttmann has many useful points to make on the putative role of the ECB as a financial regulator and lender-of-last-resort.

Bell, Chapter 8, provides an excellent résumé of the history, motivations and institutional arrangements under EMU, nicely describing the Maastricht Treaty as 'a divorce contract; it allocates various rights and responsibilities among the "divorcing" fiscal and monetary institutions' (p. 167). One of the questions that EMU has brought to the fore is whether the potential proclivity of sub-sovereign state governments to run deficits needs to be checked by constitutional constraints, for example balanced budget requirements, in the case of EMU, the Amsterdam Stability and Growth Pact Treaty, or can be left to market pressures.

Bell tends to believe that, so long as the no-bailout rule is 'seen as reasonably credible' and markets are 'well informed and efficient in their pricing of credit risk' (p. 175), the market constraint on deficit financing will bite more severely than the constitutional Amsterdam limit. I doubt that, perhaps because I also doubt the validity of the two prior conditions. We shall see. In my view the defining moment for the eurozone will arrive when a (major) country is required by the treaty to take deflationary fiscal action at a time when its economy is suffering worsening stagnation. The founding fathers of EMU must be hoping that such an occasion will not happen, or at least not for a very long time. How such a confrontation would be handled in the event is uncertain; given the delicacy of such a situation, it would hardly be possible to predict what might happen.

Let me end by returning to Perry Mehrling's penetrating review of my own analytical position. While I do see myself almost whole and clear in his brilliant mirror, he does, I believe, make me a more parochial and narrower supporter of central banks, in relation to EMU, than is justified. Thus he writes (p. 37), 'Goodhart trusts the old-fashioned nation state and especially its central banking arm, the Bank of England. He doesn't trust the newfangled federal Europe state and its central banking arm, the European Central Bank.' In fact, I do trust the ECB. I know a large number of the governing council and of their senior staff personally, and I think extremely highly of their dedication and professional skills. Mehrling here misses the point. It is not a question whether I, personally, trust the ECB, or not. The proper question is whether the *people*, the constituents of the eurozone, will be prepared to accept whatever (restrictive) policies the ECB (and the Amsterdam Treaty) may require in the interests of (price stability in the) eurozone as a whole, without concern for major national (and regional) interests. In the USA, no one would demur from the thesis that the Fed's policy, and the Federal budget, should be set in the light of overall US conditions. If a region, or state, in the USA is suffering an asymmetric problem, there are some (fiscal) palliatives, but there would be no call to leave the Union, and set up a separate state currency. Would the same be true in the eurozone? Will the individual constituents of the eurozone states trust the ECB as much as Americans trust the Fed? Mehrling is correct to see the language adopted in the eurozone as politically determined, but a political construct depends on democratic legitimacy; and it is the bedrock of such democratic legitimacy that is, to my eyes, so shaky in EMU.

Again (p. 28), Mehrling suggests that my doubts about EMU arise because 'the effect is to threaten the position of central banking – this time the threat is the replacement of national central banking with a European Central Bank and a common European currency.' This is similarly a misapprehension. I would feel no enthusiasm if the 50 US states were to split into 50 currencies each with its own central bank, nor did the separation of the former Yugoslavia or USSR make me pleased, just because there were more central banks! The number of separate central banks is *not* important; by the same token the ECB is itself an entirely adequate, professional and well-performing central banking institution. The proper and wider point is whether the conduct of monetary sovereignty is buttressed by democratic acceptability and legitimacy. In my view that remains an open question in EMU.

NOTES

1. I used to argue that EMU would represent a unique experiment, but Marc Flandreau (2001) has argued persuasively that the Austro-Hungarian empire before 1914, with a single currency but separate national budgets, had characteristics much in common with EMU.

2. The attempt to develop a role for the SDR in international exchange might seem to be a counter-example. It would be instructive to try to analyse the history and tribulations of the SDR in this intellectual context, but this lies beyond my current remit.
3. Guttmann (Chapter 7) also commented that 'The M view's emphasis on cost minimization is ... not as irrelevant as its C view opponents often claim, since new money forms – even those introduced by the state – must gain public acceptance and trust, and thus contain some degree of attractiveness.' (p. 144). Guttmann cites the development of euro-currencies and e-money, which new money forms [may have] 'profound (and often unintended) repercussions for the operation of our economic system' (p. 144). Another example will have been (by the time this book is published), the introduction of the euro as currency in the euro-zone at the start of 2002.
4. Many C theorists combine a belief that money is essentially dependent on the fiat (power) of the state with a concern whether the state will so act as to maintain the stability of the value of such money. I well recall that, to my surprise at the time, Nicky Kaldor was concerned by Nixon's repudiation of the link between gold and the US dollar at the end of the 1960s, because it removed an ultimate anchor of monetary stability. Just because one believes in the importance of the link between state power and money's acceptability, it does *not* necessarily mean that one believes that such state power will be wielded for the greater good of society; indeed not.
5. My own view is that such mismanagement was *not* the result of an intentional Kydland-Prescott, Barro-Gordon inflationary bias, but rather the unwitting result of (a) ignoring expectations in a Phillips-curve supply side context prior to the 1970s, (b) failing to appreciate, until too late, the decline in productivity after 1973–74 and (c) the oil shocks of 1973–74.

ADDITIONAL BIBLIOGRAPHY

Bell, S., (2001), 'The role of the state and the hierarchy of money', *Cambridge Journal of Economics*, 25, 149–63.
Eichengreen, B., (1992), *Golden Fetters: The Gold Standard and the Great Depression, 1919–1939*, Oxford: Oxford University Press.
Flandreau, M. (2001), 'The bank, the states and the market: An Austro-Hungarian tale for Euroland, 1867–1914', Austrian National Bank Working Paper (March).

Index